gilbert
LAW SUMMARIES

LEGAL ETHICS

Seventh Edition

Thomas D. Morgan
Professor of Law
George Washington University

HARCOURT BRACE LEGAL AND PROFESSIONAL PUBLICATIONS, INC.
EDITORIAL OFFICES: 111 W. Jackson Blvd., 7th Floor, Chicago, IL 60604

LAW SUMMARIES

REGIONAL OFFICES: Chicago, Dallas, Los Angeles, New York, Washington, D.C.
Distributed by: **Harcourt Brace & Company** 6277 Sea Harbor Drive, Orlando, FL 32887 (800)787-8717

PROJECT EDITOR
Maureen A. Mitchell, B.A., J.D.

QUALITY CONTROL EDITOR
Dawn M. Barker, B.S.

gilbert
LAW SUMMARIES

Titles Available

Administrative Law
Agency & Partnership
Antitrust
Bankruptcy
Basic Accounting for Lawyers
Business Law
California Bar Performance
  Test Skills
Civil Procedure
Commercial Paper &
  Payment Law
Community Property
Conflict of Laws
Constitutional Law
Contracts
Corporations
Criminal Law
Criminal Procedure
Dictionary of Legal Terms
Estate & Gift Tax
Evidence

Family Law
Federal Courts
First Year Questions & Answers
Future Interests
Income Tax I (Individual)
Income Tax II (Corporate)
Labor Law
Legal Ethics (Prof. Responsibility)
Legal Research, Writing,
  & Analysis
Multistate Bar Exam
Personal Property
Property
Remedies
Sales & Lease of Goods
Securities Regulation
Secured Transactions
Torts
Trusts
Wills

Also Available:

First Year Program
Pocket Size Law Dictionary
The Eight Secrets Of Top Exam Performance In Law School

**All Titles Available at Your Law School Bookstore,
or Call to Order: 1-800-787-8717**

Harcourt Brace Legal and Professional Publications, Inc.
176 West Adams, Suite 2100
Chicago, IL 60603

SUMMARY OF CONTENTS

gilbert
capsule summary
legal ethics

b. **Law students and law clerks:** Some states make exceptions for student training programs under a lawyer's supervision .... [111]

c. **Corporations:** Generally, a corporation may not represent a client directly or furnish representation through its employees who are licensed attorneys. (Exceptions exist for professional law corporations and non-profit group legal services providers) .... [115]

4. **Efforts to Prohibit Practice of Law by Nonlawyers:** Sanctions against non-lawyer practitioners include injunctions, criminal prosecution, or denial of the right to fees .... [119]

a. **Obligations of lawyers in preventing unauthorized practice:** Both the ABA Code and Model Rules require lawyers to assist in preventing the unauthorized practice. Four specific duties include: .... [120]

(1) A lawyer may not practice *in violation of the professional regulations* of the jurisdiction;

(2) A lawyer may not *"aid" a nonlawyer in the "practice of law"*;

(3) A lawyer may *not share fees with a nonlawyer*; and

(4) A lawyer may not *enter a partnership with a nonlawyer* if *any* partnership activity involves the practice of law.

II. THE CONTRACT BETWEEN CLIENT AND LAWYER

A. INTRODUCTION
The client-lawyer relationship is best understood as a contract between them. Terms are implied by custom but may be varied by agreement .... [124]

1. **Lawyer as Fiduciary:** Changes in the customary contract will be construed against the lawyer and scrutinized for fairness .... [125]

2. **Lawyer as Agent:** As an agent of his client, a lawyer is subject to limitations of the law of agency (*e.g.*, he may not be hired to perform illegal acts) ..... [126]

B. FORMATION OF LAWYER-CLIENT RELATIONSHIP—LAWYER'S DUTIES REGARDING ACCEPTING EMPLOYMENT

1. **No Obligation to Accept Every Case:** Unlike English barristers, American lawyers need not take every matter presented to them .... [127]

2. **Ethical Obligation to Provide Representation Where Needed:** Lawyers "should" accept some cases where clients cannot afford legal services, but the failure to do so does not result in discipline. Some states impose an affirmative duty to represent the defenseless or oppressed .... [128]

a. **Appointment of counsel:** Lawyers have a *moral obligation* to accept *court appointment* to represent indigent clients. Grounds for refusal of appointment are: (i) violation of a Model Rule; (ii) unreasonable financial burden; or (iii) client repugnance that would affect the lawyer's ability to adequately represent .... [131]

3. **Duty to Reject Certain Cases:** The ABA Code and Model Rules identify at least seven situations where the lawyer should refuse employment; *i.e.*, where: .... [135]

a. The client's *motive is harassment or malicious injury*;

b. The client's *legal position is unsupportable*;

c. The lawyer is *unable to act competently*;

d. The *lawyer's personal feelings interfere* (as opposed to community pressure);

e. The client is *already represented*;

f. A *disciplinary standard or other law would be violated*; or

g. The *lawyer's physical or mental condition is impaired*.

4. **Duties to a Prospective Client:** Though the lawyer-client relationship is not formed until the parties agree, some duties are owed to a prospective client

III. DUTY TO PROTECT CONFIDENTIAL INFORMATION OF THE CLIENT

A. INTRODUCTION

B. ATTORNEY-CLIENT PRIVILEGE

C. PROFESSIONAL DUTY OF CONFIDENTIALITY

IV. DUTY OF UNIMPAIRED LOYALTY—CONFLICTS OF INTEREST

V. OBLIGATIONS TO THIRD PERSONS AND THE LEGAL SYSTEM

A. COUNSELING OR ASSISTING ILLEGAL OR FRAUDULENT CONDUCT
Although a lawyer may discuss the consequences of conduct with a client and assist in acts that, in good faith, test the bounds of the law, a lawyer may not counsel

B. REGULATION OF THE MANNER OF LAWYERS SEEKING EMPLOYMENT—SOLICITATION AND ADVERTISING

TEXT CORRELATION CHART

Gilbert Law Summary Legal Ethics	Gillers Regulation of Lawyers: Problems of Law and Ethics 1992 (3rd ed.)	Hazard, Koniak The Law and Ethics of Lawyering 1990	Kaufman Problems in Professional Responsibility 1989 (3rd ed.)	Morgan, Rotunda Professional Responsibility 1991 (5th ed.)	Patterson, Metzloff Legal Ethics: The Law of Professional Responsibility 1989 (3rd ed.)	Pirsig, Kirwin Professional Responsibility Cases and Materials 1984 (4th ed.)	Schwartz, Wydick, Perschbacher Problems in Legal Ethics 1992 (3rd ed.)
I. REGULATING THE RIGHT TO PRACTICE LAW							
A. Sources of Regulation	1-6	12-14	1-30, 745-758, 765-774	11-16	57-64, 87-107	24-38	27, 36-52
B. Regulating Admission to Practice Law	536-597	862-892	603-627	31-40	774-787	57-69	27, 30-35
C. Preventing Unauthorized Practice of Law	597-608	893-906	627-637	500-512	787-791	77-110	151, 153-154, 162-170, 173-174
II. THE CONTRACT BETWEEN CLIENT AND LAWYER							
A. Introduction	42-46, 48-50	473-478		75	13-26		56-68, 87-88
B. Formation of Lawyer-Client Relationship—Lawyer's Duties Regarding Accepting Employment	46-48		51	75-77	147-171		
C. Reaching Agreement on Scope and Objectives of Representation	63-66	478		77		483-484	
D. Spheres of Authority of Lawyer and Client	56-62, 64-65, 67-68	512-536	320-331	77-79	171-183	483-497	
E. Formal Contractual Duties That Lawyers Owe to Clients	48-56, 590-593	141-184, 558-565	639-644	79, 111-122, 130-143	183-194, 211-270, 523-535	465-482, 497-516	125, 128, 140-150, 151-162
F. Obligation of Client to Lawyer—Paying a Fee for Legal Services	101-157	479-512	461-481	95-111	47-56, 93-100, 381-385, 794-805	426-453	57, 125-126, 128-140
G. Terminating the Lawyer-Client Relationship	69-70	571-579	49, 65, 80, 158, 173, 177, 193, 211, 426-427	79-80	194-199	453-465	56, 58, 69-76
III. DUTY TO PROTECT CONFIDENTIAL INFORMATION OF THE CLIENT							
A. Introduction		185-186		83	343-346	111-112	175-176, 185-197
B. Attorney-Client Privilege	17-37, 204-205	186-239	142-151, 207-244	89-95, 147-151	346-375	112-128, 133-134	175, 177-185, 197-202
C. Professional Duty of Confidentiality	32-42	239-327	142-207, 213-234	83-89, 135, 307-308	375-395	111-135	

TEXT CORRELATION CHART—Continued

Gilbert Law Summary Legal Ethics	Gillers Regulation of Lawyers: Problems of Law and Ethics 1992 (3rd ed.)	Hazard, Koniak The Law and Ethics of Lawyering 1990	Kaufman Problems in Professional Responsibility 1989 (3rd ed.)	Morgan, Rotunda Professional Responsibility 1991 (5th ed.)	Patterson, Metzloff Legal Ethics: The Law of Professional Responsibility 1989 (3rd ed.)	Pirsig, Kirwin Professional Responsibility Cases and Materials 1984 (4th ed.)	Schwartz, Wydick, Perschbacher Problems in Legal Ethics 1992 (3rd ed.)
IV. DUTY OF UNIMPAIRED LOYALTY—CONFLICTS OF INTEREST							
A. Introduction	171-174	580-581	35-41	123	271-273	136	300
B. Personal Interests That May Affect Lawyer's Judgment	174-186	565-569	89	151-158	273-281, 321-334	136-157	300-316
C. Concurrent Representation of Clients with Conflicting Interests	186-236, 445-468	581-644, 729-771	33-83, 85-88, 283-303	123-151	282-301, 321-335	169-202, 220-244, 256-271	317-321, 325-333
D. Interests of Third Persons Affecting Lawyer-Client Relationship	236-240	644-647	50-51	158-169	301-310	244-255	281-299
E. Conflict Between Interests of Current Client and Former One	247-265	648-659	89-107	169-174	310-321	203-220	317, 321-325
F. Disqualification of Other Lawyers Affiliated with Lawyer	265-277	659-692	107-116	174-183, 197-201	315-321, 335-342	208-210	319-320, 340-342
G. Limitations on Representation by Present and Former Government Lawyers	277-287	692-723	117-140	183-197	704-709, 726-735	279-289	317, 320, 333-340
V. OBLIGATIONS TO THIRD PERSONS AND THE LEGAL SYSTEM							
A. Counseling or Assisting Illegal or Fraudulent Conduct	36-37, 481-482	225-227, 254-272, 328-330, 350-357	142-151		350-358	303-304	197-198, 216-223
B. Requirement of Honesty in Communications with Others	471-488	100-132	386-407	338-369	419-421, 469-485, 597-603	269-271, 339-357	204, 216-223
C. Communicating Directly with Adverse Party	72-95	431-434	366-374	144-145, 281, 302-303, 476		347-348, 354-355, 372-375	231, 233, 251
D. Threats of Criminal Prosecution	487-488			66, 222-223		340, 355-356, 371	251-252
E. Obligation to Improve the Legal System	774-782	914-931	434-449, 665-687	540-548	576-588		
VI. SPECIAL OBLIGATIONS OF LAWYERS IN LITIGATION							
A. Duty to Reject Actions Brought Merely to Harass or Injure Third Parties	360-377	397-403, 427-428		207-208, 210-211	462-466, 622-631	290-293	56-57, 77-86
B. Limitations on Trial Publicity	749-774					378-396	240-246

TEXT CORRELATION CHART—Continued

Gilbert Law Summary Legal Ethics	Gillers Regulation of Lawyers: Problems of Law and Ethics 1992 (3rd ed.)	Hazard, Koniak The Law and Ethics of Lawyering 1990	Kaufman Problems in Professional Responsibility 1989 (3rd ed.)	Morgan, Rotunda Professional Responsibility 1991 (5th ed.)	Patterson, Metzloff Legal Ethics: The Law of Professional Responsibility 1989 (3rd ed.)	Pirsig, Kirwin Professional Responsibility Cases and Materials 1984 (4th ed.)	Schwartz, Wydick, Perschbacher Problems in Legal Ethics 1992 (3rd ed.)
C. Conduct in Court Proceedings	341-360, 378-386	431-435, 440-456	201-207, 374-386, 434-460	144-145, 220-228, 478-479	460-462	397-413	230-237
D. Limitations on Advancing Money to Client	179-180					153-157	125, 133-134, 142-144
E. Duty of Honesty	294-340, 386-391	328-330, 350-361, 381-402	142-151, 207-226, 283-303, 661-665	212-214, 229-252, 454-455	110-111, 128-139, 350-358, 419-462	291, 303-305, 329-357, 372-378, 397-417	203-208, 223-230
F. Duty to Disclose Perjury	310-335	328-381	151-207	256-278	396-417	305-329	208-223
G. Lawyer as Witness and Advocate	240-245	437-440	83-85	289-294	288-296	157-168	310-313
H. Improper Contacts with Court Officials and Jurors				288-289	636-637	417-425	231-240
I. Special Obligations of Public Prosecutors and Government Lawyers	85-94, 206-211, 244-245, 277-287, 425-428	692-723	303-319, 360-361	295-306	695-717, 726-735	272-289, 357-371	254-261, 277-278
VII. THE BUSINESS OF PRACTICING LAW							
A. Associations of Lawyers for the Practice of Law	163-168, 594-597, 709-744	900-903, 966-967, 978-981	459-460, 523-602	450-459, 483-499	766-774	43-53, 527-541	154, 170, 173-174, 281-282, 286-289
B. Regulation of the Manner of Lawyers Seeking Employment—Solicitation and Advertising	785-840	952-967	481-522	382-429	791-822	541-591	90-124
C. Regulation of Lawyer Specialization	608-609		641-644	429-446	815-822	47-49, 556-559, 563-564	
D. Division of Fees with Lawyers Outside One's Firm	165-166	499	467-476	446-450	47-56	452-453	125, 134-150
VIII. ENFORCEMENT OF LAWYERS' PROFESSIONAL OBLIGATIONS							
A. The Formal Disciplinary Process	664-689	153-154, 906-939	453-460, 665-687	41-56, 64-70	36-43, 72-77	69-77	27, 42-55
B. Personal Financial Liability (Malpractice)	611-664	142-156	639-665	56-64	66-83, 139-152, 208-209, 226-244, 621-671	497-516	151, 157-172
C. Contempt Sanction				59-60		398-413	
IX. THE SPECIAL RESPONSIBILITIES OF JUDGES A. Introduction B. General Norms	493-494, 509-510, 517-520	14, 981					350-351

TEXT CORRELATION CHART—Continued

Gilbert Law Summary Legal Ethics	Gillers Regulation of Lawyers: Problems of Law and Ethics 1992 (3rd ed.)	Hazard, Koniak The Law and Ethics of Lawyering 1990	Kaufman Problems in Professional Responsibility 1989 (3rd ed.)	Morgan, Rotunda Professional Responsibility 1991 (5th ed.)	Patterson, Metzloff Legal Ethics: The Law of Professional Responsibility 1989 (3rd ed.)	Pirsig, Kirwin Professional Responsibility Cases and Materials 1984 (4th ed.)	Schwartz, Wydick, Perschbacher Problems in Legal Ethics 1992 (3rd ed.)
C. Judge's Official Actions	511-512, 514-515, 518	458-472, 981-989	742-744	530-532	674-682	418, 425	
D. Disqualification of the Judge	497-516	981-989	709-733	520-529	682-689	417-419	351-364
E. Extrajudicial Activities of the Judge		78-79	734-472	529-530			
F. Moneymaking Activities of the Judge	494-495, 510-513			521-525	418		362-364
G. Judge's Involvement in Political Activity			695, 701-703, 705-707	535-540	418-419		366-367

approach to exams

Legal Ethics concerns the law governing legal practice. No simple secret will resolve all issues, but in analyzing Legal Ethics problems begin by asking whether the question relates to the lawyer's duties to:

1. **The client** (*see* chapters II-IV): Here you should consider primarily the duties of competence, diligence, communication, zeal, confidentiality, and loyalty. Duties to the client also include any special obligations assumed by the lawyer in a particular representation.

2. **Third parties or the court** (*see* chapters V-VI): These include the duties not to assist a crime or fraud, to deal honestly even with the opposing side, not to communicate improperly with an opposing party or witnesses, and not to abuse the processes of litigation.

3. **Other lawyers**—within a firm and throughout the legal system (*see* chapter VII): Here you may face questions about advertising and solicitation, and fee sharing both within a firm and with others.

After you have analyzed the lawyer's duties under each of these headings, don't forget to also ask what **remedies** may be invoked against the lawyer in the matter (*see* chapters I and VIII). Your primary choices will be professional discipline and malpractice, but don't forget to think about contempt of court sanctions and disqualification from participating further in a matter.

Finally, you may also get some questions about **judicial ethics**. That is a specialized area of Legal Ethics, often raised in exam questions other than those about lawyer conduct. Judges' ethics are considered in chapter IX of this Summary.

I. REGULATING THE RIGHT TO PRACTICE LAW

chapter approach

Attorneys act on behalf of clients who need help but who often are not in a position to know whether they have been well or badly represented. Thus, the practice of law is a classic subject for regulation. To protect the public, states regulate who can become licensed to practice in the state and they attempt to prevent such practice by those not licensed.

Although the topics covered in this chapter are not heavily tested in law school courses, they are nonetheless important in understanding the limitations on the right to practice law.

A. SOURCES OF REGULATION

1. **State Regulation:** [§1]   Like other professions or businesses, the practice of law affects the public interest and is therefore subject to regulation by the states. [Bates v. State Bar of Arizona, 433 U.S. 350 (1977)]

   a. **Inherent judicial power to regulate:** [§2]   Unlike other professions, however, the ultimate regulatory power over the legal profession rests with the courts rather than with the legislature. The practice of law is so intimately concerned with the administration of justice that the judicial branch is deemed to have **inherent** regulatory power over the practice of law (whether in or out of court). [Robeson v. Oregon State Bar, 632 P.2d 1255 (Or. 1981)]

      (1) **Lawyers as officers of the court:** [§3]   In recognition of the judicial source of their authority, lawyers are often called **_"officers of the court."_** This designation does not significantly alter a lawyer's obligation to a client, but it does recognize the lawyer's unique role in the judicial system. [Sams v. Olah, 169 S.E.2d 790 (Ga. 1969)]

      (2) **Regulation by state's highest court:** [§4]   The most pervasive form of regulation is that imposed by the highest court of the state in which a lawyer is licensed to practice. [Hoover v. Ronwin, 466 U.S. 558 (1984)]

      (3) **Regulation by lower courts:** [§5]   One of the most direct forms of judicial regulation is a lower court's ability to sanction a lawyer for misconduct in a case before it, in addition to or in lieu of formal disciplinary proceedings (*see infra*, §§848 *et seq.*).

   b. **Power of legislatures:** [§6]   Legislatures also have power to enact statutes regulating the legal profession. Indeed, such enactments are quite common. Nevertheless, statutory regulation is deemed in **aid** of the judiciary and does not supersede or detract from the inherent regulatory power of the courts. [Sharood v. Hatfield, 210 N.W.2d 275 (Minn. 1973)]

(1) **Admission to practice:** [§7]   Statutes commonly govern the conditions upon which persons may be admitted to the practice of law (*e.g.,* age). Such statutes, however, would not prevent the courts from demanding more than the legislature has required. [Alabama State Bar v. State, 324 So. 2d 256 (Ala. 1975)—legislature cannot prohibit judicial rule limiting number of times applicant can take state bar examination]

(2) **Lawyer discipline:** [§8]   Likewise, the statutory grounds for discipline of a lawyer are not exclusive. The courts may impose discipline for acts that are not within the statutory grounds. [Stratmore v. State Bar, 14 Cal. 3d 887 (1975)]

c. **Creation of "integrated" bar:** [§9]   A majority of states today have "integrated" bar systems, meaning that all practicing lawyers in the state are ***required*** to join the state bar association and become subject to its rules (including its rules of professional conduct). [*See, e.g.,* Cal. Const., art. VI, §9] Thus, membership in an integrated state bar association is mandatory, whereas membership in any other bar association (including the American Bar Association and all city and county bar associations) is purely voluntary.

(1) **Source of integration:** [§10]   In many states, integration of the state bar has been accomplished by statute. [*See, e.g.,* Cal. Bus. & Prof. Code §6002] But in several states (*e.g.,* Georgia), it has been ordered by the state supreme court in exercise of its inherent judicial power. [*See* Wallace v. Wallace, 166 S.E.2d 718 (Ga. 1969)]

(2) **Constitutionality:** [§11]   The compulsory membership requirement of integrated bar systems has been upheld against attacks that it violates rights of free association. [Lathrop v. Donahue, 367 U.S. 820 (1961)]

(3) **Use of membership dues:** [§12]   However, compulsory membership dues may be used only to support legislative proposals of direct interest to the bar. They may not be used to support legislation favored by a majority of the bar but unrelated to the practice of law. [Keller v. State Bar of California, 496 U.S. 1 (1990)]

d. **Regulation by multiple states:** [§13]   A lawyer is subject to regulation by ***each*** state in which the lawyer is ***admitted*** to practice, regardless of where the lawyer actually practices law. If the rules of the states in which the lawyer is admitted are in conflict, the rules to be applied are those of the state in which the lawyer ***principally practices*** or the state in which the lawyer's conduct clearly ***has its predominant effect***. [ABA Model Rule 8.5]

e. **No preemption of federal regulation:** [§14] The fact that a lawyer is qualified to practice under state law does not preclude *additional* federal regulation where the lawyer's activities are within the scope of applicable federal law. Federal regulation is generally not extensive; however, lawyers who wish to practice before some federal agencies or tribunals are required to have special qualifications (*see infra.* §74).

2. **American Bar Association as a Source of Regulation:** [§15] Although voluntary bar associations have no formal role in lawyer regulation, many standards for the practice of law come from the organized bar itself, and in particular from the American Bar Association ("ABA").

    a. **Composition of ABA:** [§16] Although the ABA is a voluntary association, it currently has about 50% of all practicing lawyers in the United States and includes lawyers from all geographic areas and types of practice.

    b. **Standards of conduct:** [§17] Since it first published Canons of Professional Ethics in 1908, the ABA has been active in the field of legal ethics and has formulated standards of conduct which serve as a guide to the various state legislatures and bar associations in passing specific regulations for the profession.

    c. **ABA Model Code of Professional Responsibility:** [§18] In 1969, the ABA enacted a comprehensive Model Code of Professional Responsibility, completely revising its earlier Canons of Ethics. Hereafter, whenever this Summary speaks of the "ABA Code," it should be understood to mean the Model Code of Professional Responsibility.

        (1) **Canons of Ethics:** [§19] The ABA Code contained nine brief Canons. These were "axiomatic norms" outlining a lawyer's general responsibilities.

        (2) **Amplification of Canons:** [§20] Each of the Canons was supplemented by two sets of principles, *Ethical Considerations* ("EC") and *Disciplinary Rules* ("DR"). These were substantially more detailed than the Canons and were designed to implement the general concepts expressed in the Canons and relate them to the situations encountered in everyday practice.

            (a) **Ethical Considerations:** [§21] The EC were *aspirational—i.e.*, they represented objectives that a lawyer should *strive* to meet in specific situations.

            (b) **Disciplinary Rules:** [§22] The DR were *mandatory* and stated the minimum level of conduct below which a lawyer could not fall without being *subject to disciplinary action.*

d. **ABA Model Rules of Professional Conduct:** [§23] In response to criticism of the ABA Code, in 1983, the ABA House of Delegates approved a completely new, "Restatement-type" format for what it called the Model Rules of Professional Conduct. Where principles discussed in this Summary are also reflected in the Model Rules of Professional Conduct, reference will be made to the relevant "Model Rule."

e. **Widespread impact of ABA Code and Model Rules on state regulation of practice:** [§24] While neither the ABA Code nor Model Rules directly regulates the legal profession in the various states, they have been designed to be adopted by state courts as a means of regulating the practice of law. [ABA Code, Preliminary Statement]

(1) **Adoption in most states:** [§25] Over 30 states have now adopted the ABA Model Rules as the authoritative standard for their lawyers—either intact or with minor revisions. Most of the other states retain some form of the ABA Code.

(2) **Source of guidance in others:** [§26] A few states have formulated or revised their own rules of professional conduct in light of the ABA Code and Model Rules. Some of these expressly *incorporate* the ABA Code or Model Rules to cover areas not covered under the local rules, while others regard them as a "source of guidance" in such areas. [*In re* Taylor, 363 N.E.2d 845 (Ill. 1977)]

(a) **Example—California:** The California Rules of Professional Conduct make no specific mention of the ABA Code (although they parallel the ABA Disciplinary Rules). However, it is stipulated that "ethics opinions and rules and standards promulgated by other jurisdictions and bar associations may also be considered." This apparently allows consideration of the ABA Code and Model Rules in areas not specifically covered under the local rules. [Cal. Rule 1-100]

(3) **Interpretation of ABA Code and Model Rules:** [§27] The ABA Code and Model Rules are in turn interpreted by *judicial opinions* on professional conduct. Moreover, the ABA Committee on Professional Ethics issues *advisory opinions* (both formal and informal) as a guide to applying the Model Code in particular fact situations. (All references herein to *"ABA Opn."* are to *Formal Opinions* published by the ABA.)

3. **Indirect Regulation Through Malpractice Liability:** [§28] Potential malpractice liability is a major concern of the practicing lawyer and thus is, for practical purposes, a major influence toward proper behavior. Indeed, many observers believe that malpractice suits will soon surpass formal disciplinary procedures in significance.

Nevertheless, at the present time, malpractice is rarely treated as an issue of "legal ethics"; thus, it will be considered in this Summary only where malpractice standards or procedures differ from those relating to professional discipline.

B. REGULATING ADMISSION TO PRACTICE LAW

1. **Admission to Practice in State Courts:** [§29]   As one method of maintaining the integrity and competence of the legal profession, states require certain standards for admission to the bar. Each state establishes its own criteria, which must be met by persons seeking to practice law within the state. The usual constitutional limitation is only that the requirements imposed have some *rational connection* with the applicant's *fitness or capacity* to practice law. [Schware v. Board of Bar Examiners, 353 U.S. 232 (1957)]

   a. **Citizenship not a valid requirement for admission:** [§30]   A state may *not* constitutionally require that a person be a United States citizen in order to be admitted to practice law within the state. [*In re* Griffiths, 413 U.S. 717 (1973)]

      (1) **Rationale:** The fact that a person is an alien bears *no rational relationship* to that person's fitness to practice law. Moreover, any discrimination against aliens as a class is "inherently suspect" under the Fourteenth Amendment Equal Protection Clause, and thus can be justified only by a "compelling" state interest; there is no such interest in excluding aliens from practicing law if they meet all other admission requirements.

   b. **Residency not a valid requirement for admission:** [§31]   The requirement that a bar applicant be a resident of the state in order to be admitted to the bar has also been struck down, this time on the ground that it violated the Privileges and Immunities Clause of the Constitution. [Supreme Court of New Hampshire v. Piper, 470 U.S. 274 (1985)]

   c. **Intellectual capability**

      (1) **Educational requirements:** [§32]   Practically all states require an applicant to complete a prescribed period of college work, followed by a period of law school study, as a means of demonstrating sufficient training to practice law.

         (a) **Accreditation:** [§33]   Many states also insist upon graduation from a law school *accredited* by the ABA. This requirement has been upheld by state and lower federal courts as bearing a "rational relationship" to fitness to practice. [Hackin v. Lockwood, 361 F.2d 499 (9th Cir. 1966); Application of Urie, 617 P.2d 505 (Alaska 1980)]

(b) **Specific courses:** [§34]   In two states, Indiana and South Carolina, supreme court rules require that law students take courses in specific fields in order to be admitted to the bar.

(2) **Examination by state bar:** [§35]   In addition to formal training, nearly all states require the candidate to pass an examination prepared and administered by the state bar. Each state adopts its own test, although the National Conference of Bar Examiners recommends standards to be followed in such examinations and also prepares the Multistate Bar Exam as part of the examination in the great majority of states today.

(a) **Constitutionality:** [§36]   The constitutionality of fairly administered exams has been repeatedly upheld by the courts. [Whitfield v. Illinois Board of Law Examiners, 504 F.2d 474 (7th Cir. 1974)]

(b) **"Diploma-privilege" exemption:** [§37]   A few states admit graduates of their own law schools to practice **without** a bar examination, whereas applicants from out-of-state law schools are required to pass an examination. This "diploma-privilege" exemption likewise has been upheld against equal protection claims. [Huffman v. Montana Supreme Court, 372 F. Supp. 1175 (D. Mont.), *aff'd,* 419 U.S. 955 (1974)]

(3) **Examination on professional responsibility:** [§38]   Over half of the states now require candidates to pass an additional examination, the Multistate Professional Responsibility Examination (MPRE), to demonstrate their knowledge of professional standards prior to bar admission. The examination tests a candidate's knowledge of the specific provisions of the ABA Code, the Model Rules, and the ABA Code of Judicial Conduct, all of which are explained in this Summary.

(a) **Note:** To be a correct answer on the MPRE, an answer must be correct under **both** the ABA Code and the Model Rules. Therefore, in this Summary, particular attention should be paid to those relatively few situations in which the two differ materially.

d. **Demonstration of "good moral character":** [§39]   A more troublesome step in the admission process involves the investigation of an applicant's moral character. The state clearly has a valid interest in insuring that persons admitted to practice possess high moral standards, including mental and emotional stability. [*See* Model Rule 8.1; EC 1-2, 1-6; DR 1-101(B)] On the other hand, the constitutional rights of applicants must also be protected against **unwarranted** infringement by the state.

(1) **Investigative procedure:** [§40]   The investigation of a candidate's moral fitness to practice law is generally conducted by a committee of bar examiners on behalf of the state bar. Usually the applicant is required

to fill out a detailed questionnaire, list a number of references, and submit fingerprints and photographs for identification purposes. The information obtained is then checked by letter or personal investigation.

(a) **Hearing before state bar committee:** [§41] If the committee feels that a question exists regarding moral fitness, the applicant is requested to appear a a hearing before the committee.

    1) **Issue same as for disbarment:** [§42] The question before the committee of bar examiners has been *equated with* the question before a *discipline* committee—namely, "is the applicant a fit and proper person to practice law?" [Hallinan v. Committee of Bar Examiners, 65 Cal. 2d 447 (1966)]

    2) **Burden of proof on applicant:** [§43] The burden of coming forward with evidence and establishing good moral character is on the applicant, who is deemed to be in the best position to know the pertinent facts. The applicant owes a *duty to cooperate* in reasonable investigations by the state bar and *to make disclosures* relevant to fitness to practice. [*In re* Anastaplo, 366 U.S. 82 (1961)]

    3) **Applicant's procedural rights:** [§44] At the same time, the applicant is entitled to procedural due process in committee proceedings—which includes the right to know the charges, to explain away derogatory information, and to confront critics or objectors. [Wellner v. Committee, 373 U.S. 96 (1963)]

(b) **Judicial review of adverse determination:** [§45] An applicant denied admission on the ground of bad moral character is also entitled to judicial review, usually by the highest court of the state.

(2) **Conduct relevant to determination of "good moral character":** [§46] The bar committee has the right (indeed the obligation) to investigate all aspects of an applicant's past conduct that may reflect upon that applicant's honesty and integrity. [Konigsberg v. Board of Bar Examiners, 353 U.S. 262 (1957)]

(a) **Any past conduct relevant:** [§47] The investigation is not limited to criminal convictions. Rather, the committee may consider *any conduct or charges* against the applicant—including mere arrest records, charges on which the applicant was *acquitted (or pardoned)*, and any civil or domestic litigation in which the applicant was involved. [Greene v. Committee of Bar Examiners, 4 Cal. 3d 189 (1971)]

1) **Example:** A personality characterized by "hypersensitivity, rigidity, unwarranted suspicion, excessive self-importance, and a tendency to blame others and ascribe evil motives to them" was sufficient to deny one applicant admission to the bar. [Application of Ronwin, 55 P.2d 1206 (Ariz. 1976)]

2) **Example:** Filing for bankruptcy so as to default on student loans three days before law school graduation was found to show a student's lack of sensitivity to his "moral responsibility to his creditors" and thus led to his inadmissibility to the bar. [*Re* G.W.L., 364 So. 2d 454 (Fla. 1978)]

(b) **Conviction of crime involving "moral turpitude":** [§48] Conviction of certain crimes may be enough by itself to show lack of good moral character. Such crimes include those involving an ***intent to defraud*** or ***intentional dishonesty for the purpose of personal gain***— *e.g.,* forgery, bribery, perjury, theft, robbery, extortion, etc. [*Ex parte* Weinberg, 201 So. 2d 38 (Ala. 1967)—desertion and nonsupport; *and see* discussion of moral turpitude in discipline cases *infra*, §§851-854]

(c) **Crimes not necessarily establishing lack of good moral character:** [§49] Many crimes do not involve "moral turpitude," and conviction of such crimes is ***not*** enough by itself to disqualify the applicant. Whether moral turpitude exists will depend on both the ***nature*** of the offense and the ***motivation of the violator***.

1) **"Adolescent misbehavior":** [§50] Thus, arrests for fistfighting and the like during youth may ***not*** be enough to establish "moral turpitude" sufficient to disqualify an applicant. Rather, this can be viewed as "adolescent behavior" which does not necessarily bear on the applicant's present fitness to practice law. [Hallinan v. Committee of Bar Examiners, *supra*, §42]

2) **Civil disobedience:** [§51] Nonviolent civil disobedience may also be insufficient grounds for denying admission to practice, since it may often be committed by "persons of the highest moral courage," and hence may not affect their qualification to practice law. [*See* Hallinan v. Committee of Bar Examiners, *supra*]

(d) **Effect of concealment:** [§52] Even though conduct by the applicant does not itself demonstrate a lack of good moral character, it still must be disclosed in response to inquiry by the bar examiners. *Concealment or false statements* by the applicant in response to such inquiry is *itself* evidence of sufficient lack of moral character to justify denial of the application. It makes no difference that the concealment is not discovered until after the applicant is admitted to practice, because a lawyer is subject to disciplinary sanctions (*e.g.*, disbarment) for making a *materially* false statement or for deliberately failing to disclose a *material* fact in her application for admission. [Model Rule 8.1; DR 1-101; *In re* Bogart, 9 Cal. 3d 743 (1973)]

    (e) **Rehabilitation as mitigating factor:** [§53]   An applicant whose past record does contain acts of moral turpitude may still gain admission by demonstrating *sufficient rehabilitation* of character. The courts seem inclined to reward self-improvement by the applicant—especially where other evidence indicates that the applicant is presently fit to practice law. [March v. Committee of Bar Examiners, 67 Cal. 2d 718 (1967)]

  (3) **Political activity:** [§54]   A lawyer is sworn to uphold the Constitution and laws of the United States and the state in which the lawyer is admitted to practice.

    (a) **Refusal to take oath to support Constitution:** [§55]   An applicant who refuses to take the *required oath* to support the federal and state constitutions may be *denied admission*, since there has been held to be a rational connection between this requirement and the practice of law. [Law Students Research Council v. Wadmond, 401 U.S. 154 (1971)]

    (b) **Membership in Communist Party:** [§56]   However, even *actual* membership in the Communist Party was held not to be a sufficient inference of "bad moral character" *per se* to permit exclusion from the practice of law. [Schware v. Board of Bar Examiners, *supra*, §29]

e. **Duty of lawyers not to aid admission of the unqualified:** [§57]   Many states require an applicant to submit letters of reference from lawyers as part of the application for admission to the bar.

  (1) **ABA Model Rules:** [§58]   The Model Rules prohibit a lawyer writing such a letter from:

    (i)   Knowingly making a false statement of material fact;

    (ii) Failing to disclose a fact necessary to correct a misapprehension known to have arisen in the matter; or

      (iii) Knowingly failing to respond to a lawful demand for nonconfidential information about an applicant.

      [Model Rule 8.1]

  (2) **ABA Code:** [§59] The ABA Code, on the other hand, states that a lawyer may not further the application of a person "known by him to be unqualified in respect to character, education, or other relevant attribute." [DR 1-101(B)]

      (a) **No investigation required:** [§60] The lawyer need not specially investigate the candidate, but must "satisfy himself" about the applicant's moral character. [EC 1-3]

      (b) **No duty to judge qualifications:** [§61] The duty of the lawyer is not to judge the applicant but to *report* "all unfavorable information" to the proper officials. [EC 1-3]

f. **Admission of lawyers licensed to practice in another state:** [§62] Conditions for admission to the bar are determined by each state. There is no constitutional duty to permit out-of-state lawyers to practice within the state. [Norfolk & Western Railway v. Beatty, 400 F. Supp. 234 (S.D. Ill), *aff'd*, 423 U.S. 1209 (1975)]

  (1) **Admission to general practice:** [§63] Requirements for an out-of-state lawyer to be admitted to general practice within a state vary widely.

      (a) **Admission by reciprocity:** [§64] A number of states admit practicing lawyers from other states without a bar examination, provided the lawyer has actively practiced in the first state for a certain period of time (usually four to six years).

        1) **Note:** Most of these states limit such admission to lawyers from *other states that allow reciprocity*, disqualifying lawyers from states that do not grant such rights. Such a limitation does not violate the Equal Protection Clause. [Goldsmith v. Pringle, 399 F. Supp. 620 (D. Colo. 1975); Hawkins v. Moss, 503 F.2d 1171 (4th Cir. 1974)]

      (b) **Separate examination:** [§65] Other states require lawyers to pass a written examination in addition to having practiced in the first state for the requisite period. [*See* Cal. Bus. & Prof. Code §6062(d); O'Neal v. Thompson, 551 F.2d 485 (2d Cir. 1977)—Nevada]

(2) **Admission to practice pro hac vice:** [§66]   Often, an out-of-state lawyer merely wishes to appear in the courts of a sister state in connection with a *particular* case ("pro hac vice").

    (a) **Normally granted as matter of comity:** [§67]   While such permission is discretionary, most courts will allow an out-of-state lawyer to appear and litigate a particular case as a matter of reciprocity or comity with the courts of the state in which the lawyer is admitted.

        1) **Note:** Such permission does *not* justify the out-of-state lawyer's opening a local office (except for the limited purpose of preparing for trial in the particular case) or engaging in any other facet of a general law practice. [Spivak v. Sachs, 16 N.Y.2d 163 (1965)]

        2) **Effect:** Once so admitted, the out-of-state lawyer is subject to local professional standards and ethical rules and can be disciplined just as any other lawyer. [State v. Kavanaugh, 243 A.2d 225 (N.J. 1968)]

    (b) **Some courts restrict:** [§68]   Some states are more restrictive than others and limit appearances pro hac vice—*e.g.*, by requiring that a local lawyer be associated in every case, by setting special qualifications (experience, etc.) for the out-of-state lawyer, or by limiting the number of appearances the lawyer can make. Such requirements are generally valid and do not raise constitutional questions. [Martin v. Walton, 357 P.2d 782 (Kan. 1960), *aff'd*, 368 U.S. 25 (1961)]

        1) **Exception—inadequate local counsel:** [§69]   However, the broad powers of state courts to limit appearances pro hac vice cannot be used to block adequate representation in local civil rights cases. Thus, *where adequate local counsel is unavailable* due to racial bias or prejudice, local rules that would effectively exclude out-of-state lawyers from appearing in such cases have been invalidated. [Sanders v. Russell, 401 F.2d 241 (5th Cir. 1968)]

        2) **Exception—no arbitrary limit on appearances:** [§70] Furthermore, the reasonable interests of the state do not justify an arbitrary numerical limit on the number of an out-of-state lawyer's appearances where that lawyer has associated with local counsel and has particular expertise in a field. [McKenzie v. Burris, 500 S.W.2d 357 (Ark. 1973)]

    3) **Exception—federal courts:** [§71] *Federal* district courts do *not* have discretion to deny admission pro hac vice to a lawyer *admitted* to and in good standing with the *state bar*, absent a showing of misconduct that would justify disbarment of one already admitted to practice before the court. [*In re* Admission of Lumumba, 526 F. Supp. 163 (S.D.N.Y. 1981)] (*See* discussion of admission to practice in federal system, below.)

2. Admission to Practice in the Federal System

a. **Separate requirements for admission:** [§72] Admission to the bar of a state does not confer the right to practice in federal courts. Rather, **each** court at **each level** of the federal judicial system independently grants admission pursuant to its own rules.

  (1) **No separate examination:** [§73] Most federal courts do not require passage of a federal bar examination in order to practice in the system. They simply require that the candidate be a member of the bar of the state in which the court sits—although a separate application for admission still must be made. [*In re* Dreier, 258 F.2d 68 (3d Cir. 1958)]

    (a) **Course requirements:** [§74] In response to concerns about the competency of trial lawyers, however, a few federal courts now require that applicants complete certain courses relevant thereto (*e.g.,* trial advocacy, professional responsibility, and federal civil and criminal procedure). [*See* Brown v. McGarr, 583 F. Supp. 734 (N.D. Ill. 1984)]

  (2) **"Reciprocity" among federal courts:** [§75] Although admission to one federal court does not automatically admit a lawyer to practice before another federal court, most court rules do permit such admission on a pro forma application by the lawyer to the second court.

b. **Validity of state regulation applied to those engaged exclusively in "federal" practice:** [§76] The question has arisen whether a person who is engaged exclusively in a "federal" practice (*e.g.,* bankruptcy, antitrust) must be admitted to the bar in the state in which she practices.

  (1) **Where specific federal regulation of practice exists:** [§77] If federal legislation provides for admission to and regulation of a particular area of practice, federal law **preempts** any state regulation of that practice.

    (a) **Example:** State statutes barring "nonlawyers" from practicing law within the state cannot be applied to a nonlawyer **patent agent** who is admitted to practice before the U.S. Patent Office and who **limits practice** to patent law. [Sperry v. State of Florida *ex rel.* Florida Bar, 373 U.S. 379 (1963)]

(b) **Example:** The same applies to any other federal administrative agency that prescribes standards for practice before the agency. Any person meeting such standards is entitled to practice before the federal agency regardless of state laws prohibiting unauthorized practice of law. [State Bar of Wisconsin v. Keller, 374 U.S. 102 (1963)]

(2) **Where no federal regulation exists:** [§78] The rule is less clear where no specific federal regulations exist. This area includes a large body of "federal law" (*e.g.*, bankruptcy, antitrust, securities regulation) which is litigated exclusively or primarily in federal courts.

(a) **Appearances pro hac vice:** [§79] Where an out-of-state lawyer appears in *federal court* on a particular matter involving federal law, the state in which the federal court is located may *not* restrict such appearances by (among other things) refusing to allow the lawyer to sue in state courts to collect her fee. [Spanos v. Skouras Theatres Corp., 364 F.2d 161 (2d Cir. 1966)—immaterial that trial in federal court required California lawyer to live in New York for over five years]

1) **Rationale:** The Privileges and Immunities Clause of the U.S. Constitution guarantees a citizen with a federal claim or defense the right to employ an out-of-state lawyer to assist in the case.

(b) **Continuous federal practice in state:** [§80] On the other hand, a state *may* properly prevent a lawyer not admitted to practice in the state from maintaining a *continuous practice* there, even though the practice is limited to "federal matters." [Ginsburg v. Kovrack, 139 A.2d 889 (Pa. 1958)—D.C. attorney admitted to practice before federal court in Pennsylvania could *not* maintain office in Philadelphia to conduct "practice of federal law"]

3. **Practice of International Law:** [§81] A foreign lawyer engaged in international practice has *no* established right to practice in a particular U.S. jurisdiction or forum.

a. **Law offices:** [§82] States may properly enjoin foreign lawyers from maintaining an office within the state and giving advice on foreign legal proceedings. [*See In re* Roel, 3 N.Y.2d 224 (1957); Bluestein v. State Bar, 23 Cal. 3d 162 (1974)]

b. **Supreme Court practice:** [§83] The United States Supreme Court rules provide that a foreign lawyer may appear before it *pro hac vice* at the discretion of the Court, and if associated with an American lawyer may be admitted to practice before the Supreme Court. [Sup. Ct. R. 6]

    c.   **State licensing:** [§84]   A few states (*e.g.,* New York) now specially license foreign lawyers as "legal consultants" to enable them to render advice as to the law of countries in which they are admitted to practice. [N.Y. Ct. Appeals R. 521]

C.   PREVENTING UNAUTHORIZED PRACTICE OF LAW

    1.   **Basic Considerations**

        a.   **Laypersons may represent themselves:** [§85]   A layperson is not required to seek legal assistance and may appear in court "in propria persona." The layperson is said to be "ordinarily exposing only himself to possible injury." [EC 3-7]

            (1)   **Criminal cases—constitutional right:** [§86]   Moreover, in criminal cases, the Supreme Court has held that defendants have a constitutional right to represent themselves. [Faretta v. California, 422 U.S. 806 (1975)]

        b.   **Only lawyers may represent persons other than themselves:** [§87]   However, lawyers are given the exclusive privilege of practicing law on behalf of others. This privilege is said to be based upon the two attributes for which persons admitted to the legal profession are examined: (i) *competence*—"the educated ability of the lawyer to relate the general body and philosophy of law to a specific legal problem," and (ii) *integrity*—the ethical standards of the profession which are vital because of the fiduciary nature of the attorney-client relationship. [EC 3-1, 3-5; Lawline v. American Bar Association, 956 F.2d 1378 (7th Cir. 1992)]

    2.   **Activities That Constitute "Practice of Law":** [§88]   The term "practice of law" is not defined by statute, and the ABA Code declares a definition to be "neither necessary nor desirable." [EC 3-5; *compare* Model Rule 5.5, Comment] The courts have therefore had to attach meaning to this term in specific situations.

        a.   **Tests applied—in general:** [§89]   Courts have generally applied one of two tests in determining whether a particular service or activity by nonlawyers constitutes the practice of law.

            (1)   **"History and custom":** [§90]   Decisions sometimes turn on whether the activity *traditionally* has been handled by lawyers. [State Bar v. Arizona Land Title & Trust Co., 366 P.2d 1 (Ariz. 1961)]

                (a)   **Criticism:** This test ignores changing conditions and focuses more upon lawyers' vested interests than clients' needs.

(2) **ABA test—"need for professional judgment":** [§91] The ABA Code purports to shift the focus from the lawyer to the client and recommends that each situation be judged by the need for a lawyer's "professional legal judgment"—*i.e.*, a judgment based upon knowledge of the general body and philosophy of law. [EC 3-5]

b. **Judicial determinations in specific areas**

(1) **Appearance in judicial proceedings:** [§92] The complexities of court procedure and the importance of having proceedings run smoothly and efficiently have been stated as the reasons for making representation in court proceedings the *sole* privilege of lawyers. [Bilodeau v. Antal, 455 A.2d 1037 (N.H. 1983)]

(2) **Appearance in administrative proceedings:** [§93] State and federal administrative agencies and boards often permit qualified laypersons to appear before them representing clients (*e.g.*, accountants are often permitted to represent clients before taxing authorities).

(3) **Settlement negotiations:** [§94] Since they are a part of adversary proceedings, settlement negotiations are also the sole province of lawyers. Thus, for example, an insurance adjuster who solicited the claims of accident victims and attempted, for a fee, to negotiate a compromise with the tortfeasor's insurer was guilty of the unauthorized practice of law. [Dauphin County Bar Association v. Mazzacaro, 351 A.2d 299 (Pa. 1976)]

(4) **Drafting documents:** [§95] The drafting of documents that *affect substantial legal rights or obligations* of others is generally considered the practice of law and the privilege of lawyers alone. This is based on the superior ability the lawyer is presumed to have as a result of general training in the law.

(5) **"Scrivening":** [§96] While drafting agreements for others is clearly the practice of law, filling in blanks in standard forms may be regarded as a clerical function (for "scriveners"), and as such may properly be performed by laypersons. The difficult issue, of course, is the point at which "scrivening" by laypersons becomes "drafting" (*i.e.*, unauthorized practice).

(a) **Real estate brokers:** [§97] It is customary for real estate brokers to fill in the blanks in offers to purchase land that they procure. Such activities do *not* constitute the practice of law as long as the contract forms are simple or standardized and the broker charges *no separate fee* (other than a commission) for such work. [Chicago Bar Association v. Quinlan & Tyson, 214 N.E.2d 771 (Ill. 1966)]

(b) **Title insurance escrow companies:** [§98]   Again, to the extent that standardized forms are used, most courts today permit title insurance and escrow companies to fill in the blanks in mortgages, deeds, etc., according to information furnished by the parties to the sale.

(6) **Giving advice:** [§99]   Giving individualized advice respecting legal rights or obligations may be regarded as the practice of law, particularly where a fee is required for such advice.

(a) **Tax advice:** [§100]   Tax advice by laypersons *may* constitute the unauthorized practice of law. The reasoning is that tax law is drawn from many other areas (*e.g.*, corporations, property, constitutional law, etc.) and thus especially requires a lawyer's general knowledge. [*See In re* Florida Bar, 355 So. 2d 766 (Fla. 1978)]

1) **Preparation of returns:** [§101]   However, an accountant *may* properly prepare *income or estate tax returns*. The courts distinguish this function from the giving of advice on the ground that any questions of law arising in connection with tax returns are merely *incidental* (whereas legal questions are the *sole* basis for tax advice).

(b) **Estate planning:** [§102]   Along the same lines, it is unauthorized practice of law for a layperson to draft a will or prepare an estate plan for another person. [Oregon State Bar v. Miller & Co., 385 P.2d 181 (Or. 1963)]

(7) **General publications:** [§103]   On the other hand, the publication by a layperson of *a book or pamphlet* containing *general* advice (*i.e.*, not calculated to apply to a particular individual) does not constitute the practice of law. [*See* New York County Lawyers Association v. Dacey, 21 N.Y.2d 694 (1967)—Dacey's "do-it-yourself" probate kit permissible because all persons have the right to represent themselves if they choose to do so]

(8) **"Do-it-yourself" divorce clinics:** [§104]   Some jurisdictions have held that low-cost advice on divorces offered by nonlawyer clinics is both the unauthorized practice of law and an interference with family relations. [*See* Florida Bar v. Furman, 451 So. 2d 808 (Fla. 1984)]

(a) **Divorce kits:** [§105]   However, the courts have split on whether the sale of "do-it-yourself" divorce *publications* constitutes unauthorized practice of law. Some cases, following the rationale in *Dacey, supra,* have upheld the right to advertise and sell such kits. Other cases are contra. [*Compare* Oregon State Bar v. Gilchrist, 538 P.2d 913 (Or. 1975), *with* Florida Bar v. Stupica, 300 So. 2d 683 (Fla. 1974)]

(9) **Prisoner legal assistance by laypersons:** [§106]   State penal systems often seek to restrict "jailhouse lawyers" (prisoners who assist fellow inmates in seeking post-conviction relief, generally through petitions for writs of habeas corpus). Such activities are usually prohibited as the unauthorized practice of law.

(a) **Necessity of alternative relief:** [§107]   In several cases, however, the Supreme Court has struck down state regulations designed to suppress this assistance, where ***the state has not provided reasonable alternative forms of legal aid for prisoners.*** Under these circumstances, inmates are free to use whatever help they can find, including assistance from other prisoners. [Wolff v. McDonnell, 418 U.S. 539 (1974); *and see* Constitutional Law Summary]

3. **Specific Classes of Persons Prohibited from Practicing Law:** [§108]   State laws typically contain a general provision that no person may practice law unless he or she is an active member of the state bar. [*See* Cal. Bus. & Prof. Code §6125] In addition, statutes in many states expressly prohibit the practice of law by certain classes of persons.

a. **Judges and court officers:** [§109]   Judges, court commissioners, and court clerks are usually prohibited from practicing law, ***whether or not*** they are also licensed attorneys. In the case of judges, the prohibition may be constitutional as well as statutory. (*See infra,* §995 for Code of Judicial Conduct prohibition.)

(1) **Exception—inferior courts:** [§110]   A limited exception is sometimes made for judges of the lowest state courts of record, provided they do not practice before these same courts. [*See* Cal. Gov't Code §68083— exception for judge of justice court]

b. **Law students and law clerks:** [§111]   Clerks or students not admitted to practice may perform research or administrative tasks in a law firm, but they may not do any acts that would constitute the practice of law (such as advising clients or appearing in court).

(1) **Exception for student training programs:** [§112]   Several states have authorized law students to engage in a variety of legal activities. These often include preparation of pleadings or briefs, interviewing clients and

witnesses, participation in negotiations, and appearances in court. [*See* Ill. Sup. Ct. R. 711]

(a) **Lawyer's supervision required:** [§113] Such activity must take place under the guidance and supervision of a licensed lawyer, and the lawyer must assume *personal* responsibility for the student's work.

(2) **Further exception for "nonadvocate" court appearances:** [§114] Courts in some states also permit both law students and law clerks to respond in court to a calendar call or present ex parte orders for signature by the court. [People v. Alexander, 202 N.E.2d 841 (Ill. 1964)]

c. **Corporations:** [§115] The general rule in most states is that a corporation cannot practice law; *i.e.*, it cannot represent a client directly or furnish representation through its employees who are licensed attorneys. Thus, an insurance company usually may not use an in-house lawyer to represent one of its insureds. [Gardner v. North Carolina State Bar, 341 S.E.2d 517 (N.C. 1986)]

(1) **Rationale:** The reason for this limitation is said to be the *relationship of trust and confidence* essential between lawyer and client. When the lawyer owes primary allegiance to the corporation (as the lawyer's immediate employer), there is a substantial risk that the lawyer's loyalty to the client may be incidental or divided.

(2) **Exceptions—group legal services and professional law corporations:** [§116] Two important exceptions to this general rule exist for corporations providing group legal services on a nonprofit basis (*see infra*, §§772-777) and for professional law corporations (*see infra*, §743).

(3) **No corporate self-representation:** [§117] A corruption of the above rationale in many states also prohibits a corporation from representing *itself*; *i.e.*, it may not appear in court through its officers and directors. Thus, for example, a corporation must hire a lawyer to file suit to collect its bills. [Remole Soil Service v. Benson, 215 N.E.2d 678 (Ill. 1966); *but see contra*, Cal. Civ. Proc. Code §116.530—small claims court]

(4) **Collection agencies:** [§118] Most courts hold, however, that collection agencies may sue in their own name to enforce debts *assigned* to them for collection. This is not considered unlawful practice of law because assignment of the debt confers *legal title* thereto upon the agency, thus making it the "real party in interest" for purposes of litigation. [Cohn v. Thompson, 128 Cal. App. 783 (1932)]

4. **Efforts to Prohibit Practice of Law by Nonlawyers:** [§119]   Sanctions against a nonlawyer practitioner include *injunctions, criminal prosecution, or denial of the right to fees* for the unauthorized services.

    a. **Obligations of attorney in preventing unauthorized practice:** [§120]   ABA Model Rule 5.5 and ABA Code Canon 3 require lawyers to "assist in preventing the unauthorized practice of law." The Rules impose four specific duties in this regard:

        (1) *A lawyer may not practice law in violation of professional regulations* in that jurisdiction (*e.g.*, in a state where the lawyer is not admitted to practice). [Model Rule 5.5(a); DR 3-101(B)]

        (2) *A lawyer may not "aid" a nonlawyer* in activities that constitute the "practice of law." [Model Rule 5.5(b); DR 3-101(A)]

        (3) *A lawyer may not* (with certain limited exceptions) *share legal fees with a nonlawyer.* [Model Rule 5.4(a); DR 3-102; *and see infra*, §§753-759]

        (4) *A lawyer may not enter a partnership with a nonlawyer* if *any* of the partnership activities include the practice of law. [Model Rule 5.4(b); DR 3-103; *and see infra*, §750]

    b. **Bar opinions on what constitutes unauthorized practice:** [§121]   Traditionally, the bar's unauthorized practice committees have stipulated what is and is not the unauthorized practice of law, and lawyers have felt constrained to follow these decisions.

        (1) **Extending availability of legal services:** [§122]   Related to the expansion of activity by nonlawyers is the increasing public demand for services historically considered to be the "practice of law." Such services may range from appearances before courts or administrative agencies to counseling on leases, contracts, and other legal instruments. The bar has been justly criticized for devoting more attention to unauthorized practice issues than to the need for legal help among large groups of citizens.

        (2) **Antitrust violation:** [§123]   Indeed, one federal district court has held that unauthorized practice opinions issued by voluntary bar associations can violate the antitrust laws in that the lawyers' response to them is a "group boycott" of the firms engaged in the alleged unauthorized practice. [Surety Title Insurance Agency v. Virginia State Bar, 431 F. Supp. 298 (E.D. Va. 1977)]

II. THE CONTRACT BETWEEN CLIENT AND LAWYER

chapter approach

This chapter covers the lawyer-client relationship from its beginning to end.

Important points to remember about the **formation** of the relationship include:

1. The lawyer need **not accept** every case and should **reject** some cases, *e.g.*, those brought for harassment, unsupportable by law or a good faith argument for changing the law, where lawyer is not competent to effectively represent the client, where a disciplinary standard would be violated, etc.

2. The lawyer should reach an agreement with the client on the **scope and objectives** of the representation.

During the representation, issues arise about:

1. The appropriate **spheres of authority**. Recall that the **client** makes the ultimate decisions on matters such as settlement, compromise, or dismissal; the **lawyer** has control over the procedural matters of the case.

2. The **lawyer's duties** to the client:

    a. **Duty of competence**—The lawyer must have the ability to handle the case and perform those services with care.

    b. **Duty of diligence**—The lawyer must act with reasonable promptness in representing the client.

    c. **Duty of communication**—The lawyer must keep the client informed about the case.

    d. **Duty of zealous representation**—The lawyer is an advocate and must present the client's position zealously but within the bonds of the law.

    e. **Duty of confidentiality**—The lawyer must keep the client's secrets (*see* Chapter III).

    f. **Duty of loyalty**—The lawyer must avoid conflicts of interests (*see* Chapter IV).

    g. **Duty to safeguard client's property**—The lawyer must keep the client's funds and property safe and separate from the lawyer's assets.

3. The **client's duty**: In return for the lawyer's duties, the client owes the lawyer the duty to **pay a reasonable legal fee**.

Regarding the termination of the relationship, keep in mind that the *client* can fire the lawyer at any time (although may be liable for some or all of the fee) but the *lawyer* generally may not terminate the relationship unless circumstances justify it and steps are taken to protect the client.

A. INTRODUCTION [§124]

The relationship between client and lawyer is best understood as a contract between them. The terms of that contract are implied by custom, but, with few exceptions, the terms may be varied by agreement between client and lawyer.

1. **The Lawyer as Fiduciary:** [§125]   A lawyer stands in a fiduciary relationship to a client. That does not change the contractual character of their relationship, but it means that changes in the customary contract will be construed against the lawyer and closely scrutinized for fairness.

2. **The Lawyer as Agent:** [§126]   It is also often helpful to see a lawyer as an agent of the client, subject to the limitations imposed by the law of agency. Thus, for example, a lawyer may not be hired to perform an illegal act for a client any more than the client could hire any other agent to do something illegal.

B. FORMATION OF LAWYER-CLIENT RELATIONSHIP—LAWYER'S DUTIES REGARDING ACCEPTING EMPLOYMENT

1. **No Obligation to Accept Every Case:** [§127]   Unlike English barristers (who *must* accept cases within their areas of experience upon tender of a proper fee), American lawyers need not take every matter presented to them. [EC 2-26—"A lawyer is under no obligation to act as adviser or advocate for every person who may wish to become his client"]

2. **Ethical Obligation to Provide Representation Where Needed:** [§128] Nevertheless, the freedom of lawyers to select their clients does not override the interest of each person in obtaining legal representation when needed.

    a. **ABA standards:** [§129]   Both the ABA Code and the Model Rules assert that each lawyer has a personal obligation to serve persons who could not normally afford legal services. However, failure to meet the obligation is not a disciplinable offense under either standard. [Model Rule 6.1; EC 2-25]

    b. **State standards:** [§130]   Some state regulations go even further and make it a positive *duty* for lawyers to represent "the causes of the defenseless or the oppressed," the breach of which could result in suspension or disbarment. [*See* Cal. Bus. & Prof. Code §§6068(h), 6103]

c. **Appointment of counsel:** [§131]   A lawyer's duty to represent a client when the lawyer would not choose to do so is most apparent where the client has a *constitutional right to counsel* (*e.g.*, in a criminal trial) but cannot afford to hire a lawyer. Most courts now have paid public defenders or panels of lawyers who volunteer for such cases, but in their absence, it is the *moral obligation* of every lawyer to accept court appointment to represent an indigent client. [Model Rule 6.2; EC 2-29; State v. Richardson, 631 P.2d 221 (Kan. 1981)]

(1) **Grounds for rejecting an appointment:** [§132]   While lawyers are reluctant to offend a judge who seeks to appoint them in such cases, Model Rule 6.2 identifies three situations in which an appointment may be refused; *i.e.*, where there is:

(a) *A violation of a Model Rule*—*e.g.*, where the representation would involve a conflict of interest;

(b) *An unreasonable financial burden*—*i.e.*, a burden "so great as to be unjust" (this standard is affected by §133, below); or

(c) *Client repugnance* that would affect lawyer's ability to represent client adequately.

(2) **Right of lawyer to payment if lawyer is appointed to represent client:** [§133]   Contrary to prior tradition, however, some cases have now held that it is unconstitutional to require a lawyer to represent an indigent client without compensation by some public agency. [Stephan v. Smith, 747 P.2d 816 (Kan. 1987); DeLiso v. Alaska Superior Court, 740 P.2d 437 (Alaska 1987)]

(3) **Duty in civil cases:** [§134]   While a federal court may "request" a lawyer to represent an indigent client in a civil case, the Supreme Court has held that 42 U.S.C. section 1915 does not permit the court to order that the lawyer do so. The Court left open whether a federal court has "inherent authority" to so order. [Mallard v. United States District Court, 490 U.S. 296 (1989)]

3. **Duty to Reject Certain Cases:** [§135]   The ABA Code and the Model Rules specify seven situations in which the lawyer *should refuse* employment:

a. **Where client's motive is harassment:** [§136]   A lawyer may not bring an action, conduct a defense, assert a position in litigation, or take other steps where the client's motive is to *harass* or *maliciously injure* any person. [Model Rule 4.4; DR 2-109(A)(1)]

b. **Where client's legal position is unsupportable:** [§137] A lawyer may not present a claim or defense in litigation that is neither warranted under existing law nor supportable by "good faith argument" for a change in the law. [Model Rule 3.1; DR 2-109(A)(2)]

c. **Where lawyer is unable to act competently:** [§138] A lawyer may not accept a case that the lawyer is too *busy* or too *inexperienced* to handle competently. [Model Rule 1.1; EC 2-30]

d. **Where lawyer's personal feelings interfere:** [§139] If a lawyer's personal feelings (as distinguished from community pressure) about a prospective case or client are so strong that they might impair her effective representation of that client, then the lawyer should decline the case. [Model Rule 6.2(c); EC 2-30]

e. **Where client is already represented:** [§140] A lawyer who knows that the client has already retained counsel may accept the case only if the other counsel approves, withdraws, or has been discharged by the client. [EC 2-30]

f. **Where disciplinary standard would be violated:** [§141] If representation of a client would force the lawyer to violate any disciplinary standard or other law, the lawyer must decline the case. [Model Rule 1.16(a)(1)]

g. **Where lawyer's physical or mental condition is impaired:** [§142] If the lawyer's physical or mental condition would materially impair the lawyer's ability to represent the client, the lawyer must decline the case. [Model Rule 1.16(a)(2)]

4. **Duties to a Prospective Client:** [§143] Finally, although ordinarily no lawyer-client relationship is formed until both lawyer and client agree, the lawyer owes some duties even to a prospective client who consults the lawyer about obtaining legal assistance.

a. **Duty not to mislead prospective client into believing lawyer-client relationship has been formed:** [§144] Prospective clients are of varying degrees of sophistication and experience with lawyers. If a client manifests an intent that lawyer act for the client and the lawyer fails to negate the client's expectation, an obligation to so act may be found even if the lawyer did not in fact consent to do so. [Togstad v. Vesely, Otto, Miller & Keefe, 291 N.W.2d 686 (Minn. 1980)]

b. **Duty to protect confidential information:** [§145] As explained more fully later in this Summary, a lawyer must protect the confidential information revealed by a prospective client as fully as that revealed by a client. (*See infra*, §§326-327.)

(1) **Caution:** Some law firms have found themselves disqualified from acting on behalf of other clients in later matters because of what they are told in meetings with prospective clients. Thus, the ABA has advised lawyers to require prospective clients to reveal as little confidential information as possible in the initial inteview with a lawyer. [ABA Opn. 90-358]

c. **Duty to give competent legal advice:** [§146] Even if a lawyer declines a case, the lawyer may not give the prospective client misleading information about the law or the prospective client's need for legal services. [Miller v. Metzinger, 91 Cal. 3d 31 (App. 1979)—lawyer must warn prospective client that statute of limitations is about to expire]

C. REACHING AGREEMENT ON SCOPE AND OBJECTIVES OF REPRESENTATION

1. **In General:** [§147] A lawyer's obligation to a client is to act in a manner reasonably calculated to advance the client's lawful objectives.

2. **Definition of Scope and Objectives of Representation:** [§148] Consistent with the contractual nature of the lawyer's relationship with a client, the scope and objectives of a given representation may be defined and limited by agreement between lawyer and client. [Model Rule 1.2(c); DR 7-101(A)(1)]

   a. **In absence of agreement:** [§149] In the absence of other agreement, a lawyer is to pursue a client's objectives, as defined in client communications with the lawyer, in all reasonably available legal ways.

   b. **Limitation of representation to particular subjects:** [§150] A lawyer and client may agree that the lawyer will undertake to address some but not all legal needs of the client. For example, the lawyer may undertake to incorporate the client's business, but not to give the client income tax advice.

   c. **Limitation on legal remedies to be pursued in representation:** [§151] A lawyer and client may similarly agree that the lawyer will seek to resolve a matter short of litigation or will not pursue remedies against particular persons.

3. **Informed Consent of Client Required to Limit Scope or Objectives:** [§152] In general, the law assumes that a client wants to pursue all lawful objectives in all lawful ways. Thus, informed client consent is required for decisions to limit the scope and objectives of representation.

   a. **Lawyer's role in counseling about alternatives:** [§153] The lawyer has a fiduciary relationship with a client and one of the lawyer's roles is to ensure that the client understands the advantages and risks associated with any limitations on the representation. [Model Rule 1.2(c)]

b. **Lawyer should document agreement with client:** [§154] While agreements limiting the scope or objectives of representation need not be in writing, in any subsequent litigation, the burden of proving the contents of such an agreement with the client will be on the lawyer; thus, a written agreement is advisable.

D. SPHERES OF AUTHORITY OF LAWYER AND CLIENT

1. **In General:** [§155] The fact that a lawyer is retained to represent the client does *not* mean that the lawyer assumes complete control over the case. The client remains the party in interest and, with some exceptions, must be allowed to make ultimate decisions on the merits. [Model Rule 1.2(a); EC 7-7]

2. **Matters Within Authority of Client:** [§156] The decision on any matter that will substantially affect the client's rights must be made by the client. When such matters arise, the lawyer has a duty to advise the client on particular courses of action, but the decision itself rests with the client. [Model Rule 1.2(a); EC 7-7]

   a. **Settlement or compromise of action:** [§157] The lawyer may *not* settle or compromise a civil action without the authorization of the client. The same rule applies *a fortiori* to the entry of a plea in a criminal case. [Model Rule 1.2(a)]

      (1) **Effect of unauthorized settlement or compromise:** [§158] Most courts take the position that a lawyer is *presumed* to have the client's authority to negotiate a settlement or compromise. However, the presumption is rebuttable. [56 A.L.R.2d 1290 (1957)]

      (2) **Ratification by client:** [§159] The client may, however, *ratify* an unauthorized compromise or settlement agreed to by the lawyer. Indeed, such ratification may be *implied* unless the client disavows the compromise within a *reasonable time* after learning of it. [Yarnell v. Yorkshire Mills, 87 A.2d 192 (Pa. 1952)]

         (a) **Example:** Without Client's knowledge, Lawyer negotiates a settlement of Client's claim against Defendant and absconds with the proceeds. If Client promptly disavows the unauthorized settlement, Client's claim against Defendant is not affected. However, if Client brings suit against Defendant to recover the misappropriated monies, Client *thereby ratifies* the settlement, and is left with a claim only against the dishonest lawyer. [Navrides v. Zurich Insurance Co., 5 Cal. 3d 698 (1971)]

   b. **Dismissal or abandonment of case:** [§160] The client also has the sole power to authorize dismissal or otherwise to end a case on its merits.

(1) **Client may dismiss at any time:** [§161]   The client has the power to dismiss the case at any time regardless of the lawyer's wishes to proceed, even if the client signed a retainer expressly agreeing **not** to dismiss without the lawyer's consent. However, the client's dismissal of the case or direct settlement with the opposing party may entitle the lawyer to whatever fee was provided for in the retainer agreement in event of settlement.

(2) **Dismissals "without prejudice":** [§162]   A lawyer clearly has **no** authority to dismiss an action "**with** prejudice" (*i.e.*, barring relitigation) unless the client has authorized such dismissal. However, he may have implied authority to dismiss a case "**without** prejudice" (*i.e.*, no bar to relitigation) if the dismissal is **in the client's interest**—*e.g.*, when some tactical advantage may be gained by refiling the suit elsewhere, and the dismissal would not jeopardize the client's case (no problem of statute of limitations, etc.). [Northwest Realty v. Perez, 119 N.W.2d 114 (S.D. 1963)]

3.   **Matters Within Lawyer's Authority:** [§163]   While the substantive action (or defense) is the client's, the court proceedings to resolve the controversy are deemed within the primary control of the lawyer. Hence, the client usually may **not** act directly with respect to the details of litigation.

a.   **Procedural matters:** [§164]   As to most procedural matters, the **client has no formal authority**; and normally if the client does intervene, her actions will be disregarded by the court.

(1) **Rationale:** The orderly conduct of a case is best handled by lawyers. Moreover, it would invite chaos to allow an adversary to deal directly with the client so as to override the lawyer representing the client.

(2) **Scope:** [§165]   Within the scope of procedural matters are decisions as to: what suit to maintain; the court in which to file; the nature and content of pleadings, motions, discovery, etc.; and the making of **stipulations** affecting procedural matters (as distinguished from stipulations affecting the cause of action itself).

(3) **Exception—jury trial:** [§166]   It is for the **client** to decide whether or not to waive trial by jury. [Graves v. P.J. Taggares Co., 605 P.2d 348 (Wash. 1980)]

b.   **Admissions**

(1) **"Judicial admissions":** [§167]   Admissions of fact made by a lawyer in the pleadings or in the course of narrowing the issues for trial (*e.g.*, at the pretrial conference) are deemed "judicial admissions." As such they are **conclusive** and bind the client, unless the court permits them to be amended or withdrawn. (*See* Evidence Summary.)

(2) **Other admissions:** [§168] The rule is different, however, as to other admissions of fact made by the lawyer (*e.g.*, in negotiations or correspondence). These are not *conclusive* as to the client, but they are admissible in evidence against the client *if* the lawyer was authorized to speak for the client with respect to the subject in question. (*See* "vicarious admissions" in Evidence Summary.)

(3) **Relief for mistake or negligence:** [§169] Even where a lawyer's admission is binding on the client, the client may seek relief therefrom by moving promptly after discovering the matter and showing that the lawyer was unauthorized or mistaken. The court may, in the exercise of its *discretion*, set aside any judgment or order based on the unauthorized admission. If the court refuses such relief, the client's only remedy would be a *malpractice* action against the lawyer for any harm or loss resulting from the admission.

4. **Special Problem—Decision Making by Mentally Impaired Client:** [§170] Lawyers sometimes represent clients who are "under a disability," *i.e.*, whose "ability to make adequately considered decisions" is impaired, typically by old age. Insofar as possible, the lawyer is to maintain a normal relationship with such clients, including consulting with them about major decisions. [Model Rule 1.14(a); EC 7-12]

   a. **Appointment of guardian:** [§171] If the lawyer concludes that the client cannot adequately act in his own interest, the lawyer may seek appointment of a legal guardian to act for the client. [Model Rule 1.14(b)]

   b. **Application of these principles to representation of minors:** [§172] Because the law often treats minors *as if* they were mentally impaired, these principles apply to their representation as well. A lawyer must consult with a minor client and let the minor decide most matters within any client's authority to decide, but the lawyer must see that a guardian is appointed to decide matters for the minor where the law so requires.

E. FORMAL CONTRACTUAL DUTIES THAT LAWYERS OWE TO CLIENTS

1. **Duty of Competence:** [§173] The duty to represent a client competently has at least two components: (i) the *ability*—the knowledge and skill to perform the required services for the client, and (ii) *care*—the necessary thoroughness and preparation in performing the services. These combine as the first principle of the Model Rules. [Model Rule 1.1; DR 6-101]

   a. **Ability to represent client:** [§174] A lawyer may not attempt to handle a legal matter which she knows *or should know* she is not competent to handle, without *associating* a lawyer who is competent in the matter. [DR 6-101(A)(1); Lewis v. State Bar of California, 28 Cal. 3d 683 (1981)]

(1) **Exception—where competency anticipated:** [§175] A lawyer *may* accept such employment if that lawyer in good faith expects to become qualified to perform the necessary services. [EC 6-3] In this respect, the lawyer must diligently undertake whatever work or study is required to attain proficiency in the matter. [EC 6-4]

    (a) **Limitation:** Attempting to gain the requisite competency is *not* a proper course of action if it would result in *unreasonable delay or expense* to the client. [EC 6-3]

(2) **Association of competent counsel:** [§176] The appropriate solution when a lawyer faces a problem outside that lawyer's own area of competence is to associate another lawyer who is already proficient in the area. This is the *only proper course*, short of declining employment, when the lawyer is not and does not expect to become personally qualified. The association of co-counsel, of course, requires the client's consent. [EC 6-3; Horne v. Peckham, 97 Cal. App. 3d 404 (1979)]

(3) **Judicial criticism of lawyer competence:** [§177] On several occasions in recent years, former Chief Justice Burger accused the "majority of lawyers who appear in court" of not being sufficiently skilled to perform competently. He called for development of a specialized trial bar, perhaps analogous to British barristers. The proposal is unlikely to be adopted soon but promises to keep the public sensitive to and concerned about lawyer competence.

b. **Care in representing the client:** [§178] Even where the lawyer is capable of performing required services for the client, or where competent counsel is associated, the services must be performed *properly*. The Ethical Considerations urge a broader standard of care than the bare minimum of "nonnegligence." The lawyer should be motivated by *professional pride*, rather than by fear of malpractice suits or discipline. [EC 6-5]

(1) **Preparation:** [§179] The ABA Code and Model Rules state that a lawyer must not handle a matter without *adequate preparation*. [DR 6-101(A)(2); Model Rule 1.1]

(2) **Thoroughness:** [§180] A lawyer must also act with thoroughness appropriate to the complexity of each matter. [Model Rule 1.1]

c. **Incompetence as a basis for malpractice liability:** [§181] While professional discipline is possible in cases of incompetent representation, by far the most common remedy is a suit for professional malpractice against the lawyer. (*See infra*, §§899 *et seq.*)

d. **Incompetence as ground for setting aside judgments or convictions:** [§182] When the losing party seeks to have a judgment or conviction set aside because of the negligence or incompetence of that party's attorney, a conflict arises between the policy of *res judicata* (finality of judgment) and the goal of *justice in the individual case*.

(1) **Criminal cases:** [§183]   The arguments for setting aside a judgment for incompetency of counsel are strongest in a criminal case. Among other factors, the consequences of the incompetency are severe (loss of liberty or even life), and the stated goal of the criminal process is to obtain *justice* rather than merely convictions.

    (a) **Few convictions set aside:** [§184]   Relatively few cases have set aside a criminal conviction because of incompetency of counsel, and then only where the errors of defense counsel were so shocking that they deprived the accused of the constitutional right to *effective* counsel. [*See* McMann v. Richardson, 397 U.S. 759 (1970)]

    (b) **Present standard of "effective assistance":** [§185]   Today the standard of "effective assistance" is tougher. The old "farce and mockery" standard of *McMann v. Richardson* has been rejected. Under the new standard, a defendant must show that counsel's acts or omissions "were outside the wide range of professionally competent assistance." Furthermore, they must have caused *"actual prejudice,"* not just some "conceivable effect" on the outcome. [Strickland v. Washington, 466 U.S. 668 (1984)]

    (c) **Criminal appeals:** [§186]   The Supreme Court has also held that a criminal defendant is also entitled to effective assistance of counsel on appeal, at least on the first appeal as of right. [Evitts v. Lucey, 469 U.S. 387 (1985)]

(2) **Civil proceedings:** [§187]   Courts have been more reluctant to set aside *civil* judgments on the basis of negligence of counsel. The standard doctrine is that the client as principal is charged with the errors or incompetency of his lawyer-agent in a civil case. There are some qualifications, however.

    (a) **Default judgments:** [§188]   Where the lawyer's negligence results in entry of a default judgment against the client (*e.g.*, the lawyer failed to file answer within statutory period), courts are frequently willing to set aside the default judgment if there is a *reasonable excuse* for the lawyer's error (as opposed to the "busy lawyer" alibi). Here, the policy in favor of resolving litigation on the merits outweighs the policy that binds a client by the lawyer's errors. [Rudd v. Rogerson, 424 P.2d 776 (Colo. 1963)]

    (b) **Minority requires "justice in individual case":** [§189]   And there are a *few* decisions that argue for a client's right to "competent" representation in any proceeding—civil or criminal. These decisions hold that if the incompetence of counsel is so grievous as to deny justice in the individual case, a new trial should be granted the client. [Coerber v. Rath, 135 P.2d 228 (Colo. 1967)—setting aside default judgment and ordering new trial on merits where default had resulted from *inexcusable* neglect by counsel]

2. **Duty of Diligence:** [§190] In addition, the ABA Model Rules require a lawyer to "act with reasonable diligence and promptness in representing a client." [Model Rule 1.3] This provision was added to the Model Rules largely because "no professional shortcoming is more widely resented than procrastination." [Model Rule 1.3, comment]

   a. **ABA Code provision:** [§191] Ethical Consideration 6-4 of the ABA Code required lawyers to "give appropriate attention to" legal work, so the Model Rules do not constitute a change in policy, but a lawyer's lack of diligence is now a basis upon which professional discipline may be imposed.

3. **Duty of Communication:** [§192] Similarly, the ABA Model Rules require a lawyer to:

   (i) *Keep each client informed* about the status of the client's matters;

   (ii) *Comply promptly with reasonable client requests for information*; and

   (iii) *Provide clients with information* reasonably necessary to make informed decisions about the representation.

   [Model Rule 1.3]

   a. **Right to withhold certain information:** [§193] If disclosure of certain information would be likely to be "imprudent" (*e.g.*, where the information is a diagnosis that the client is mentally ill), such disclosure may be "delayed." However, the lawyer may not withhold information to serve the lawyer's own interest or convenience. [Model Rule 1.3, Comment]

   b. **No ABA Code counterpart:** [§194] Again, this rule has no counterpart in the ABA Code, although presumably lawyers have always been understood to have a duty to assist their clients to make informed decisions in the course of their cases.

4. **Duty of Zealous Representation**

   a. **ABA standards:** [§195] The ABA Code does not define "zealous representation" and the Model Rules do not use the term, but they require that the lawyer not "fail to seek the lawful objectives of the client through reasonably available means." [DR 7-101(A); *compare* Comment to Model Rule 3.1—"The advocate has a duty to use legal procedure for the fullest benefit of the client's cause"]

(1) **In litigation matters—doubts to be resolved in favor of client:** [§196] The lawyer must act as an *advocate* in *litigation* matters. This means that any doubts about the facts of the case or the bounds of the law applicable thereto should be resolved in favor of the client. As long as a good faith argument for the client's position can be made, the lawyer should make it—even if the lawyer does not personally believe that it will or should prevail. [Model Rule 3.1; EC 7-3, 7-4]

    (a) **Compare—greater detachment owed in nonadversary matters:** [§197] In contrast, the lawyer acts as an *adviser* in *nonlitigation* matters and owes the client a greater detachment. The lawyer should inform the client of possible adverse consequences of the facts and should give the client the benefit of the lawyer's professional judgment in charting the client's *future* dealings or conduct. In short, the adviser should make known possible pitfalls in advance so that the client may act accordingly. [Model Rule 2.1; EC 7-5]

b. **Lawyer need not adopt client's viewpoint personally:** [§198] The duty to provide "zealous" representation as an advocate does not obligate a lawyer personally to approve or adopt a client's viewpoints. Thus, a lawyer may properly take positions on public issues and espouse legal reforms that are *contrary* to the client's position, although the lawyer should do this "with circumspection" so as not to prejudice the client's rights. [Model Rule 1.2(b); EC 7-17]

c. **Duty to assert "technicalities":** [§199] To the extent that the client's interests are *advanced* or protected by reliance on "technicalities," the lawyer usually *owes a duty* to assert them. (For example, it would be incompetency for the lawyer to fail to plead the Statute of Frauds as a defense to a suit on an oral land sale contract.)

(1) **Exception—waiver in client's best interests:** [§200] On the other hand, it is not improper to waive or fail to assert a technicality where, in *the exercise of the lawyer's professional judgment*, this is in the client's best interests. Moreover, such a waiver is *not* a ground for a malpractice action against the lawyer. [DR 7-101(B)(1)]

    (a) **Example:** Where the opposing party has delayed in filing a pleading so that a default could be entered, the lawyer may conclude that it best serves the client's interests to call the oversight to the attention of the opposing party—rather than have the default entered and then try to resist a motion to set aside, which will likely be granted.

d. **Duty of lawyer for criminal defendant:** [§201] There is a strong public interest in seeing that *all* persons accused of a crime have the services of counsel. The fact that counsel is court-appointed, rather than privately retained, does not reduce the lawyer's obligation to provide *zealous* representation to an accused in a criminal case.

(1) **Conflicts of conscience:** [§202] Counsel for an accused may have personal doubts about the innocence of the client. Nevertheless, the lawyer fails to provide zealous representation—and may well deprive the client of constitutional rights—if the lawyer allows such feelings to affect the presentation of the client's case.

    (a) **Example:** Where a lawyer failed to submit relevant jury instructions and waived final argument because he *disbelieved* his client's story, the court granted habeas corpus, holding that the client had been denied his constitutional right to the "undivided allegiance and faithful service" of counsel. [Johns v. Smyth, 176 F. Supp. 949 (E.D. Va. 1959)]

    (b) **Compare—no duty to present perjury:** [§203] The lawyer's duty of zeal does not extend so far as to require or permit presentation of perjured evidence. Thus, where a client sought to change his planned truthful testimony to a lie and the lawyer threatened to tell the trier of fact if he did so, the lawyer was held not to have denied his client the effective assistance of counsel. [Nix v. Whiteside, 475 U.S. 157 (1986)]

(2) **Questionable appeals:** [§204] Similar problems may arise when counsel is appointed for an appeal requested by the defendant. The lawyer must recognize that his duties are those of an *active advocate supporting the appeal* to the best of his ability, as opposed to those of an "amicus curiae" advising the court on the merits of the appeal. [Anders v. California, 386 U.S. 738 (1967)]

(3) **Plea bargaining:** [§205] If the lawyer concludes after a full investigation that conviction of the client is likely, zealous representation requires seeking the permission of the client to engage in plea bargaining. [ABA Standards Relating to the Defense Function §6.1]

    (a) **Federal courts:** [§206] Some courts (including federal courts) will accept a guilty plea where the accused merely admits that there is a "factual basis" for the charge, but does not admit actual guilt.

        1) **Note:** There is no constitutional requirement that an accused admit guilt in pleading guilty. A plea of guilty is constitutionally valid even though accompanied by protestations of innocence. [North Carolina v. Alford, 400 U.S. 25 (1970); *and see* Criminal Procedure Summary]

    (b) **Admission of actual guilt:** [§207] Other courts, however, require the accused to admit actual guilt in order to plead guilty. If the lawyer believes the client innocent, the lawyer has a serious dilemma. Some authorities argue that the duty of zealous representation requires the lawyer to help the client make the best deal, honest or not. The better view, however, seems to be that the duty of zealous representation does not compel or permit the lawyer to falsely admit the client's guilt or help the client to do so.

5. **Duty of Confidentiality:** [§208] The duty of confidentiality is such a central obligation of a lawyer that it is considered in detail in Chapter III (*see infra*, §§325 *et seq.*).

6. **Duty of Loyalty:** [§209] The duty of loyalty—*i.e.*, the duty to avoid conflicts of interest—is of such importance that it too merits a full chapter. It is described in detail in Chapter IV, *infra*, §§383 *et seq.*

7. **Lawyer Duties with Regard to Client Property:** [§210] As another part of the broad fiduciary duties owed each client, a lawyer must keep the funds and property of clients *safe and entirely separate* from the lawyer's own assets. [Model Rule 1.15; DR 9-102; Cal. Rule 4-100]

   a. **Separate bank accounts:** [§211] All funds belonging to the client that are received by the lawyer must be deposited in one or more *separately identified* bank accounts (usually called "trust accounts" or "clients' funds accounts"). [Model Rule 1.15(a); DR 9-102(A)] It is proper to have only one separate trust account containing monies of various clients.

      (1) **No commingling:** [§212] In general, the lawyer must not deposit any personal funds in these bank accounts. [Model Rule 1.15(a); DR 9-102(A)]

         (a) **Bank charges:** [§213] A limited exception to this rule allows an attorney to deposit in the trust account amounts necessary to pay the *bank charges* thereon. [DR 9-102(A)(1)] However, the lawyer may *not* keep any sum of personal money in the trust account for other purposes (*e.g.*, as protection against bounced checks, etc.). [*See* Silver v. State Bar, 13 Cal. 3d 134 (1974)]

      (2) **Expenses advanced by client:** [§214] Under the ABA Code, a lawyer *need not* deposit in these accounts monies advanced by the client to cover *costs or expenses*. [DR 9-102(A)] However, some state rules are more restrictive and require such advances to be deposited in the trust account. [*See, e.g.,* Cal. Rule 4-100]

   b. **Withdrawals from joint funds:** [§215] A lawyer who receives money that belongs in part to the client and in part to the lawyer (*e.g.*, a settlement in a contingent fee case) must deposit the *entire* sum in the client's trust account.

      (1) **Undisputed fee:** [§216] If the lawyer's portion is undisputed and the amount is fixed, the lawyer must *withdraw it as soon as possible* (to prevent commingling with clients' funds). [*See* Cal. Rule 4-100; Black v. State Bar, 57 Cal. 2d 219 (1961)]

(2) **Disputed funds:** [§217]   But if the client *disputes* the lawyer's right to receive all or any portion of the funds, the disputed *portion* may not be withdrawn until the controversy is resolved. [Model Rule 1.15(c); DR 9-102(A)(2)]

c. **Disbursements from clients' funds:** [§218]   A lawyer holds the client's funds in a fiduciary capacity and cannot distribute them except as authorized by the client. Thus, without authorization, the lawyer cannot disburse funds even if the lawyer determines that the client owes the money involved (*e.g.,* paying the client's doctor or other creditors—including the lawyer—with proceeds from settlement). [*Jackson v. State Bar,* 15 Cal. 3d 372 (1975)]

d. **Duties regarding custody of clients' property (other than funds):** [§219]   As a fiduciary, the lawyer must identify and label securities and other property of the client upon receipt thereof, and must deposit such property at once in a *safe deposit box or other suitable storage facility*. [Model Rule 1.15(a); DR 9-102(B)]

e. **Other duties:** [§220]   The lawyer must also:

(i) *Notify the client* promptly upon receiving funds (*e.g.,* settlement check) or property for the client from a third party;

(ii) *Keep full and accurate records* of all funds and other property held for clients;

(iii) *Render periodic accountings* to clients of funds and property held on their behalf; and

(iv) *Promptly pay over* any funds or property a client requests and is entitled to receive.

[Model Rule 1.15(b); DR 9-102(B); Cal. Rule 4-100(B)]

F.   OBLIGATION OF CLIENT TO LAWYER—PAYING A FEE FOR LEGAL SERVICES

1. **Minimum Fee Schedules:** [§221]   In the past, some state and local bar associations published schedules of minimum fees for various kinds of legal services. In some instances, the fees in the schedules were offered merely as a "suggestion" of the "going rate" for particular services, but in other instances, lawyers were threatened with discipline if they regularly undercut the fees stated in the schedules.

a. **Violation of antitrust laws:** [§222]   In *Goldfarb v. Virginia State Bar* (*infra,* §781), the United States Supreme Court held that a fee schedule that had the *effect* of creating uniform fees for legal work connected with interstate commerce was illegal as price fixing under section 1 of the Sherman Act.

b.   **Fees a matter of private contract or legal decree:** [§223] The result of *Goldfarb* is that specific fees are no longer a matter for bar association determination or review. Fees are either the product of private negotiation between lawyer and client or are established by controlling legislation or court order.

2.   **Time at Which Agreement Is To Be Made:** [§224] Good practice dictates that fee arrangements be agreed upon *at the outset* of the attorney-client relationship. As a practical matter, it is not always easy for a lawyer to set a fee in advance of the work, but at least the *basis* of the fee should be agreed upon in advance (per hour, per diem, etc.). [EC 2-19]

a.   **Model Rules requirement:** [§225] At least when the lawyer has not regularly represented a client, the Model Rules *require* that the client be told the basis or rate of the fee before or within a reasonable time after commencing the representation. [Model Rule 1.5(b)]

b.   **Presumption of undue influence attaches where fee agreement entered into later:** [§226] If no fee arrangement is made at the outset, the lawyer may have problems enforcing whatever fee arrangement is subsequently reached with the client. In many states, a lawyer is presumed to have a power of undue influence over the client so that any fee agreement entered into *after* the commencement of the attorney-client relationship is presumptively unfair to the client. The result is that the burden is on the lawyer to prove the fairness of the agreement or else it will not be enforced. [13 A.L.R. 3d 731 (1967)]

c.   **Agreements to increase fees:** [§227] Agreements to *increase* the lawyer's fees above those originally agreed upon are likely to be held invalid—because of the presumption of undue influence, because of elements of economic duress, or sometimes on contractual principles (no consideration for client's promise to pay more). [Bonougias v. Peters, 199 N.E.2d 809 (Ill. 1964)]

3.   **Form of Agreement:** [§228] A fee agreement, unless for a contingent fee, is enforceable whether oral or written. However, good practice dictates that the agreement be in writing to avoid future misunderstandings. [Model Rule 1.5(b); EC 2-19] Furthermore, in the event of litigation, any ambiguity or uncertainty will be *construed against the lawyer*—on the rationale that she has superior skill and knowledge and is usually responsible for the form of the agreement.

4.   **Requirement that Fees Be Reasonable:** [§229] Courts may refuse to enforce a fee agreement against a client and may impose professional discipline upon a lawyer where the fees charged are found to be "unreasonable." [Model Rule 1.5(a)] The corresponding terms in other lawyer codes are "clearly excessive" [DR 2-106(A)] or "unconscionable" [Cal. Rule 4-200].

a.   **Determining "reasonableness":** [§230] The "reasonableness" of a fee agreement depends upon *all relevant circumstances*. In this respect, the interests of both clients and lawyers must be considered; *i.e.*, excessive fees would deter the use of legal services, while inadequate compensation might undermine effective representation. [EC 2-17, 2-18]

(1) **Relevant factors:** [§231]   The following factors are relevant, although not necessarily conclusive, in determining the "reasonableness" of fees charged: (i) the *time, labor, and skill* required; (ii) the likelihood of *interference with or preclusion of other employment* of the lawyer; (iii) the amount involved and the *results obtained*; (iv) the *experience*, reputation, and ability of the lawyer; (v) the *time pressures* imposed upon the lawyer; (vi) the *customary fees* for such services; (vii) the *nature of the fee* (*i.e.*, fixed or contingent); and (viii) the *nature and length of the attorney-client relationship*. [Model Rule 1.5(a); DR 2-106(B)]

(2) **Bargaining position of client:** [§232]   Where the client is aged or infirm, or otherwise *susceptible to overreaching*, courts are more prone to find the fee arrangement "unreasonable" or *lacking in informed consent*. [*In re* Schanzer's Estate, 7 App. Div. 2d 275 (1959); *and see* Cal. Rule 4-200(B)(2)]

b. **Fee arbitration:** [§233]   Several states allow clients who are dissatisfied with their bills for legal services to have them reviewed by an arbitrator. Most such plans are voluntary, but proposals are being made to make them mandatory, and the comment to Model Rule 1.5 exhorts lawyers to submit to arbitration.

5. **Recovery in Quantum Meruit for "Reasonable" Fee:** [§234]   The lawyer is entitled to recover in quasi-contract for the reasonable value of services rendered whenever (i) the fee *agreement* calls for the client to pay a "reasonable" fee (no fixed price agreed upon); (ii) there is *no agreement* at all regarding fees (so that a promise to pay a "reasonable" fee is implied in law); *or* (iii) the fee agreement is held *invalid* (*e.g.*, unconscionable) but valuable services have been rendered thereunder.

a. **Benefit to client required:** [§235]   Where quantum meruit is the basis for recovery, it must always be shown that the services had some "reasonable value" *to the client*. In such cases, the court may properly evaluate not only hours expended by the lawyer but also the *results obtained*. [Shelley v. Bixby, 80 Cal. App. 2d 102 (1947)—no recovery where lawyer failed to defend a client with proper skill]

6. **Legislative Regulation of Fees:** [§236]   Congress and some state legislatures have set *maximum* fees for certain types of legal services. Typical examples include legal services rendered in connection with probate of a decedent's estate, guardianships, workers' compensation claims, Social Security claims, and representation of indigents in criminal proceedings.

a. **Strict application of fee limitations:** [§237]   In general, state courts adhere rigorously to these legislative "ceilings" on legal fees. Moreover, disciplinary action may be taken against lawyers who attempt to avoid the limitation.

(1) **Example:** [§238] Where a lawyer obtained an award of $5,000 and a lifetime annuity of $50 per month for a disabled veteran, it was held that the lawyer's fee was properly limited to the $10 statutory maximum applicable to the proceedings. [*In re* Shinberg's Estate, 238 App. Div. 74 (1933)]

(2) **Effect on right to counsel:** [§239] Furthermore, it has been held that the $10 statutory fee limitation on claims before the Veteran's Administration did not violate a veteran's right to due process or equal protection—even though the limitation effectively prevented him from being able to obtain counsel. [Walters v. National Association of Radiation Survivors, 473 U.S. 305 (1985); *but see* National Association of Radiation Survivors v. Derwinski; 778 F. Supp. 1096 (N.D. Cal. 1991)]

b. **"Ordinary" vs. "extraordinary" services:** [§240] Some statutes are drafted to mitigate the above problem by specifying a ceiling only for the lawyer's "ordinary" services in handling the case, and also empower the court (or tribunal) hearing the claim to award *additional* reasonable fees for "extraordinary" services. [Bias v. Oklahoma, 568 P.2d 1269 (Okla. 1977)]

7. **Setting Fees in Class Actions, Derivative Suits, and Certain Civil Rights Actions:** [§241] In some kinds of cases involving multiple plaintiffs or fees paid by the losing party, the rules provide for judicially established attorneys' fees. Traditionally courts awarded fees based on a percentage of the *fund* recovered, but this often resulted in exorbitant fees, bearing little relation to the time and effort required.

a. **Lodestar approach:** [§242] Under the most common approach now used, the court establishes a "lodestar": the number of hours spent multiplied by the lawyer's reasonable hourly rate. [Lindy Brothers v. American Radiator, 487 F.2d 161 (3d Cir. 1973)] The lodestar is then *adjusted* up or down by one or more multipliers to reflect complexity of the case, amount recovered, uncertainty of result, and the like. [City of Detroit v. Grinnell Corp., 495 F.2d 448 (2d Cir. 1974)]

(1) **Criticism of approach:** This approach has it own disadvantages. Critics assert that basing fees primarily on time spent instead of results achieved encourages lawyers to spend excessive time on unproductive discovery and research. [*In re* Fine Paper, 98 F.R.D. 48 (E.D. Pa. 1983)]

b. **Substantial benefit rule:** [§243] Fee awards are not now limited to cases where a "fund" is recovered. Under the "substantial benefit" rule, attorneys' fees may also be awarded where some substantial *nonpecuniary* benefit has been conferred on the class. [Fletcher v. A.J. Industries, 266 Cal. App. 2d 313 (1968)]

c. **Proportionality not required:** [§244] Furthermore, the fee may be substantially in excess of the amount recovered if necessary to reward the lawyer for efforts on the plaintiff's behalf. [*City of Riverside v. Rivera*, 477 U.S. 561 (1986)]

8. **Special Problems with Contingent Fee Agreements:** [§245] Contingent fees depend upon success in the controversy; *i.e.*, by agreement, the lawyer is to receive only a percentage of whatever the client recovers in settlement of the litigation (and nothing if the client loses).

   a. **General considerations:** [§246] Contingent fees are *prohibited* in England and most European countries, and in this country contingent fees have been criticized.

      (1) **Objections to contingent fee arrangements:** [§247] The principal objection is that such arrangements tend to *stir up litigation*. Other objections are that contingent fee agreements permit the lawyer to charge *excessive fees* and that they tend to prolong litigation and induce unprofessional conduct by lawyers bent on achieving maximum monetary recovery.

      (2) **Factors supporting use of contingent fees:** [§248] On the other hand, contingent fees have the advantage of enabling poor clients with meritorious claims to enforce them without compromising for a small fraction of their total value. It is also urged that such arrangements help to support and encourage a body of independent lawyers ready to challenge wrongs done to their clients from any source.

   b. **Propriety of contingent fee agreements:** [§249] In this country, the problem of contingent fees has been resolved in favor of permitting their use, subject to regulation designed to prevent abuses. [*See* Model Rule 1.5; EC 2-20, 5-7; DR 5-103(A)(2)]

      (1) **Discouraged where client able to pay fee:** [§250] As an ethical consideration, lawyers are *urged* to decline employment on a contingent fee basis where the client is able to pay a reasonable fixed fee. However, it is not improper to accept contingent fee employment where the client has been "fully informed of all relevant factors" and still desires the lawyer's representation on this basis. [EC 2-20]

      (2) **Model Rules approach:** [§251] The Model Rules are more protective of clients than the ABA Code but less so than some cases. Under Model Rule 1.5(c), the contingent fee agreement must:

         (a) *Be in writing*;

         (b) *State the method by which the fee is to be determined*, including the lawyer's percentage in the event of settlement, trial, or appeal;

(c) *Identify expenses to be deducted* from the recovery and whether they are before or after the lawyer's percentage is calculated; and

(d) *Be followed up after the case with a written statement* accounting for disposition of the recovery.

(3) **"Rarely justified" in domestic relations cases:** [§252] Because of the human relationships involved and the unique character of the proceedings, contingent fee arrangements are "rarely justified" in domestic relations cases (divorce, guardianship, adoption, etc.). [EC 2-20]

(a) **Model Rules prohibit contingent fees in divorce case:** [§253] The Model Rules go further and flatly *prohibit* a lawyer from accepting a fee *contingent upon obtaining a divorce, property settlement, or support.* The rationale is that the contingent fee might interfere with the possibility of reconciliation. [*In re* Smith, 254 P.2d 464 (Wash. 1953); Model Rule 1.5(d)(1)]

(b) **Compare—post-divorce matters:** [§254] Once a divorce has been *granted*, and the current proceedings involve only collection of a debt (*e.g.*, past due alimony), some courts permit contingent fee arrangements. [Krieger v. Bulpitt, 40 Cal. 2d 97 (1953)]

(4) **Prohibited in certain cases:** [§255] Furthermore, there is an *absolute prohibition* on contingent fee arrangements in certain cases:

(a) **Criminal cases:** [§256] A lawyer is prohibited from taking any criminal case on a contingent fee basis, on the asserted ground that legal services in such cases do not yield the client any fund or property with which to pay the fee. [Model Rule 1.5(d)(2); EC 2-20; DR 2-106(C)]

(b) **Securing favorable legislation:** [§257] Likewise, contingent fees are unlawful where their payment depends upon the lawyer's securing passage of legislation or other governmental action. The rationale is that possible harm might result from the lawyer's use of extreme measures to achieve success. [Trist v. Child, 88 U.S. 441 (1874)]

(5) **Recovery permitted in quantum meruit:** [§258] Where a contingent fee arrangement is void for reasons of public policy, the courts usually permit the lawyer to recover the *reasonable value* of his services (assuming the services rendered were otherwise lawful); *see supra*, §234. [Hay v. Erwin, 419 P.2d 32 (Or. 1966)]

c. **Regulation to prevent "overreaching" by lawyer:** [§259] Even where contingent fee contracts are allowed, courts have carefully scrutinized such arrangements to prevent overreaching by lawyers. This is especially true in the case of *personal injury claims* or in other situations involving helpless or inexperienced plaintiffs.

(1) **Minors' claims:** [§260] In most states, any contract with a minor for litigation services is void unless approved by the court; and the same applies to any contract with the parents "on behalf of" the minor.

    (a) **Note:** The proper procedure is for the parents to be appointed "guardians ad litem" by the court and then to seek *court approval* of a contingency fee contract.

(2) **Maximum limits:** [§261] In a few states, *court rules* fix maximum percentages that may be charged by lawyers under contingent fee contracts. (Usually, the maximum declines as the size of the recovery increases; *e.g.*, 50% of the first $1,000; 40% of the next $2,000; 30% of the next $5,000, etc.). Such schedules have been upheld against attacks that they constitute unconstitutional interference with lawyers' freedom to contract. [American Trial Lawyers Association v. New Jersey Supreme Court, 316 A.2d 19, *aff'd*, 330 A.2d 350 (N.J. 1974)]

    (a) **Additional fees in "extraordinary" circumstances:** [§262] Often a procedure is provided whereby a lawyer may apply to the court for approval of a larger fee "where extraordinary circumstances warrant." [American Trial Lawyers Association v. New Jersey Supreme Court, *supra*]

    (b) **Disclosure requirement:** [§263] Some courts go even further and require a lawyer handling a case on a contingent fee basis to disclose this fact to the court in which the action is pending and to *justify* any fee greater than the maximum suggested in the court rules. [Gair v. Peck, 6 N.Y.2d 97 (1959)]

9. Protecting Lawyer's Right to Compensation

a. **Lawyer's duties in collecting fees:** [§264] According to the ABA standards, lawyers are obliged to be "zealous" in their efforts to avoid controversies with clients over fees and should attempt to resolve amicably any differences that arise. [EC 2-23]

(1) **Self-help remedies:** [§265] A lawyer who uses self-help remedies in collecting a fee must be very careful not to overreach the client. For example, a lawyer can be disciplined for withholding services in a case until the client pays the fees. [State v. Mayes, 531 P.2d 102 (Kan. 1975)]

(2) **Litigation to be avoided if possible:** [§266] EC 2-23 states that a lawyer should not sue a client for a fee "unless necessary to prevent fraud or gross imposition by the client."

    (a) **Application:** As a practical matter, however, courts do not require lawyers to abstain from litigation over fees. As long as the fee claim is asserted in good faith, and prior demand for payment has been made, it is not improper for a lawyer to file suit against the client to collect the fee.

b. **Retaining (possessory) lien:** [§267]   In most states (but not California), a lawyer has, by statute or judicial decision, a possessory lien on all property, documents, and funds belonging to the client that come into the lawyer's possession by reason of the employment.

   (1) **Applicable to all fees incurred:** [§268]   This retaining lien protects *all* fees owed by the client to the lawyer for work *on any matter*; *i.e.*, it is not limited to the matter concerning which the money, property, or documents were submitted to counsel. [Norrell v. Chasan, 4 A.2d 88 (N.J. 1939)]

   (2) **Limited to property acquired as attorney:** [§269]   Note, however, that a retaining lien attaches *only* to property that comes into the lawyer's possession in the lawyer's capacity *as attorney* for the client. Hence the lien does *not* apply to documents or other materials received by a lawyer while acting as trustee, escrow holder, director, etc., for the client. [Brauer v. Hotel Associates, Inc., 192 A.2d 831 (N.J. 1963)]

   (3) **Retaining lien on needed files void:** [§270]   Note also that even if there is a written agreement by which the lawyer has a retaining lien on a client's papers and files as security for the fees, such lien will not be upheld as applied to files the client needs to pursue her case. [People v. Altvater, 78 Misc. 2d 24 (1974)]

   (4) **Retaining lien not affirmatively enforceable in court:** [§271]   The basic value of the retaining lien lies in the *inconvenience* that the client or the client's successors experience in being denied access to the property. The retaining lien *cannot* be sued upon by the lawyer (although it can be asserted as a *defense* to a suit by the client demanding return of his property).

c. **Charging (nonpossessory) lien:** [§272]   In most states, in addition to the general retaining lien, a lawyer has, by statute or judicial decision, a "charging lien." This lien gives the lawyer the right to have *any fund or recovery* obtained for the client serve as security for the attorney's fees and disbursements in that matter. For example, a lawyer who prosecutes a contingent fee case to judgment is recognized as having a lien on the judgment for the amount of the contingent fee and expenses. [3 A.L.R.2d 148 (1949)]

   (1) **Charging lien created by contract:** [§273]   In some states, including California, the common law charging lien is *not* recognized. In such states, however, the lawyer and client may, by *express* agreement, create a lien on the client's prospective recovery to secure the attorney's fees and expenses. In general, the express lien is subject to the same rules and limitations as the common law lien.

(2) **Advantages over retaining lien:** [§274] The charging lien has several distinct advantages over the general retaining lien:

    (a) **Charging lien is nonpossessory:** [§275] This lien applies even though the lawyer does not have possession of any fund. In contrast, the retaining lien reaches only things that come into the lawyer's "possession," and hence would not apply to a judgment rendered by a court. (Nor would it reach the *proceeds* of the judgment, even if actually paid to the lawyer, because the lawyer receives such proceeds as a *trustee* for the client, and hence they are exempt from the retaining lien; *see* above.)

    (b) **Enforcement:** [§276] The major advantage of the charging lien over the retaining lien is that the charging lien can be *affirmatively enforced*. If the client fails or refuses to pay the agreed fee, the lawyer can file a legal action to foreclose the lien on the client's judgment (or whatever fund or recovery has been obtained). [Noel v. Missouri Pacific Railroad, 74 S.W.2d 7 (Mo. 1934)]

(3) **Limitations on charging liens:** [§277] At the same time, the charging lien is subject to several limitations:

    (a) **Limited to fees in particular case:** [§278] The lien is limited to the fees and costs incurred by the client in connection with the particular action in which the judgment or settlement is obtained. It does *not* secure other fees owed by the same client on other matters (unlike the retaining lien, *supra*).

    (b) **No lien for fees in defense:** [§279] In addition, a lawyer does not have a charging lien on property involved in litigation where the lawyer merely *defeats* a claim against the client. The lien applies only where there is some recovery or affirmative relief. [Snitow v. Jackson, 4 Misc. 2d 351 (1956)]

(4) **Time at which charging lien attaches:** [§280] Most states permit the lawyer to assert a charging lien against the client's interest only when a judgment or settlement is obtained. A number of states, however, have *expanded* the scope of charging liens and permit them to attach at earlier stages in the proceeding, thus preventing the client from settling the case without paying the lawyer.

(5) **Lien not defeated by direct settlement of case:** [§281] Provided the lawyer gives the defendant *notice* of the contingent fee interest, and provided further that the lien is held to attach to the *cause of action* (*see* above), the client may not defeat a charging lien by settling the claim directly with the defendant.

(a) **Effect:** In most states, the defendant in this situation *remains personally liable* to the plaintiff's lawyer for the fees due; *i.e.*, a defendant who has *notice* of the lien may end up paying twice if he settles directly with the plaintiff. [Downs v. Hodge, 413 S.W.2d 519 (Mo. 1967)]

(b) **But note:** The settlement itself is *effective*. Even where the lien attaches to the cause of action (*see* above), most courts hold that the lawyer has *no right to continue the case to judgment* (in hopes of getting a larger recovery and hence a bigger fee).

(6) **Lien not defeated by discharge of lawyer:** [§282] The charging lien also protects a lawyer employed on a contingent fee basis in the event of discharge by the client.

(a) **Example:** An express lien in the contingent fee agreement survives the lawyer's discharge and allows payment out of the client's recovery for any services performed prior to discharge. [Weiss v. Marcus, 51 Cal. App. 3d 590 (1975)]

(b) **But note:** A lien upon anticipated recovery can be enforced only *after* actual recovery by the client, and only through an independent action brought by the lawyer. [Bandy v. Mt. Diablo Unified School District, 56 Cal. App. 3d 230 (1976)—lawyer may not intervene in former client's suit to have the lien established]

d. **Caveat—lawyer's fiduciary duties:** [§283] The ABA Code states that a lawyer may assert legally recognized liens to secure payment of fees and expenses. [DR 5-103; EC 5-7] But the Code and all states impose *strict* fiduciary obligations upon lawyers in possession of their clients' money or property (*see supra*, §§210-220). Any lawyer who seeks the protection of lawyers' liens must comply in every respect with these fiduciary duties. [People v. Radinsky, 512 P.2d 627 (Colo. 1973)]

10. Financing of Legal Fees

a. **Traditional view prohibited:** [§284] Earlier opinions held that it was improper for a lawyer to participate in plans for financing legal fees. The theory was that use of such plans would encourage the lawyer to overbill the client so as to offset whatever charges the lawyer incurred in the financing plan. Furthermore, such plans were viewed as involving some division of fees with nonlawyers (the bank or lender).

b. **Credit card financing now permitted:** [§285] However, the modern view is contra. Provided there is no increased charge to the client, it is not improper for a lawyer to accept credit card charges for legal fees or to participate in legal fee financing plans (*e.g.*, where the fees receivable are assigned to local banks where client's credit has been established). [ABA Opn. 338]

    c. **Bank financing:** [§286] A lawyer may likewise participate in a bar association plan that allows clients to borrow money to pay their legal fees. [ABA Opn. 320]

    d. **Interest-bearing notes:** [§287] And although it is ordinarily unwise for the lawyer to become a client's "banker," it has been held proper for the lawyer to take an unsecured, interest-bearing promissory note in payment of a fee. [Walton v. Broglio, 52 Cal. App. 3d 731 (1967)]

G. TERMINATING THE LAWYER-CLIENT RELATIONSHIP [§288]

The attorney-client relationship typically concludes when a matter is resolved and the lawyer has performed all necessary legal services. However, either the lawyer or the client may also seek to terminate the relationship *before* completion of the matter.

1. **Withdrawal by Lawyer:** [§289] Even where there is no formal contract of employment between the lawyer and the client, once the lawyer undertakes to represent the client, she may not simply withdraw from (or otherwise terminate) their relationship at will.

    a. **Requirements—in general:** [§290] A lawyer's decision to withdraw from a case should be made only on the basis of "compelling circumstances" and after careful consideration. The lawyer should make every effort to minimize possible adverse effects on the client. [Model Rule 1.16(d); EC 2-32]

        (1) **Duty to withdraw:** [§291] Under certain circumstances, the lawyer has an *obligation* to withdraw from employment.

            (a) **Client's purpose is harassment or malicious prosecution:** [§292] Where the lawyer knows or it is obvious that the client wishes to use the lawyer's services merely to harass or maliciously injure another, the lawyer *must* withdraw. [DR 2-110(B)(1)]

            (b) **Employment is violative of rules of professional conduct:** [§293] Likewise, the lawyer has a duty to withdraw when she knows (or should know) that continued employment will result in violation of a standard of professional conduct. [Model Rule 1.16(a)(1); DR 2-110(B)(2)]

            (c) **Personal inability to continue employment:** [§294] If the lawyer's mental or physical condition makes it "*unreasonably* difficult" for her to provide effective representation, she must withdraw. [Model Rule 1.16(a)(2); DR 2-110(B)(3)]

(d) **Discharge by client:** [§295] The lawyer must of course withdraw if discharged by the client. [Model Rule 1.16(a)(3); DR 2-110(B)(4); *and see* below]

(2) **Permissive withdrawal:** [§296] Where withdrawal is not *required*, the lawyer is under a general duty to continue the employment to its natural conclusion. However, there are specific exceptions that *permit* a lawyer to withdraw from a matter.

(a) **Actions by client:** [§297] Where the client refuses reasonable cooperation or otherwise makes it unreasonably difficult for the lawyer to act effectively, the lawyer may properly seek to withdraw. [Model Rule 1.16(b)(5); DR 2-110(C)(1)(d)] *Examples:*

1) Withdrawal is permitted if the client insists upon pressing an *unwarranted* claim or defense, or seeks to have the lawyer engage in *conduct prohibited under the rules of professional conduct* (or if the client seeks to pursue an illegal course of conduct). [Model Rule 1.16(a)(1); DR 2-110(C)(1)(a), (b), (c)]

2) In an office matter (as opposed to litigation), the lawyer may withdraw if the client insists that the lawyer engage in *conduct contrary to the lawyer's own judgment and advice*, even if such conduct is neither illegal nor unethical. [Model Rule 1.16(b)(3); DR 2-110(C)(1)(e)]

3) The lawyer need not continue to represent the client if the client *deliberately disregards* an agreement or obligation concerning *attorneys' fees and expenses*. [Model Rule 1.16(b)(4); DR 2-110(C)(1)(f)]

(b) **Potential violation of Disciplinary Rules:** [§298] A lawyer who believes that continued employment is *likely* to violate a Disciplinary Rule (*e.g.*, likely to create a potential conflict of interest) may also seek to withdraw. [DR 2-110(C)(2)]

(c) **Inability to work effectively with co-counsel:** [§299] If the lawyer cannot work effectively with co-counsel, there is a sufficient ground for withdrawal. [DR 2-110(C)(3)]

(d) **Consent of client:** [§300] When the client *freely and knowingly consents* to termination of employment, a lawyer may withdraw. [DR 2-110(C)(5)]

(e) **Other grounds satisfactory to court:** [§301] Finally, a lawyer may seek permission to withdraw when the lawyer believes in good faith that the court will find good cause for withdrawal. [Model Rule 1.16(b)(6); DR 2-110(C)(6)]

(3) **General obligations of lawyer in withdrawing from employment:** [§302] Whether withdrawal is mandatory or permissive, the lawyer has a duty to *safeguard the rights and interests* of the client. [Model Rule 1.16(d)]

    (a) **Approval of court in litigation matters:** [§303] When a matter is pending before a court or other tribunal, the lawyer may have to obtain *permission from the court* to withdraw. (*See infra*, §307.)

    (b) **Notice to client in every case:** [§304] In *all* matters, the lawyer cannot withdraw until the client has been given sufficient notice so that other counsel can be retained. [DR 2-110(A)(2)]

    (c) **Refund of unearned attorney's fees:** [§305] Upon withdrawal from employment, the lawyer must *refund* any fees the client paid in advance which the lawyer has not earned. [DR 2-110(A)(3)]

    (d) **Delivery of clients' materials:** [§306] The lawyer must also promptly return to the client *all papers and property* to which the client is entitled. [DR 2-110(A)(2)]

b. **Judicial requirements for withdrawal:** [§307] Once a lawsuit is filed, the rules of most courts require the lawyer to continue providing services unless released by the client or the court. [Model Rule 1.16(c); DR 2-110(A)(1); Smith v. Bryant, 141 S.E.2d 303 (N.C. 1965)] The decision by a court to allow withdrawal is a *discretionary* one.

2. **Discharge by Client:** [§308] Unlike the limitations on a lawyer's freedom to withdraw from employment, the right of a *client* to terminate the attorney-client relationship is virtually unconditional.

a. **Right to discharge lawyer:** [§309] The client has a unilateral right to discharge the lawyer and terminate the relationship *at any time, with or without just cause*. [McLeod v. Vest Transportation Co., 235 F. Supp. 369 (N.D. Miss. 1964)]

    (1) **Rationale:** There is a need for *continuing client confidence* if the attorney-client relationship is to succeed. Once such confidence ends—for whatever reason—the relationship is best terminated.

    (2) **Provision for "irrevocability" invalid:** [§310] It follows that any provision in a retainer agreement that purports to make the lawyer's employment irrevocable is *void*. [Richette v. Solomon, 187 A.2d 910 (Pa. 1963)]

    (3) **Judicial refusal to allow discharge in exceptional cases:** [§311] In some instances, courts may *refuse* to permit the discharge of a lawyer in the interests of justice. For example, where a client seeks to discharge a lawyer

during trial in order to make a "flaming" personal address to the jury, the court may refuse to honor such a request. [Dennis v. United States, 183 F.2d 201 (2d Cir. 1950)]

b. **Continuing fiduciary duty of lawyer:** [§312]   The fact that a lawyer is discharged without cause does *not* relieve the lawyer of fiduciary obligations to the client. As in the case of withdrawal, the lawyer is still prohibited from revealing confidential information or from representing conflicting interests (*see infra*, §§325 *et seq.*).

c. **Liability of client to lawyer for wrongful discharge:** [§313]   While the client is free to discharge the lawyer for any reason, the client may still be *contractually* liable to the lawyer in the event the client terminates the relationship *without cause*.

(1) **Fixed fee:** [§314]   If a fixed fee agreement was involved (a set amount for the particular case or transaction), the lawyer may be entitled to recover on a *quantum meruit basis* for the work done but may not recover more than the amount set in the agreement.

(2) **Contingent fee—measure of recovery:** [§315]   There is a split of authority as to the proper measure of recovery where the case was being handled on a contingent fee basis.

    (a) **Recovery of full contingent share:** [§316]   Some courts have held that the discharged lawyer is entitled to the *full share* of any recovery ultimately obtained by the client. [*See* Dombey v. Detroit Toledo & Ironton Railroad, 351 F.2d 121 (6th Cir. 1965)—same rule applies where client settles case *without* discharging lawyer]

        1) **Rationale:** The client got what she bargained for (the status of legal representation); the client's own wrongful conduct (firing the lawyer without cause) excuses the lawyer from rendering the services contemplated.

        2) **Effect:** However, the impact of protecting the lawyer's right to a full share is that if the client retains new counsel to handle the case, the client may end up having to pay a *double contingent fee* (one to the former lawyer and one to the replacement). [Carter v. Dunham, 117 P. 533 (Kan. 1919)]

    (b) **Recovery in quantum meruit:** [§317]   Other courts have held (and this is believed to be the better view) that the contingent fee contract is *not enforceable* where the client discharges the lawyer (even if the discharge was wrongful). *Rationale:* To enforce the contingent fee contract would significantly deter clients from exercising *their essential right to change lawyers*. These courts permit the discharged lawyer to recover only the *reasonable value of services actually rendered*. [Fracasse v. Brent, 6 Cal. 3d 784 (1972)]

1) **Measure of recovery:** [§318] Courts following this approach are themselves divided over the proper measure of recovery.

a) **Lower percentage:** [§319] Some courts hold that the proper remedy is to award the discharged lawyer *some percentage* of the final recovery, albeit less than the percentage provided in the contract. [Tonn v. Reuter, 95 N.W.2d 261 (Wis. 1959)]

b) **"Reasonable fee":** [§320] Others award the discharged lawyer a "reasonable fee" based on the general standards for determining "reasonableness" (*see supra*, §230). Of particular importance are the nature and *amount of the claim*, the *work performed* to date, the *results* accomplished to date, and the reasonable value of the *work remaining* to be done. [Fracasse v. Brent, *supra*]

c) **Recovery requirement:** [§321] Under either approach, however, the lawyer generally gets *nothing* unless and until the client *recovers* on the claim, either by settlement or judgment. [*See* Plaza Shoe Store v. Hermel, 636 S.W.2d 53 (Mo. 1982)]

d. **Liability of third parties for inducing discharge:** [§322] A lawyer is also afforded protection against third parties who induce the client to discharge the lawyer without good cause. In this situation, the lawyer may seek damages from the third person for *interference with contractual relations*. (*See* Torts Summary.)

(1) **Example:** Insurance Company induced Claimant to "get rid of" Claimant's lawyer by promising that a "satisfactory settlement would be arranged without paying the attorney's fees. Lawyer may recover damages against Insurance Company. [Herron v. State Farm Mutual, 56 Cal. 2d 202 (1961)]

(2) **Interference by another lawyer:** [§323] Where another lawyer is guilty of soliciting the case and inducing the client to discharge present counsel without good cause, *professional discipline* (as well as tort damages) may be imposed on the soliciting lawyer (*see supra*, §140). [Oklahoma Bar Association v. Hatcher, 452 P.2d 150 (Okla. 1969)]

(a) **Exception—law firm clientele:** [§324] This rule probably does not prevent an associate in a firm from informing clients for whom the associate does work that they may follow him to the associate's new firm, but it does prohibit their encouraging them to do so (*see supra*, §813).

III. DUTY TO PROTECT CONFIDENTIAL INFORMATION OF THE CLIENT

chapter approach

A general rule of agency is that no agent may reveal confidential information of the principal without the principal's consent. This rule is especially important in the practice of law, given the sensitivity of issues with which lawyers often deal and the importance of getting the client to give the lawyer truthful information necessary for effective representation. Two doctrines govern a lawyer's dealing with confidential client information: the attorney-client privilege and the professional duty of confidentiality. For exam purposes, it is important to remember:

1. The ***attorney-client privilege*** is the narrower of the two doctrines. It applies only to ***communications*** (not documents or physical evidence) made to the lawyer ***in confidence*** (the privilege may be lost if third parties are present).

2. The ***duty of confidentiality*** (sometimes called the duty to preserve secrets) is broader. Under the ABA Code, the lawyer may not disclose ***any*** information learned ***in representing the client*** that might embarrass the client or that the client wants kept secret. The Model Rules provision is broader still: The lawyer may not disclose any information ***related to representing the client*** learned from ***any source and under any circumstances***. (Thus, the presence of third parties at the time the lawyer learns the information is irrelevant.)

3. There are ***exceptions*** to these rules. For example, watch for issues concerning consent, lawyer self-defense or fee collection, and the client's intention to commit a ***future*** crime or fraud.

A. INTRODUCTION

1. **Two Basic Legal Doctrines:** [§325]   The two related but quite different doctrines that govern a lawyer's dealing with confidential client information are:

    (i) *The attorney-client privilege*, a rule of evidence that protects certain information from disclosure by a lawyer *even* in judicial proceedings. The ABA Code calls such privileged information a client's "*confidences*" [DR4-101(A)]; and

    (ii) *The professional duty of confidentiality*, a rule of legal ethics requiring that a lawyer not disclose a much larger body of nonprivileged information *unless* ordered by a court to do so. The ABA Code calls this information "*secrets*" of the client [DR 4-101(A)].

The *Model Rules* do not distinguish between these two classes of information, but the courts draw a distinction between privileged and unprivileged information even in states that have adopted the Model Rules. [*See* Model Rule 1.6]

2. **Period During Which Duty and Privilege Apply:** [§326]   Both the professional duty and the legal privilege of nondisclosure extend *beyond* the lawyer's actual employment.

    a. **Prior to employment:** [§327]   Confidential information disclosed to a lawyer by a potential client in discussions *preliminary* to any actual employment is nonetheless protected by the attorney-client privilege and the ethical obligation. This is true even though no agreement was reached regarding representation, and even though the lawyer refused to take the case (*i.e.*, even though no "client" relationship developed). [EC 4-1]

        (1) **Rationale:** This encourages potential clients to discuss the facts of their cases freely when they first consult a lawyer—*i.e.*, without concern that the lawyer may later testify against them or use information so obtained in representing an adversary. Furthermore, it helps the lawyer get all the facts needed to decide whether to take the case. [Taylor v. Sheldon, 173 N.E.2d 892 (Ohio 1961)]

        (2) **May affect right to accept employment from opposing side:** [§328]   Where preliminary discussions disclose *confidential* information, the lawyer may thereafter be prevented from representing the opposing side. [Autry v. State, 430 S.W.2d 808 (Tenn. 1968); *and see infra*, §§468-470]

    b. **After employment ceases:** [§329]   The duty to preserve confidential information also continues after the lawyer is no longer employed by the client. [EC 4-6]

3. **Prohibition of Use as Well as Disclosure:** [§330]   It is a standard principle of agency law that an agent must neither reveal confidential information nor use it for the agent's own gain, even if that use would not be adverse to the interest of the principal. That rule is reiterated in the ABA Code. [DR 4-101(A)(2)]

    a. **Model Rules distinction:** [§331]   The Model Rules retain the prohibition of a lawyer's personal *use* of confidential client information when it would be *detrimental* to the interest of the client. [Model Rule 1.8(b)]

        (1) **But note—nonadverse use permitted:** [§332]   Under the Model Rules, the lawyer would be permitted to use information for the lawyer's benefit where the use would not adversely affect the client. The distinction is worth noting, but because of the lawyer's general fiduciary obligations to the client, a lawyer would be ill-advised to seek to profit personally from a client's confidential information even in a Model Rules jurisdiction.

4. **Permitted Disclosures**

a. **Disclosure to others in law firm:** [§333]   Unless the client specifies otherwise, a lawyer may properly discuss the client's affairs with partners or associates, as this conforms to ordinary law firm procedures in which members usually work together in representing a client. Furthermore, the lawyer may make such disclosures to secretaries, investigators, and other employees of the firm as reasonably required. [EC 4-2; *and see* comments to Model Rule 1.6]

b. **Disclosure to outside personnel:** [§334]   The lawyer may even give limited information from her files to persons outside the law firm for *bookkeeping, accounting*, or other legitimate purposes, provided the client does not object. [DR 4-101(D)]

c. **Duty to control:** [§335]   However, the lawyer owes a duty to exercise reasonable care to prevent employees and associates from disclosing confidential information obtained from a client. Specifically, the lawyer is charged with *selecting and training* responsible persons, and with *supervising their access* to clients' files. [Model Rules 5.1, 5.3(a); DR 4-101(D); EC 4-2, 4-3]

B. ATTORNEY-CLIENT PRIVILEGE [§336]

The *legal* privilege of nondisclosure governs the extent to which a lawyer may be compelled to disclose in *court* proceedings what a client has revealed to the lawyer in confidence. The privilege is based on the need to insure that every person may freely and fully confide in his lawyer so as to be adequately represented. [Upjohn Co. v. United States, 449 U.S. 383 (1981)]

1. **Scope of the Privilege:** [§337]   The privilege is discussed in detail in the Evidence Summary. Briefly, however, four basic elements are necessary for the attorney-client privilege to apply:

(i)   The holder must be (or have sought to become) *a client*;

(ii)   The person to whom the communication was made must be *an attorney acting as such at the time*;

(iii)   The communications must be made *in confidence* (without strangers present); and

(iv)   The communications must be made *for the purpose of obtaining legal assistance*.

In addition, there must be *no waiver* of the privilege by the client.

a. **Revealing incriminating physical evidence received from client:** [§338]   The privilege applies only to *"communications"* from the client. It does *not* protect incriminating documents or physical evidence turned over to the lawyer by the client, or evidence discovered by the lawyer on his own while investigating the case (*e.g.*, the murder weapon or the stolen property).

(1) **Example:** Although the fact that it was the client who delivered the evidence may be privileged, the evidence itself is not. [State v. Olwell, 394 P.2d 681 (Wash. 1964); *In re* January 1976 Grand Jury, 534 F.2d 719 (7th Cir. 1976)]

(2) **Note:** It has been held that a lawyer's *duty as an officer of the court* makes it incumbent upon him to *turn over* to the prosecution or court evidence that he *knows* or realizes constitutes the "instrumentalities" of a crime. [Morrell v. State, 575 P.2d 1200 (Alaska 1978)]

(3) **And note:** Quite apart from ethical obligations, a lawyer who secretes or disposes of evidence that he *knows* the prosecution is seeking may be guilty of a criminal act—suppression of evidence. [*See* Cal. Penal Code §135]

b. **Requirement that communication be made "in confidence":** [§339] The usual communication between lawyer and client takes place in the lawyer's office with the door closed. If the communication takes place under less than such confidential circumstances, however, the entire privilege may be lost.

(1) **Third party in a position to overhear:** [§340] If the client's statement is made when it is clearly possible for someone other than the lawyer or lawyer's employee to hear it, the statement is not privileged. [People v. Harris, 57 N.Y.2d 335 (1982)]

(a) **Example:** An Illinois ethics opinion reminded lawyers that the privilege may be lost if the communication takes place over a cellular telephone because of the possibility that such calls may be easily monitored by third parties. [Illinois Bar Opinion 90-7 (1990)]

(2) **Waiver by subsequent disclosure:** [§341] The privilege may later be lost if the client does not treat the communication as confidential, such as where the client discloses the lawyer's opinion in the course of business negotiations with a third party. [Jonathan Corp. v. Prime Computers, Inc., 114 F.R.D. 693 (E.D. Va. 1983)]

c. **Information shared by clients with common interest:** [§342] If two or more clients have a common interest in a matter, they and their lawyers may share the information each provides in the course of preparing their common case without losing the privilege. [Eisenberg v. Gagnon, 766 F.2d 770 (3d Cir. 1985)]

(1) **Privileged against third parties:** [§343] Any one of the clients may assert the privilege against the government or any other third party who attempts to compel disclosure of the communication. [Hunydee v. United States, 355 F.2d 183 (9th Cir. 1965)]

(2) **Not privileged in later dispute among clients:** [§344] However, if the clients later have a falling out, each may use the disclosure of the others against them in the subsequent litigation. [Ohio-Sealy Mattress Manufacturing Co. v. Kaplan, 90 F.R.D. 21 (N.D. Ill. 1980)]

d. **Corporation as "client":** [§345] The privilege against disclosure of confidential communications extends to *corporate* as well as personal clients. [Radiant Burners v. American Gas Association, 320 F.2d 314 (7th Cir. 1963); Upjohn Co. v. United States, *supra*, §336]

  (1) **Privilege applicable to all legal counsel:** [§346] The attorney-client privilege of corporations applies to confidences made both to in-house counsel and to independent attorneys retained by the corporation.

  (2) **Not available to avoid legitimate discovery:** [§347] However, like a personal client, a corporation may not use the attorney-client privilege as a means of avoiding discovery. Thus, where the corporation simply "funnels" papers and files to its lawyers, the privilege does not apply. [Radiant Burners v. American Gas Association, *supra*]

  (3) **No privilege for nonlegal communications:** [§348] And as with individual clients, the professional relationship necessary to invoke the privilege does not exist when the corporate client seeks *business or personal* advice as opposed to legal assistance. [United States v. Bartone, 400 F.2d 459 (6th Cir. 1968)]

   (a) **"Mixed" communications within privilege:** [§349] Nevertheless, the privilege is *not* lost simply because relevant nonlegal advice is contained in communications that involve legal advice. Otherwise, the corporate client would be under an impossible burden in deciding what it could or could not disclose to its lawyers. [Upjohn Co. v. United States, *supra*]

  (4) **Not applicable to protect personal confidences of corporate officials:** [§350] However, the lawyer for the corporation is normally *not* the lawyer for corporate officials, even if they think such is the case. Thus, a corporate officer's "confession" of wrongdoing to the corporate lawyer might be privileged in a case where the *corporation* is the defendant, but *not* where the officer is tried *as an individual*. [*In re* Grand Jury Proceedings, 434 F. Supp. 648 (E.D. Mich. 1977)]

2. **Exceptions to Privilege of Nondisclosure:** [§351] In addition to the above situations in which disclosure may be compelled, there are certain *general exceptions* to the privilege protecting confidential communications.

a. **Consent by client:** [§352] When the client *consents* to the disclosure of confidential information, the lawyer may properly reveal such information.

b. **Disclosure of future crime or fraud:** [§353] The attorney-client privilege does not cover a communication in which the client seeks the services of a lawyer to further the planning or commission of a future crime or fraud. [Cal. Evid. Code §956]

   (1) **Example:** C asks Lawyer L to help her prepare false documents to defraud X. C's request is not covered by the privilege; both C and L could be compelled to testify about the request.

   (2) **Disclosure by lawyer:** [§354] This exception also gives the lawyer the ***right, but does not impose the duty***, to make voluntary disclosure of the client's intention to commit a ***future*** crime and to supply the information necessary to prevent its commission.

      (a) **Compare:** California takes the position that a lawyer should ***avoid disclosure*** of an intended crime unless the crime is one likely to cause serious damage to members of the public ***and*** its commission is imminent. [Los Angeles County Bar Association Opn. 353; *compare* Tarasoff v. Regents of University of California, 17 Cal. 3d 425 (1976)—psychotherapist liable for failing to warn killer's intended victim]

   (3) **Compare—past crime or fraud:** [§355] The attorney-client privilege ***does protect*** confidential communications in which the client reveals the ***previous*** commission of a crime or other unlawful act.

      (a) **Example:** Where a lawyer was appointed to defend a client charged with murdering P, and the client admitted to the lawyer in confidence that he had also murdered S and told the lawyer where S's body was buried, the lawyer could ***not*** disclose this information to the prosecuting authorities, the court, or anyone else (even when asked by S's parents, who thought she was still alive, and even though burial statutes required disclosure of such information). [People v. Belge, 41 N.Y.2d 60 (1976)]

      (b) **Example:** Similarly, where a client admits to having committed perjury in a ***prior*** judicial proceeding, this is privileged information which the lawyer must not disclose. (*See infra*, §§664 *et seq.*)

c. **Disclosure for lawyer self-protection:** [§356] A lawyer may also reveal sufficient confidential information to defend himself, his associates, or employees against charges of ***negligence or misconduct***, or to collect a fee owed to the lawyer. [Meyerhofer v. Empire Fire & Marine Insurance Co., 497 F.2d 1190 (2d Cir. 1974)]

   (1) **Example:** A lawyer in a malpractice case may reveal what the client's instructions were or the nature of the services the client expected the lawyer to perform. [ABA Opn. 250]

3. **Responsibilities of Lawyer in Asserting the Attorney-Client Privilege:** [§357] A lawyer has a duty "to advise the client of the attorney-client privilege and timely to assert the privilege unless it is waived by the client." [EC 4-4]

   a. *Some courts hold that an attorney must refuse to disclose* privileged information *regardless of the personal consequences.* [Cal. Bus. & Prof. Code §6068(e)] For example, it has been suggested that a lawyer ordered to testify under threat of a citation for contempt should *go to jail* rather than disclose confidential information without the consent of the client. [People v. Kor, 129 Cal. App. 2d 436 (1954)—lawyer should accept punishment and "take his chances on release by a higher court"]

   b. *However, the ABA seems to impose a less rigorous duty* upon the lawyer in this situation. DR 4-101(C) states that a lawyer *may* reveal the confidences and secrets of a client when "required by . . . *court order.*"

   c. *Where the propriety of the court's disclosure order is questionable*, the best solution would seem to be for the lawyer to allow himself to be placed in contempt so as to get the matter tested on appeal. If the order is sustained on appeal, then the information has been found *not privileged* and the lawyer must disclose it. [*Compare* Comments to Model Rule 1.6—"lawyer must comply with final order of a court requiring the lawyer to give information . . ."]

C. PROFESSIONAL DUTY OF CONFIDENTIALITY [§358]

Besides the attorney-client privilege, which protects certain client information from legally compelled disclosure by a lawyer, lawyers also have a *professional duty* not to reveal a much larger body of confidential client information. [Model Rule 1.6(a); DR 4-101(B)]

1. **Professional Duty Broader Than Privilege:** [§359] The description of the professional duty is stated slightly differently in the ABA Code and Model Rules, but in both the duty of nondisclosure covers considerably more information than is protected by the privilege.

   a. **Model Rules formulation—information relating to representation:** [§360] The Model Rules require a lawyer not to disclose *any* information relating to the representation—no matter from whom learned or under what circumstances. [Model Rule 1.6(a)]

   b. **ABA Code formulation—information gained in professional relationship that would embarrass client or that client requests be kept confidential:** [§361] The ABA Code makes the duty of confidentiality turn on how the lawyer learned the information, the client's wishes, and the likely impact that disclosure could have on the client. [DR 4-101(A)]

      (1) **Example:** At a dinner party, a third party who does not know that Lawyer represents Client tells Lawyer that Client has prior convictions that would be relevant at the time of sentencing in a current criminal case. Under

the ABA Code, the information is not technically a "secret" because it was not "gained in the professional relationship." Under the Model Rules, however, Lawyer must not voluntarily disclose the information because it "relates to the representation."

(2) **Example:** While investigating a tort case for Client, Lawyer learns from a third party witness that Client is contemplating divorce. Under the ABA Code, the information must be protected; it was both learned in the course of the professional relationship and its disclosure is likely to be something that would embarrass the client. Under the Model Rules, however, it does not relate to the current representation and thus is not required to be kept confidential.

c. **Duty not affected by presence of strangers:** [§362] Whereas the attorney-client privilege does not apply to communications made in the presence of third parties (and thus not "in confidence"), the professional duty of nondisclosure applies even to information learned where third parties were present.

(1) **Example:** Information about a client's net worth is disclosed by the client's banker in the presence of a friend of the client. The lawyer is required to treat it as within the professional obligation of confidentiality.

2. **Exceptions to Duty of Confidentiality:** [§363] Some exceptions to the professional duty to protect the client's secrets are identical to exceptions to the attorney-client privilege, *e.g.*, client consent, lawyer self-defense, and collection of the lawyer's fee. However, there are some significant differences in the exceptions.

a. **Court may compel lawyer's testimony about secrets:** [§364] By definition, a court will not compel a lawyer to disclose information protected by the attorney-client privilege even if it is highly relevant to the resolution of a contested issue in a case. However, relevant information subject to the lawyer's professional duty but not legally privileged *may be compelled* to be disclosed in a deposition or at trial. [Fellerman v. Bradley, 493 A.2d 1239 (N.J. 1985)]

b. **Generally known information:** [§365] Because the scope of information required to be protected is otherwise so broad, the Model Rules wisely suggest that the lawyer need not protect information once it has become "generally known." [Model Rule 1.9(b)]

c. **Affirmative revelation of future crime or fraud:** [§366] While information about a client's future crime or fraud is not privileged and testimony about it could be compelled, the information is rarely known by a third party who could seek such compelled testimony. Instead, the practical question is whether or when a lawyer may come forward to warn potential victims about the client's plans.

(1) **ABA Code—intention of client to commit a crime:** [§367]   The ABA Code permits a lawyer to reveal the intention of the client to commit any crime (*e.g.*, shoplifting) and the information necessary to prevent that crime. [DR 4-101(C)(3)]

(2) **Model Rules—only to prevent client's committing criminal act likely to result in death or substantial bodily harm:** [§368]   The Model Rules permit significantly *less* disclosure. If the client's planned criminal act does not threaten someone's imminent death or substantial bodily harm, the lawyer may not reveal the client's intention to commit it. [Model Rule 1.6(b)(1)]

(3) **Example:** Client reveals to Lawyer his plans to commit a criminal securities fraud that will cost investors millions of dollars. The information is not privileged because it concerns both a future crime and fraud. The ABA Code would allow Lawyer to reveal Client's plan to the S.E.C. or to potential investors so as to prevent the future harm. Under the Model Rules, however, the plan may *not* be disclosed because the crime involves financial loss and not imminent death or substantial bodily harm.

3. **Applications of the Concepts of Confidences and Secrets**

a. **Identity of client:** [§369]   In most cases, the name or identity of a client is *not* a "communication" and hence is not privileged. However, the fact that the client had consulted a lawyer might be embarrassing or required to be kept confidential. If so, it would be a "secret" and could not be disclosed.

(1) **Identity held privileged where it might incriminate client:** [§370]   It has been held that the government may not compel a lawyer to disclose the name of the client on whose behalf the lawyer was acting in paying a large sum of unreported income taxes. The effect of compelling the lawyer to disclose the client's identity would be to *incriminate* the client for nonpayment of the taxes. [Baird v. Koerner, 279 F.2d 623 (9th Cir. 1960)]

(2) **Identity a secret where it might endanger client:** [§371]   A lawyer reporting information regarding political corruption and graft to an investigating commission should withhold the informant's identity. In such instances, the client's identity is a "secret" and should not be disclosed. [*In re* Kaplan, 8 N.Y.2d 214 (1961)]

b. **Whereabouts of client:** [§372]   Absent other circumstances, a lawyer is *privileged* not to disclose a client's address, if supplied by the client in confidence and for the *purpose* of allowing the lawyer to *communicate* with the client. [*Ex parte* Schneider, 294 S.W. 736 (Mo. 1927)]

(1) **Rationale:** Compelling disclosure in this situation might prevent the frank communication between lawyer and client necessary to protect properly the client's interests. [ABA Opn. 23]

(2) **Whereabouts may be a secret:** [§373]   Whether or not the client's address is privileged, the lawyer must not disclose it if disclosure could harm or embarrass the client.

(3) **Compare—disclosure compelled where violation of court order:** [§374]   However, when a lawyer applies for a court order on behalf of a client, the lawyer impliedly represents to the court that the client will abide by the terms and conditions of the order. Therefore, as an officer of the court, the lawyer **must** advise the court of the client's whereabouts (*i.e.*, no privilege) **if** the lawyer learns that the client has violated the order **and** cannot persuade the client to cease the violation. [ABA Opn. 156]

   (a) **Example:** A lawyer must disclose the address of a client who absconds with his child after visitation rights were granted by the court. [Dike v. Dike, 448 P.2d 490 (Wash. 1968)]

c. **Fee arrangements with client**

(1) **Privilege not applicable:** [§375]   Information regarding the fees paid or owed by a client to a lawyer is generally **not** protected by the attorney-client privilege. [United States v. Haddad, 527 F.2d 537 (6th Cir. 1975)]

   (a) **Exception:** [§376]   There are some extraordinary cases in which fee information may be held **privileged**, where to reveal the fee would **incriminate** the client. *Example:* Lawyer defending client accused of stealing $45 in silver and $5 in gold is privileged to refuse to answer whether client paid his fee by giving $45 in silver and $5 in gold. [State v. Dawson, 1 S.W. 827 (Mo. 1886)]

(2) **Ethical obligation applies:** [§377]   The fact that fee information is generally not legally privileged does **not** necessarily mean that a lawyer is **ethically** free to disclose fee arrangements since they may constitute a secret.

   (a) **Compare:** The lawyer may, however, reveal such confidences or secrets of the client as are necessary to **establish and collect the lawyer's fee** (*e.g.*, nature of work performed for client). [Model Rule 1.6(b)(2); DR 4-101(C)(4)]

d. **Physical evidence:** [§378]   The attorney-client privilege and the duty to preserve client secrets both apply only to information about the client. They do not require or permit the lawyer to take possession of or help secrete fruits or instrumentalities of a crime.

(1) **Duty to turn over to police:** [§379]   When the lawyer takes possession of physical evidence, he must turn it over to the police even if it thereby incriminates the client. [State v. Olwell, 394 P.2d 681 (Wash. 1964)]

(2) **Mere information handled differently:** [§380] If the lawyer merely knows the whereabouts of physical evidence but has not taken possession of it, the information is protected as a privilege or secret. [People v. Meredith, 29 Cal. 3d 682 (1981)]

e. **Possible claims against corporate client:** [§381] Lawyers generally have an ethical obligation not to reveal client's contingent liabilities—*i.e.*, unasserted possible claims against the client. Although such information in most cases is not a privileged "confidence," it is a "secret" since disclosure might be embarrassing to the client or might *cause* the potential claimants to assert the claims.

(1) **Auditor's inquiries into contingent liabilities:** [§382] However, S.E.C. disclosure requirements put pressure on auditors to disclose contingent liabilities, and auditors in turn ask corporate lawyers to reveal "unasserted possible claims" against their clients. A compromise has been worked out with the Financial Accounting Standards Board under which lawyers do *not* have to disclose contingent liabilities. However, they must certify that they have *told* their clients of contingent liabilities that the *client* should disclose—*i.e.*, claims (i) that are "*probable* of assertion," (ii) that if asserted, there is a "reasonable possibility" of losing, and (iii) that are large enough to be "material." [62 A.B.A.J. 1572 (1976)]

IV.   DUTY OF UNIMPAIRED LOYALTY— CONFLICTS OF INTEREST

__*chapter approach*__

In addition to duties such as competence and confidentiality, a lawyer owes a client a duty of unimpaired loyalty. Thus, the lawyer may not represent a client when the lawyer has an actual or potential conflict of interest, unless the client gives informed consent.

The four major kinds of conflicts of interest are:

1.   Conflicts between the *lawyer's personal interest and the interest of the client* (*e.g.*, the lawyer wishes to enter into business transactions with the client, receive a gift from the client, etc.).

2.   Conflicts between the interests of *two or more clients* that the lawyer is *concurrently representing*. This is especially a problem in litigation matters but can also arise in nonlitigation situations.

3.   Conflicts between the *client's interest and that of a third party to whom the lawyer owes obligations*. Here you should watch out for facts showing a third party paying the lawyer's fee, *e.g.*, a lawyer for the insurer representing the insured.

4.   Conflicts between the *lawyer's duties to a present client and the lawyer's continuing duties to a former client*.

Keep in mind that when a lawyer is disqualified due to a conflict of interest, it is likely that others associated with the lawyer will also be disqualified.

A.   INTRODUCTION

1.   **Model Rules—No Direct Adversity and No Material Limitation on Lawyer's Responsibilities to Client:** [§383]   The Model Rules state the general rule against conflict of interest as a prohibition of a lawyer's representing one client in a manner *"directly adverse"* to another client, or under circumstances causing the lawyer's representation of the client to be *"materially limited"* by other responsibilities or interests. [Model Rule 1.7]

2.   **ABA Code—No Adverse Effect on Lawyer's Professional Judgment on Behalf of Client:** [§384]   The ABA Code makes the same point in different words. A lawyer may not take a case in which the lawyer's "professional judgment" *may or is likely to be compromised*. [DR 5-101(A); DR 5-105(A), (B)]

3. **Exception—Client Consent:** [§385]   Under either statement of the general rule, a lawyer may represent a client *in spite of a conflict* if but only if:

   (i)   The lawyer can do so *without adverse effect* on the representation; and

   (ii) The client gives *informed consent*.

   [Model Rule 1.7; DR 5-101(A); DR 5-105(C)]

B. PERSONAL INTERESTS THAT MAY AFFECT LAWYER'S JUDGMENT [§386]

Whether the interest predates the representation or arises later, a lawyer must not allow a personal interest to detract from the lawyer's duty of loyalty to the client. [Model Rule 1.7(b); DR 5-101(A)]

1. **Prohibition on Acquiring Interest in Subject Matter of Employment:** [§387]   A lawyer is prohibited from purchasing or otherwise acquiring any interest in the claim or property that is the subject matter of the litigation being conducted for the client. *Rationale:* The lawyer's own financial interest might cause her to "stir up litigation." Because courts are interested in not stirring up litigation, client consent is *not* enough to eliminate this prohibition. [Model Rule 1.8(j); DR 5-103]

   a. **Example:** It is improper for a lawyer to acquire an interest in land that is the subject of a lawsuit the lawyer is handling. This ban applies both to an ownership interest and a lien (mortgage).

   b. **Example:** Likewise, a lawyer may not purchase property (directly or through any intermediary) at a probate, foreclosure, or judicial sale in an action in which the lawyer or any member of her law firm appears as attorney for a party, or in which the lawyer is acting as executor, trustee, etc. Again, the potential for a conflict of interest disqualifies the lawyer as a purchaser. [*See* Cal. Rule 4-300]

   c. **Exception—security for fees:** [§388]   The ABA Code and the Model Rules specifically recognize that a lawyer may acquire a financial interest in the subject of litigation to secure fees and costs, *e.g.*, the lawyer may charge a contingent fee and may enforce an attorney's lien (*see supra*, §§267-282).

2. **Acquiring Pecuniary Interest Adverse to Client:** [§389]   It is likewise improper for a lawyer to purchase or otherwise knowingly acquire any property or financial interest adverse to the client, unless the client expressly consents.

3. **"Kickbacks" from Third Parties:** [§390]   Similarly, without client consent, a lawyer may not accept "kickbacks" or any other form of compensation from third parties with whom the lawyer is dealing on behalf of the client (*e.g.*, a title insurance company involved in the purchase of property that the lawyer is handling for client). [Model Rule 1.8(f); DR 5-107(A)(2)]

a. **Rationale:** Again, the receipt of such benefits may affect the lawyer's independent judgment; *i.e.,* it may induce the lawyer to involve the client with persons or companies who will pay the lawyer the largest "kickback," rather than those who will best serve the client's interest. [ABA Opn. 304]

b. **Remedy:** Where it is shown that a lawyer received any such compensation without the client's knowledge, the lawyer will be held to be a ***constructive*** trustee on behalf of the client.

4. **Business or Financial Transactions with Client:** [§391]   When a lawyer acquires an interest in a client's business or property or otherwise enters into a financial transaction with the client, the lawyer's professional judgment may be affected. This possibility, together with the lawyer's fiduciary duty to avoid any hint of overreaching or undue influence, has caused the courts to examine such transactions with great care. [Committee on Professional Ethics v. Mershon, 316 N.W.2d 895 (Iowa 1982)]

a. **Presumption of undue influence:** [§392]   Courts generally hold that a lawyer who enters into a business transaction with a client must overcome a presumption of overreaching or undue influence by ***affirmative evidence*** to the contrary. Failure to present such evidence is grounds for ***setting aside the transaction***, regardless of the legal sufficiency of the consideration. [Benson v. State Bar, 13 Cal. 3d 581 (1975)]

b. **ABA Code standard:** [§393]   The ABA Code flatly states that a lawyer may not, absent client consent following full disclosure, enter into a business transaction with a client in which their interests ***differ*** if the client expects the lawyer to protect the client's interest. [DR 5-104(A)]

c. **Model Rules approach:** [§394]   The Model Rules and some state regulations are even more restrictive and bar a lawyer from entering into a business transaction with a client unless: (i) the terms are ***fair and reasonable*** and have been ***disclosed in writing*** to the client in an ***understandable*** form; (ii) the client is given a reasonable opportunity to seek the advice of independent counsel; and (iii) the client ***consents in writing*** thereto. [Model Rule 1.8(a); Cal. Rule 5-101; *and see In re* Brown, 55 P.2d 884 (Or. 1977)—failure to obtain consent in writing led to discipline]

5. **Gifts or Bequests to Lawyer:** [§395]   Lawyers are particularly susceptible to a charge of undue influence or overreaching when they accept gifts or bequests from their clients. It is improper under ***any*** circumstances for a lawyer to ***suggest*** that a gift be made to her or for her benefit. Even where the client voluntarily offers to make a gift, the conditions on which a lawyer may accept are carefully circumscribed. [Model Rule 1.8(c); EC 5-5]

a. **ABA standard:** [§396] Before accepting a significant gift, a lawyer should urge the client to obtain the *disinterested advice of a competent third person*.

   (1) **Beneficiary:** [§397] Except in extraordinary circumstances, a lawyer must insist that *any instrument* (including a will) naming the lawyer as a beneficiary be prepared by a different lawyer of the client's own choosing. [Model Rule 1.8(c); EC 5-5; State v. Horan, 123 N.W.2d 488 (Wis. 1966)]

   (2) **Executor, trustee, counsel:** [§398] Along the same lines, a lawyer should not knowingly influence a client to name her executor, trustee, or counsel in an instrument. [EC 5-6; State v. Gulbankian, 196 N.W.2d 733 (Wis. 1972)]

b. **Exception—drafting wills for personal friends or relatives:** [§399] Most courts *do* permit a lawyer to prepare wills for the lawyer's family, friends, or relatives even though the will names the lawyer (or members of the lawyer's family) beneficiary, *provided* that there is no hint of overreaching and that the bequest is "reasonable under the circumstances." [*See* Model Rule 1.8(c); State v. Horan, *supra*]

   (1) **Compare:** A few courts prohibit the preparation of wills even in this situation if the lawyer would receive anything more under the will than that to which she would be entitled as an intestate heir (without a will). [State v. Collentine, 159 N.W.2d 50 (Wis. 1968)]

c. **Presumption of undue influence:** [§400] Quite apart from the *ethical* problem, there may be a presumption made by the probate court of undue influence if any gift is made to the lawyer who drafted the will; *i.e.*, the lawyer may not be entitled to receive the gift unless she can produce *independent evidence* showing that the testator chose to make the gift freely and independently. (*See* Wills Summary.)

6. **Publication Rights Concerning Subject Matter of Employment:** [§401] Prior to the conclusion of *all* aspects of a case, a lawyer may not acquire publication rights from the client as to the subject matter of the lawyer's employment (*e.g.*, a lawyer representing a defendant in a notorious criminal case cannot accept employment on the basis that the lawyer will have the right to publish a biography of the defendant's escapades). [Model Rule 1.8(d); DR 5-104(B); Maxwell v. Superior Court, 101 Cal. App. 3d 735 (1980)]

   a. **Possible effect on lawyer's judgment:** [§402] This prohibition is based on the *possibility* that the ownership of such rights might have an adverse effect on the lawyer's exercise of independent professional judgment. For example, great media interest in a sensational case might influence the lawyer—consciously or unconsciously—to conduct the case in a manner that would enhance the value of the publication rights but prejudice the client's position. [EC 5-4]

7. **Personal Interests Affecting Association of Co-Counsel:** [§403]   The lawyer is duty-bound to associate co-counsel to provide expertise in any field in which the lawyer is not qualified to provide competent *representation for the client* (*see supra*, §§174, 176). A lawyer must not let personal interests (*e.g.*, the possibility of having to share fees with another lawyer) influence her judgment on whether she is qualified to handle the case alone. [EC 5-11]

C. CONCURRENT REPRESENTATION OF CLIENTS WITH CONFLICTING INTERESTS [§404]

The lawyer's obligation to exercise independent judgment on behalf of *each* client can be severely tested where the interests of more than one client are involved. Problems arise whenever a lawyer seeks to represent *two or more* clients with *differing* interests, whether the interests are "conflicting, inconsistent, diverse, or otherwise discordant." [EC 5-14]

1. **General Standards:** [§405]   The lawyer must *decline* employment by a client whose interests conflict with or differ from an existing client's. If the conflict of interest becomes apparent only after employment has begun, the lawyer must *withdraw* from representing the client. In close cases, the lawyer must resolve any doubt by *declining representation*. [Model Rule 1.7; DR 5-105(A), (B)]

    a. **In litigation:** [§406]   The lawyer should never represent multiple clients whose interests are *directly opposed* in a litigated proceeding. The same rule applies even though the clients' interests are only *potentially* differing, because later withdrawal—if the interests became actually conflicting—could create serious hardship. [Model Rule 1.7(a); EC 5-15]

    b. **In nonlitigation matters:** [§407]   Where litigation is not involved, the rule is less restrictive. The lawyer may, in some circumstances, properly represent several clients whose interests differ.

        (1) **Requirements:** [§408]   The lawyer may represent several clients in a nonlitigation matter where there is:

            (a) **Disclosure and consent:** [§409]   The lawyer must make a full and complete disclosure of the potential conflict to the clients and give them the chance to obtain separate counsel, and the lawyer must obtain each client's consent to the dual representation (which in some states must be in writing). [Model Rule 1.7; DR 5-105(C); Cal. Rule 3-310]

            (b) **No adverse effect on client:** [§410]   In addition to disclosure and consent, the lawyer must make a *separate* determination that continuing to act will not adversely affect the client. That must be "obvious" under the ABA Code [DR 5-105(C)], and "reasonably believed" under the Model Rules [Model Rule 1.7].

(2) **Withdrawal if conflict develops:** [§411] If conditions change (*e.g.,* clients' potentially differing interests later develop into an ***actual*** conflict), the lawyer ***must*** reevaluate the situation, get new consent from the clients, or possibly withdraw. [EC 5-15]

(3) **Lawyer's liability for nondisclosure**

    (a) **Discipline:** [§412] If the disclosure was less than candid, the consent was not freely and knowingly given, or the lawyer continued the multiple representation after an actual conflict arose, the lawyer is subject to discipline. [DR 5-105; Cal. Rule 3-310]

    (b) **Malpractice liability:** [§413] In addition, a lawyer who undertakes multiple representation without making full disclosure runs a risk of civil liability to a client who suffers a loss caused by such lack of disclosure. [Crest Investment Trust, Inc. v. Comstock, 327 A.2d 891 (Md. 1974)]

    (c) **Decision of client final and binding:** [§414] In analyzing the interests of two or more clients (in either a litigation or nonlitigation matter), the lawyer may conclude that such interests are neither actually nor potentially differing. Even so, the lawyer should disclose and discuss multiple representation with the clients. If a client decides (for whatever reason) that the arrangement is undesirable, the lawyer must defer to that opinion and withdraw—despite the lawyer's own belief in the propriety of the representation. [EC 5-19]

2. **Application of Standards—Litigation Matters:** [§415] The likelihood of impaired judgment and prejudice to the client is greatest when the lawyer seeks to represent several clients in the same litigation.

    a. **Criminal proceedings—constitutional considerations:** [§416] The problem of differing interests frequently arises when a lawyer is appointed to represent several indigent defendants in the same criminal proceeding. If the defendants' interests are in fact divergent, there is more than an ethical problem: Each accused is ***constitutionally*** entitled to the assistance of his own counsel; it is the ***duty of the court*** to appoint separate counsel whenever differing interests appear. [Holloway v. Arkansas, 435 U.S. 475 (1978); Cuyler v. Sullivan, 446 U.S. 335 (1980)]

        (1) **Accusations by one client against another:** [§417] If one defendant accuses a co-defendant of the crime, their interests are clearly adverse, and representation of both by the same appointed counsel is unconstitutional. This is true regardless of whether the accusing defendant denies guilt or admits it. [White v. United States, 396 F.2d 822 (5th Cir. 1968); Commonwealth v. Westbrook, 400 A.2d 160 (Pa. 1979)]

(2) **Differences in strength of case:** [§418] Common representation may also be unconstitutional where the defenses available to one client-defendant are **stronger** than those available to the others. The defendant with the stronger case may well be prejudiced by failure of the shared lawyer to establish or emphasize relevant defenses, and vice versa. [Campbell v. United States, 352 F.2d 359 (D.C. Cir. 1965)]

(3) **Compare—privately-retained counsel:** [§419] Where the two defendants are not indigent and have jointly retained **private** counsel, it is their shared counsel's duty to advise them of any potential conflict of interest. On appeal, however, they cannot complain of a conflict of interest unless their joint counsel's representation amounted to actual inadequate assistance. [People v. Cook, 13 Cal. 3d 663 (1975); *but see* Aetna Casualty & Surety Co. v. United States, 438 F. Supp. 886 (W.D.N.C. 1977)]

(4) **"Inherent" conflicts from shared representation?** [§420] Some courts have suggested that shared counsel may **inevitably** involve conflicts sufficient to disqualify such representation in criminal cases even by privately-retained counsel. These courts contend that the additional burden of representing another party may impair the lawyer's overall effectiveness—regardless of any differences between the parties. [Abraham v. United States, 549 F.2d 236 (2d Cir. 1977)]

   (a) **Example:** The fact that one defendant cannot take the stand to exonerate the other without risking prejudice to the defendant's own case (by cross-examination) may affect counsel's presentation of both cases (*i.e.,* counsel's decision whether to put either or both on the stand).

b. **Personal injury litigation:** [§421] Several persons injured in the same mishap may seek to retain a single lawyer to represent them in jointly litigating their respective claims. Such claimants may well have potentially differing interests which could make multiple representation improper, absent informed consent. [EC 5-17]

   (1) **Plaintiff and cross-defendant:** [§422] Where one of several plaintiffs is **also** named as a cross-defendant (*e.g.,* plaintiffs A and B sue D; D cross-complains against A claiming A was jointly liable in causing injury to B), a lawyer **cannot** represent the co-plaintiffs. *Rationale:* The lawyer would in effect be representing both sides in an adversary action, where interests must necessarily differ. [Jedwabny v. Philadelphia Trust Co., 135 A.2d 252 (Pa. 1957)]

   (2) **Driver and passenger:** [§423] Similarly, it may be improper for a lawyer to represent **both driver and passenger** in a negligence action against a common defendant, at least where the driver's contributory negligence could be imputed to bar the passenger's claim. [DuPont v. Southern Pacific Co., 366 F.2d 193 (5th Cir. 1966)]

(a) **Rationale:** The lawyer must contend on behalf of the passenger that the driver's contributory negligence is not a defense. If this argument is strongly advanced, it may prejudice the claim of the driver by implying that contributory negligence actually exists.

c. **Other civil matters:** [§424]   While criminal and personal injury cases account for most instances of shared representation in litigation, conflicts of interests among clients may exist in other matters as well.

   (1) **Divorce proceedings:** [§425]   If a state's divorce proceedings require a determination of "fault," the prohibition on joint representation of both spouses clearly applies. [McDonald v. Wagner, 5 Mo. App. 56 (1878)]

      (a) **"No fault" dissolution:** [§426]   Even where such proceedings are no longer adversary in nature (*e.g.*, the California "dissolution" proceeding, which eliminates any determination of fault), potentially differing interests over subjects like *property and child custody* make separate representation essential in most cases.

      (b) **Nonlitigation matters:** [§427]   But it is not improper for a lawyer to *counsel* spouses who are contemplating a separation or dissolution as to their mutual rights and obligations in a nonlitigation setting.

         1) **Note:** After *full disclosure* of the conflicting interests and with the *express consent* of both spouses, it is permissible for the lawyer to prepare a written separation agreement providing for division of property, support and child custody, which can then be submitted to the court in an *uncontested* proceeding.

         2) **And note:** Even where parties have a present dispute over one area (*e.g.*, child support), it has been held proper for one lawyer to help them determine and set forth the areas on which they do agree. [Klemm v. Superior Court, 75 Cal. App. 3d 893 (1977)]

   (2) **Adoption proceedings:** [§428]   Courts have approved joint representation of the consenting mother and the adopting parents in an adoption proceeding, provided again that full disclosure has been made to all parties concerned of the potential conflicts of interest. [Arden v. State Bar, 52 Cal. 2d 310 (1959)]

   (3) **Liquidation and reorganization proceedings:** [§429] Regardless of whether individual bankruptcies or major corporate receiverships are involved, such proceedings usually involve diverse and conflicting interests which make multiple representation improper.

      (a) **Basic categories of parties:** [§430]   There are usually three main classes of parties to such proceedings: *creditors, stockholders, and management groups,* each with its own particular interests. And within each class there may also exist various subclasses whose interests are similarly divergent (*e.g.*, secured and unsecured creditors, preferred and common stockholders).

(b) **Joint representation strictly scrutinized:** [§431] Courts have insisted upon the unimpaired loyalty of lawyers who represent parties to such proceedings. For example, a lawyer for "junior" claimants (*e.g.*, general creditors or common stockholders) may *not* also represent "senior" claimants (*e.g.*, bondholders or preferred stockholders). [Woods v. City National Bank, 312 U.S. 262 (1947)]

(c) **Denial of compensation where multiple representation is improper:** [§432] Moreover, the courts have repeatedly held that lawyers who place themselves in a dual role in bankruptcy or reorganization proceedings do so *at the risk of their fee*, should their clients be found to have conflicting interests.

d. **Representing opposing clients in unrelated matters:** [§433] The prohibition on representing opposing sides in adversary proceedings applies even where the adversary proceedings are unrelated. For example, absent client consent, a lawyer employed by a client to provide legal services in a lawsuit may *not* simultaneously agree to represent another party in a different lawsuit against that same client. [Grievance Committee v. Rottner, 203 A.2d 82 (Conn. 1964)]

(1) **Avoiding appearance of divided loyalty:** [§434] No actual conflict of interest is necessary. The prohibition is designed to maintain *public confidence in the bar* by assuring existing clients that they will have the *undivided loyalty* of their lawyers throughout the duration of employment. [Jeffrey v. Pounds, 67 Cal. App. 3d 6 (1977)]

(2) **Strict application:** [§435] The prohibition applies even where the second proceedings may *aid* the interests of the existing client. For example, without the consent of both clients, the lawyer for a judgment creditor in a civil action against debtor, D, *cannot* represent D in an unrelated criminal proceeding—even though a successful defense on D's criminal charge might improve the creditor's chances of collection. [*In re* Kushinsky, 247 A.2d 665 (N.J. 1968)]

e. **Lump sum settlement for several clients:** [§436] A lawyer who *is* able to represent more than one client in litigation proceedings may face divergent interests when a "lump sum" settlement is offered by the other side. Here, again, the lawyer must carefully preserve independent judgment and loyalty to *each* client.

(1) **Consent of each client after full disclosure:** [§437] To prevent conflicting interests, *each client* must consent to the aggregate settlement after being advised of (i) the existence and nature of all claims involved in the proposed settlement, (ii) the total amount of the settlement, *and*

(iii) the participation of each person in the settlement. [Model Rule 1.8(g); DR 5-106]

(2) **Application to criminal defendants:** [§438] The Model Rules extend this requirement to situations where a lawyer represents multiple criminal defendants considering nolo contendere or guilty pleas that might have an impact on the other defendants. [Model Rule 1.8(g)]

3. **Application of Standards—Nonlitigation Matters:** [§439] As discussed earlier, representing multiple clients in nonlitigation matters is still a conflict but often is permitted, even though the clients have *potentially* differing interests, if the conflict is waived. [EC 5-15]

   a. **Examples**

      (1) **Sale of property:** [§440] A lawyer for the seller of real property may not also represent the buyer in closing title, unless full disclosure has been made to the buyer of the possible pitfalls of such dual representation. [*In re* Kamp, 194 A.2d 236 (N.J. 1963)]

      (2) **Borrower and lender:** [§441] The same problems may arise where a lawyer purports to represent both borrower and lender on a mortgage or other security. Again, such representation is improper without full disclosure to both sides of the potential conflicts, and the parties' mutual consent. [*In re* Greenberg, 121 A.2d 520 (N.J. 1956)]

      (3) **Trustee and testator:** [§442] Provided the testator fully understands the relationship and its implications (*e.g.*, fees), a lawyer who represents a bank may properly draw a will for a testator that names the bank as executor and trustee. [ABA Opn. 243]

   b. **Advantages of multiple representation:** [§443] In matters such as the drafting of contracts, joint representation may actually be *preferable* to retaining separate counsel. Some courts have compared this to the advantages that conciliation and negotiation have over litigation in reaching agreements. [Hobart's Administrator v. Vail, 66 A. 820 (Vt. 1907)]

   c. **Model Rules approach:** [§444] The Model Rules explicitly recognize this role of the lawyer and call it acting as an "intermediary" [*see* Model Rule 2.2], applying the following conditions:

      (1) *The potential conflict must be fully explained*, and the clients given a chance to retain separate counsel;

      (2) *The clients must give their full knowledgeable consent* (in writing, in some states);

(3) **The lawyer must make an independent judgment** that each client can be **adequately represented**; and

(4) **No actual conflict must later arise** (if it does, the lawyer must withdraw).

4. **Special Problems of Corporate Counsel:** [§445] The lawyer for a corporation or other complex organization faces an inherent conflict of interest situation. Stockholders, officers, and directors of the corporation often have differing interests, and the lawyer may not seem to be able to serve each totally in a given situation.

    a. **ABA Code—entity theory:** [§446] The ABA Code takes the traditional view that the interests of the corporate entity are to be favored over those of any constituent part. [EC 5-18]

    b. **Model Rules—more complex duties for lawyer:** [§447] The Model Rules treat the corporate counsel more extensively than does the ABA Code, although the basic duty to the entity is said to be the same. [Model Rule 1.13(a)]

    (1) **If a lawyer learns that someone within the organization** is now violating or intends to **violate a legal obligation** to the organization or one that may be imputed to the organization, and which is likely to result in **substantial injury** to the organization, then the lawyer shall proceed as **"reasonably necessary"** in the best interests of the organization. Measures may include asking reconsideration of the matter, getting a separate opinion, or referral higher in the organization, even ultimately to the Board of Directors. [Model Rule 1.13(b)]

    (2) **If the lawyer is unsuccessful in getting the matter resolved** by the "highest authority" in the organization, the lawyer's option under an earlier version of the Model Rules was to go outside the organization—*e.g.*, to the S.E.C. As adopted by the ABA, however, the Model Rules give the lawyer only the option to **resign**. [Model Rule 1.13(c)]

    (3) **A lawyer may represent both the organization and persons within it** but only if there is no actual conflict of interest. [Model Rule 1.13(e)]

    (4) **Where interests do conflict,** the lawyer must take care to let officers, directors, and the like, know that the lawyer represents the organization and not them. [Model Rule 1.13(d)]

D. INTERESTS OF THIRD PERSONS AFFECTING LAWYER-CLIENT RELATIONSHIPS [§448]

The lawyer is under a duty to disregard the desires or interests of any third person that would **impair the lawyer's independent judgment and loyalty** to the client. [Model Rule 1.7(b); EC 5-11; DR 5-107(B)]

1. **Compensation from Third Parties for Representing Client:** [§449]   A lawyer may not accept any form of compensation from a third person for services to the client, *except with the full knowledge and consent* of the client. *Rationale:* Even the appearance of divided interests is to be avoided. [Model Rule 1.8(f); DR 5-107(A)]

2. **Employment by Lay Intermediary:** [§450]   Nor may a lawyer accept employment by a corporation or anyone else who would have the *right to direct or control* the lawyer's professional judgment in representing clients. [Model Rule 5.4(c); DR 5-107(B)]

   a. **Example:** A lawyer should decline to defend the accused in a criminal case where the accused's boss will pay the attorney's fees if the client will not cooperate with the prosecution. The lawyer's loyalty might be divided between the boss (the source of the fee) and the client (whose best interests might call for cooperation with the prosecution). [Matter of Abrams, 266 A.2d 275 (N.J. 1970)]

3. **Representing Liability Insurer and Insured:** [§451]   Liability policies usually provide that the insurance company will indemnify the insured against liability to third persons up to the monetary limits of the policy, and that the company will provide a lawyer (selected and paid by the company) to represent the policyholder in any lawsuit filed against her. The insured agrees to "cooperate" in defending against claims covered by the policy.

   a. **Nature of problem:** [§452]   When a claim is brought against an insured under the liability policy, differing interests may arise. The insured wants the dispute settled without personally incurring liability, whatever the cost may be to the insurance company. On the other hand, the company wishes to pay as little as possible in resolving the case—whether in the form of payment to the opposing party *or* in its costs of litigation.

   b. **Propriety of joint representation:** [§453]   Despite these potential conflicts, the insurance company's furnishing a lawyer to defend the insured is an essential ingredient of liability insurance and is deemed socially useful. Hence, it is both proper and quite common for the lawyer selected by the insurance company to represent both the company's interest and that of the policyholder in defending claims brought against the insured.

   c. **Duty of lawyer to avoid conflicting interests:** [§454]   However, the lawyer selected by the company to represent the insured *still* has a professional obligation to avoid conflicting interests and impaired loyalty. The lawyer may be subject to both disciplinary action and civil liability for failing to do so (*see* below).

   d. **Possible areas of conflict**

      (1) **Policy coverage in dispute:** [§455]   Insurance policies often cover certain contingencies (*e.g.*, negligence) but *exclude* others (*e.g.*, intentional harm).

The insured naturally wishes any liability to be covered under the policy, while the insurer is best served if liability is found to be in the excluded area. If a dispute arises between the insured and the insurance company as to whether the claim is covered under the policy, the lawyer clearly may **not** represent both. (As a practical matter, the insurance company often agrees to defend the action "with a reservation of rights"—meaning that it will only litigate the issue of policy coverage with the insured if the insured is held liable on the claim.) [Parsons v. Continental National American Group, 535 P.2d 17 (Ariz. 1976)]

(2) **Settlement proposals—policy limits cases:** [§456]   The interests of the insurance company and the insured defendant may also conflict where a settlement demand is made by the plaintiff that is **within or close to the policy limits**. *Example:* P sues D (insured) claiming personal injury damages of $100,000; D's liability insurance is limited to $10,000; later P offers to settle the case for $10,000 (policy limits).

(a) **Conflict of interests:** [§457]   The insured (D) naturally wants the insurance company to accept the settlement offer—to avoid the risk of a judgment against D personally in excess of the policy limits. On the other hand, the insurance company has nothing to lose and everything to gain by litigating the matter—it may be lucky and get a lower verdict.

(b) **Obligation of the insurer:** [§458]   The insurer must take care to protect the interests of the insured. When a settlement offer close to the policy limits is made, the insurer must evaluate the offer as though its liability exposure was for the whole of plaintiff's claim, not just part of it. If the insurer rejects the offer negligently or in bad faith, it will be liable for **all** of a subsequent judgment—even that portion in excess of the policy limits. [Crisci v. Security Insurance Co., 66 Cal. 2d 425 (1967)]

(c) **Obligation of lawyer:** [§459]   A lawyer representing both the insurer and insured who is faced with such a settlement offer should advise both clients of the conflict of interest involved. The lawyer is obliged not only to inform the insurer of its duty to the insured regarding settlement but also to use all best efforts to see that the interests of the insured are protected. Lawyers who regard themselves as primarily lawyers for the insurance company, and act accordingly, risk liability to the policyholder.

1) **Example:** If a lawyer continues to represent both the insurer and insured, and negligently or in bad faith counsels rejection of the settlement offer, the lawyer's conduct is not only unethical but may cause the lawyer to be held **personally liable** for any damage caused to the insured (*i.e.,* the amount of any judgment returned against the insured in excess of the policy limits). [Lysick v. Walcom, 258 Cal. App. 2d 136 (1968)]

(3) **Collusion or failure to cooperate by insured:** [§460]   In certain instances, especially those involving liability claims against the insured by members of her own family, the policyholder refuses to give adequate cooperation in defending against the claim. (For example, Son claims he slipped and fell in driveway as result of insured Mother's negligence in failing to remove grease.)

    (a) **Duty to insured in withdrawing from the case:** [§461]   The lawyer who suspects collusion or lack of cooperation by the insured may (i) recommend to the insured that she seek independent counsel, and (ii) withdraw from the proceedings altogether. If suit is pending, however, the lawyer may withdraw only with leave of court and after giving the insured reasonable time to obtain a new lawyer. [Thomas v. Douglas, 2 App. Div. 2d 885 (1957)]

4. **Juvenile Court Proceedings:** [§462]   A lawyer retained or appointed to defend a juvenile in delinquency or criminal proceedings owes a duty to act as *advocate* for the juvenile. It is the courts function, not the lawyer's, to decide whether the child needs punishment, rehabilitation, parental care, or the like. The lawyer's primary responsibility is to the client (juvenile), and this means rigorously asserting all possible defenses for acquittal. [116 Pa. L. Rev. 1156 (1968)]

    a. **Disclosure and decision making:** [§463]   As with any other client, the lawyer owes a duty to disclose all relevant considerations and submit all important decisions to the juvenile. [*Compare* Model Rule 1.14—decision making by someone under a "disability"]

    b. **No client responsibility to parent:** [§464]   Even if the fee is being paid by the parents, the lawyer's obligation is to the child (the client). Thus, for example, the lawyer must refuse to disclose to the parents information revealed in confidence by the child, and the attorney-client privilege pertains to the child and not the parents. Likewise, the lawyer must follow the child's decisions as to the case, rather than the parents' (*see supra*, §448).

    c. **Potential conflicts of interest with parents:** [§465]   There may be cases where the parents' interests actually conflict with those of the child (*e.g.*, where a child is cited for delinquency because of parental neglect). In such cases, the lawyer may *not* represent both the parents and the child.

5. **Service on Board of Legal Services Organization:** [§466]   A lawyer who serves on the board of a legal services organization has fiduciary duties to persons represented by that organization. Service on such a board is not per se prohibited, but the lawyer may not knowingly participate in a decision or action of the organization that would (i) conflict with the lawyer's duty to a private client, or (ii) have an adverse effect on an organization client whose interests are adverse to the lawyer's other clients. [Model Rule 6.3]

E. CONFLICT BETWEEN INTERESTS OF CURRENT CLIENT AND FORMER ONE [§467]

The final traditional conflict of interest is not really a problem of divided loyalties. Here, the former client is simply someone who is owed some residual duty by the lawyer. At the very least, the lawyer has a continuing duty to protect the former client's confidential information. This is a subject on which the ABA Code has few specific provisions; case law and the Model Rules, however, deal with it directly.

1. **Prohibition on Representation in Same Matter:** [§468] The lawyer may ***not*** successively represent opposing parties in the ***same*** litigation. [Model Rule 1.9(a)] *Examples:*

    a. **Defense lawyer becomes prosecutor:** [§469] It is improper—and a denial of ***due process***—for a lawyer hired to represent an ***accused in a criminal case*** thereafter to accept an appointment as prosecutor and represent the state against the accused on the same charge. [Corbin v. Broadman, 6 Ariz. App. 436 (1967)]

    b. **Representing both parties to a divorce:** [§470] Representing first one spouse and then the other in the same divorce proceeding is prohibited. This ban also extends to a successive representation in ancillary proceedings in the same matter. Thus, a lawyer may not represent the husband in a divorce action and subsequently appear for the wife in an action to increase support payments. [Ennis v. Ennis, 276 N.W.2d 341 (Wis. 1979)]

2. **Prohibition on Representation in "Substantially Related" Matters:** [§471] The bar to a lawyer's later representation also applies where the lawyer would be taking a position materially adverse to a former client in a matter ***closely related factually or legally*** to the prior one, or where there is some other substantial risk that the lawyer will ***use confidential information*** obtained in the prior representation against the former client. [Model Rule 1.9(b), (c)] *Examples:*

    a. **Cases related factually:** [§472] A lawyer who has defended medical malpractice cases for a hospital may not thereafter represent a patient in a malpractice suit against the hospital, at least where the facts arose during the period when the lawyer was representing the hospital. [Crawford Long Hospital of Emory University v. Yerby, 373 S.E.2d 749 (Ga. 1988)]

    b. **Case involving contract lawyer drafted:** [§473] A lawyer who has drafted employment contracts for a client may not thereafter represent an employee suing to construe or challenge the contract. [NCK Organization, Ltd. v. Bregman, 542 F.2d 128 (2d Cir. 1976)]

    c. **Other cases in which former client's confidential information may be at risk**

        (1) **Former general counsel of company:** [§474] It was held improper for a lawyer who had been general counsel of a company to represent a client suing the company. The lawyer knew no specific confidential

information relating to the case but knew general confidential information about company operations. [Chugach Electric Association v. United States District Court, 370 F.2d 441 (9th Cir. 1966)]

   (2) **Former client now a witness in present case:** [§475] Because the interest to be protected is that of the former client, even if that client is not a party to the new case the lawyer will be disqualified if the former client will be an essential witness for the other side and confidential information might be used by the lawyer to impeach the former client. [United States v. Iorizzo, 786 F.2d 52 (7th Cir. 1986)]

  d. **Actual disclosure of confidential information not required:** [§476] The court is not required to determine what confidential information might have been disclosed or used against the former client; to do so would require the former client to disclose that which it had a right to protect. [T.C. Theatre Corp. v. Warner Bros. Pictures, Inc., 113 F. Supp. 265 (S.D.N.Y. 1953)—case in which the "same or substantially related" test was first announced]

  e. **However, former client must have had an expectation that information would be held confidential:** [§477] Where a lawyer had represented two clients in a joint venture and there had been complete sharing of business information, it was not improper for the lawyer to represent one of the firms in the bankruptcy of the other. [Allegaert v. Perot, 565 F.2d 246 (2d Cir. 1977)]

3. **Consent of Affected Clients Can Waive Conflict:** [§478] As in the case of other kinds of conflicts of interest, a lawyer may undertake "conflicted" representation if the former client gives informed consent. If conditions are imposed by the former client on conduct of the new matter (*e.g.*, in order to protect sensitive information), informed consent of the new client to the continuation of the representation is also required. [Model Rule 1.10(c)]

F. DISQUALIFICATION OF OTHER LAWYERS AFFILIATED WITH LAWYER [§479]

The prohibition on representing clients because of a conflict of interests extends to persons affiliated with the lawyer. [Model Rule 1.10(a); DR 5-105(D)]

1. **Private Law Firms:** [§480] The most common application of this principle is to persons affiliated as partners, associates, and other lawyers in a private law firm.

  a. **Offices in multiple cities:** [§481] The rule even applies where one firm has offices in different cities. Thus, if a client is represented by lawyer A in one city, A's partners in another city are disqualified from representing clients in an unrelated suit against A's client. [Cinema 5, Ltd. v. Cinerama, Ltd., 528 F.2d 1384 (2d Cir. 1976); Westinghouse Electric Corp. v. Kerr-McGee Corp., 580 F.2d 1311 (7th Cir. 1978)]

b. **Affiliated persons or firms:** [§482]   Even other firms that have been working on a case with a disqualified firm may themselves be disqualified pursuant to this rule. The factual question will be whether the relationship between the firms was close enough to warrant concern that prohibited confidential information may have passed between them. [Fund of Funds, Ltd. v. Arthur Andersen & Co., 567 F.2d 225 (2d Cir. 1977)—firm disqualified; American Can Co. v. Citrus Feed Co., 436 F.2d 1125 (5th Cir. 1971)—no disqualification]

c. **Persons other than lawyers with disqualifying information:** [§483]   Similar problems can arise if a law firm hires, for example, a secretary (or a law student) who had worked for the firm on the other side of a major case; but imputed disqualification is less automatic in such cases. [*See* Heron v. Jones, 637 S.W.2d 569 (Ark. 1982)—secretary could be "walled off" from case at new firm]

d. **When disqualified person has left law firm:** [§484]   If a lawyer who would have had a personal conflict of interest has permanently ceased association with a law firm, leaving no records and no person in the firm who would be similarly disqualified, the firm is no longer prohibited from undertaking a representation. [Model Rule 1.10(b)]

2. **Other Practice Organizations:** [§485]   The statement of the disqualification rule in the ABA Code and the Model Rules is very broad. For example, it clearly covers lawyers in a corporate legal office, but its application to organizations with no common economic interest is less clear.

a. **Lawyers sharing office space:** [§486]   When lawyers share office space but otherwise do not work on each other's cases or share revenue from them, imputed disqualification will not be imposed if each lawyer's confidential information is adequately protected. [United States v. Bell, 506 F.2d 207 (D.C. Cir. 1974)]

b. **Government legal offices:** [§487]   The practical effect of potentially making it impossible for an entire government legal office to act has caused courts to disqualify such offices only where there is a clear possibility of harm arising from the conflict. [State v. Jones, 429 A.2d 936 (Conn. 1980)—refusal to disqualify prosecutor's office]

c. **Legal services agencies:** [§488]   The same result should be reached in the case of nonprofit legal services agencies, but courts have seemed to be more willing to find imputed disqualification in cases where such agencies seek to represent persons with conflicting interests. [Flores v. Flores, 598 P.2d 893 (Alaska 1979)]

3. **Lawyers Related as Spouses:** [§489]   When one spouse works for one firm and the other spouse for another, a danger of making inadvertent disclosures is created that could compromise the interests of clients. Thus, while the firms for which

spouses work are not automatically barred from representing opposing interests, the two related lawyers may not themselves represent clients who are "directly adverse" unless their clients give informed consent. [Model Rule 1.8(i)]

a. **Other related lawyers:** [§490] Similar problems are created by parent-child and sibling relationships, and the rules pertaining to disqualification are the same. [Model Rule 1.8(i)]

4. **Interlocutory Appeals of Disqualification:** [§491] A very practical issue in the disqualification/imputation area has been the right to an interlocutory appeal of a grant or denial of a motion to disqualify. Now it is clear that *neither* a grant nor denial of such a motion may be appealed until the case reaches final judgment. [Firestone Tire & Rubber Co. v. Risjord, 449 U.S. 368 (1981)—denial of motion in civil case; Richardson Merrill, Inc. v. Koller, 469 U.S. 915 (1985)—grant of motion in civil case; Flanagan v. United States, 465 U.S. 259 (1984)—grant in criminal case; United States v. White, 743 F.2d 488 (7th Cir. 1984)—denial in criminal case]

5. **Use of Work Product:** [§492] However, if one firm *is disqualified* from acting as counsel in a matter after beginning work, its work product *may be used* by successor counsel to the extent it is not tainted by the use of confidential information. [First Wisconsin Mortgage Trust v. First Wisconsin Corp., 584 F.2d 201 (7th Cir. 1978)]

G. LIMITATIONS ON REPRESENTATION BY PRESENT AND FORMER GOVERNMENT LAWYERS [§493]

When a lawyer leaves or enters government service, special conflict of interest questions are presented.

1. **ABA Code:** [§494] The ABA Code prohibits a lawyer from accepting private employment in any matter in which that lawyer had *"substantial responsibility"* while a public employee. [DR 9-101(B)]

a. **Matter defined:** [§495] For purposes of this rule, the same "matter" is the "same lawsuit" or "representation concerning some issue of fact involving the same parties." [ABA Opn. 342]

b. **No claim of improper influence:** [§496] In addition, no lawyer may claim or imply the ability to improperly influence a government official. [DR 9-101(C)]

2. **Model Rules:** [§497] The Model Rules distinguish four different problems involving present and former government lawyers.

a. **"Personal and substantial" involvement:** [§498] Consistent with DR 9-101(B), a former government lawyer may not represent a private client in any matter in which the lawyer "participated personally and substantially" while in government, unless the appropriate government agency consents. [Model Rule 1.11(a); *and see* Model Rule 1.12(a)—former judge, law clerk, or arbitrator]

(1) **Matter defined:** [§499]   Here, the word "matter" means any "judicial . . . proceeding, application, request for a ruling, . . . contract, claim, controversy, . . . or other particular matter involving a specific party or parties." Among the things *excluded* from this definition is the drafting of legislation or regulations. [Model Rule 1.11(d)]

(2) **Imputation to partners and associates:** [§500]   A former government lawyer's *firm* is *not* disqualified if the tainted lawyer (i) is *screened from any participation* in the matter, (ii) *shares no fees* earned from the case, and (iii) *written notice* is promptly given to the appropriate government agency. [Model Rule 1.11(a); *and see* Model Rule 1.12(e)—former judge, law clerk, or arbitrator]

b. **Confidential government information:** [§501]   Even if the lawyer's work on a matter was not "personal and substantial" while in government, the lawyer may not represent a private client adverse to another private party about whom the lawyer learned "confidential government information" without the consent of that adverse party. [Model Rule 1.11(b)]

(1) **Definition:** [§502]   "Confidential government information" is information obtained under government authority and which, at the time the rule is invoked, the government may not disclose or which is otherwise not available to the public. [Model Rule 1.11(e)]

(2) **Imputation:** [§503]   Once again, the tainted lawyer's firm may only handle the matter if the tainted lawyer is adequately screened. [Model Rule 1.11(b)]

c. **Lawyer coming to government from private practice:** [§504]   A lawyer in government service may not participate in work on any matter in which the lawyer was involved while in nongovernmental employment unless, by law, no one else may act in the lawyer's stead. [Model Rule 1.11(c)(1)]

d. **Negotiating for private employment:** [§505]   A government lawyer may not negotiate for private employment with any person involved in a matter on which the government lawyer is working. [Model Rule 1.11(c)(2); *and see* Model Rule 1.12(b)—judge or law clerk negotiating employment]

3. **Federal Statute:** [§506]   The Federal Conflict of Interest Act, originally passed in 1963, imposes substantial *criminal sanctions* for certain representation of private parties after government service, whether or not the government service was as a lawyer.

a. **Permanent bar:** [§507] A lawyer who has participated "personally and substantially" in a matter is barred *forever* from *contacting the government about it* on behalf of a private client. [18 U.S.C. §207(a)(1)]

b. **Two year bar:** [§508] A lawyer is barred for *two years* from contacting the government about any matter within the lawyer's "official responsibility" while in government, even if the lawyer did no personal work on it at all. [18 U.S.C. §207(a)(2)]

c. **No imputation:** [§509] Unlike the ABA Code and Model Rules provisions, these disqualifications are personal and not imputed to the lawyer's firm. Indeed, the former government lawyer may work on the cases as long as she does not contact the government orally or in writing. [18 U.S.C. §207(a)]

V. OBLIGATIONS TO THIRD PERSONS AND THE LEGAL SYSTEM

chapter approach

Although the duties of a lawyer to the client are the beginning of any analysis of legal ethics, the law imposes important _limitations_ on what a lawyer may do on the client's behalf and imposes _affirmative duties_ to other parties. The important limitations and duties include:

1. **No counseling or assisting illegal or fraudulent conduct:** The lawyer may not help a client commit a crime or fraud, or cover it up or avoid detection, but the lawyer _may discuss_ the legal consequences of proposed conduct.

2. **Being honest in communicating with others:** Although the lawyer must represent the client zealously, this does not allow the lawyer to make false statements of _material fact or law._ Sometimes too the lawyer must affirmatively disclose matters to the court or other party.

3. **Communicating with appropriate party:** If the adverse party is represented by counsel, the lawyer must communicate directly with counsel on any subject of the controversy. If the adverse party has no counsel, the lawyer must be careful not to advise the party or to take "unfair advantage" of him.

4. **No threatening of criminal prosecution:** A lawyer may not try to use the threat of criminal prosecution to gain an advantage in a civil case.

5. **Improving the legal system:** Lawyers have a duty to support and improve the legal system by becoming involved in public service, supporting judges and the judicial system, etc. Also, a lawyer representing a client before a legislative body has duties both to the client and the legislative body.

Note that these limitations and duties apply regardless of whether the matter is in litigation.

A. COUNSELING OR ASSISTING ILLEGAL OR FRAUDULENT CONDUCT

1. **In General:** [§510]   A lawyer may not counsel a client to engage in conduct that the lawyer knows is illegal or fraudulent. [Model Rule 1.2(d); DR 7-102(A)(7), (8)] _Examples:_

    a. **Making illegal bribes:** [§511]   Advising and assisting clients to make illegal bribes to union agents can subject lawyers to both personal criminal liability and disbarment. [Disciplinary Counsel v. Stern, 526 A.2d 1180 (Pa. 1987)]

b. **False tax returns:** [§512] Similarly, a lawyer who knowingly assists in preparation of a client's fraudulent income tax returns both violates the criminal law and is subject to professional discipline as a lawyer. [West Virginia State Bar Association v. Hart, 410 S.E.2d 714 (W. Va. 1991)]

2. **Discussing Legal Consequences of Conduct:** [§513] Of course, lawyers often are asked about conduct that if undertaken would be illegal. In such cases, a lawyer may discuss the legal consequences of proposed conduct with a client as long as the lawyer does not advocate the client's undertaking it or counsel the client how to avoid detection or escape arrest. [Model Rule 1.2(d); EC 7-5]

3. **Good Faith Testing of Bounds of the Law:** [§514] A lawyer *may* assist a client to commit an act that will, in good faith, test the validity, scope, meaning, or application of the law. [Model Rule 1.2(d); *compare* DR 7-106(a)—good faith testing of court order]

4. **Lawyer's Refusal to Assist Arguable Crime or Fraud:** [§515] Under the ABA Code, a lawyer may refuse to assist a client in conduct the lawyer believes to be illegal even if the conduct is arguably legal. [DR 7-101(B)(2); *compare* Model Rule 1.16(b)(1)—lawyer's right to withdraw in such a case]

B. REQUIREMENT OF HONESTY IN COMMUNICATIONS WITH OTHERS

1. **Basic Obligation of Truthfulness:** [§516] A lawyer may not knowingly make a false statement of material fact or law to a third person in the course of representing a client, even if that might seem to serve the client's interest. [Model Rule 4.1(a); DR 7-102(A)(5)]

   a. **Example:** A lawyer who misleads doctors by saying that the client lacks the money to pay their bills is subject to professional discipline. [Florida Bar v. McLawhorn, 505 So. 2d 1338 (Fla. 1987)]

   b. **Comment:** This obligation, of course, is consistent with the lawyer's broader duty to avoid "conduct involving dishonesty, fraud, deceit, or misrepresentation." [Model Rule 8.4(c); DR 1-102(A)(4)]

2. **Duty to Come Forward with Information:** [§517] A lawyer sometimes even has an obligation to correct a misapprehension of material fact by a third person, but the scope of this obligation is much more controversial than the lawyer's duty personally to tell the truth.

   a. **Model Rules requirement:** [§518] The Model Rules say that a lawyer may not "knowingly fail to disclose a material fact to a third person when disclosure is necessary to avoid assisting a criminal or fraudulent act by a client, unless disclosure is prohibited by Rule 1.6 [the duty to protect confidential client information]." [Model Rule 4.1(b)]

b. **ABA Code provision:** [§519] The ABA Code is even more general. A lawyer may not "conceal or knowingly fail to reveal that which he is required by law to reveal," thus leaving open what the law requires to be revealed. [DR 7-102(A)(3)]

3. **Lawyer's Duty in Negotiations Generally:** [§520] Most commonly, issues of honesty and affirmative disclosure arise in the context of negotiations. In general, a lawyer has *no duty* to do the other side's fact research nor any *right* to reveal facts that would undermine the client's position.

a. **Puffing and other subjective assertions:** [§521] It is part of the essence of negotiation that the lawyer tries to magnify the strength of the client's position, and a reasonable hearer would not take many of a lawyer's statements as worthy of reliance. [*See* Model Rule 4.1, Comment]

(1) **Example:** A lawyer's statement that "any jury would award my client at least a million dollars" would ordinarily constitute permitted puffing, not prohibited dishonesty.

b. **No duty to correct misapprehensions not involving deceit by lawyer or client:** [§522] Furthermore, a lawyer who believes that an opponent is underestimating the strength of its position has no duty to correct that belief unless the lawyer or client has caused the underestimation. [Brown v. County of Genessee, 872 F.2d 169 (6th Cir. 1989)—opponent miscalculated amount of her lost pay]

c. **Where disclosure was required:** [§523] In some cases, a lawyer is required to disclose information. *Examples:*

(1) Settlement of a case was *set aside* when the plaintiff's lawyer failed to disclose to the defendant that the plaintiff, a potentially strong witness, had died. [Virzi v. Grand Trunk Warehouse, 571 F. Supp. 507 (E.D. Mich. 1983)]

(2) A prosecutor was held to have a *duty to tell* a criminal defendant, prior to accepting a guilty plea, that physical evidence of the defendant's guilt had been accidentally destroyed. [Fambo v. Smith, 433 F. Supp. 590 (W.D.N.Y. 1977)]

d. **Possible exception—the passive lawyer:** [§524] Some cases that say that a lawyer may transmit fraudulent information to a third party, as long as the information was prepared by the client and the lawyer does not separately vouch for its accuracy. [Schatz v. Rosenberg, 943 F.2d 485 (4th Cir. 1991)]

(1) **Caution:** While such a defense might suffice in a case where the lawyer's actual knowledge of the fraud were in doubt, a lawyer might be held to have aided and abetted the client's fraud if he in fact knew of it.

4. **Specially Assumed Duty of Candor in Communication—Lawyer as Evaluator:** [§525] In the interest of time or reducing cost, a lawyer may be asked by the party on the other side of a transaction to certify facts on which the other party may rely. Unless contrary to the interest of the lawyer's client, the lawyer may do so. [Model Rule 2.3]

   a. **Common examples:** Lawyers frequently agree to make such certifications for the benefit of third parties. For example, they give opinion letters (*e.g.*, "the client is validly incorporated"), and make title examinations of property the client wants to sell or mortgage.

   b. **Model Rule requirements:** [§526] The Model Rules call this making an "evaluation for use by third persons." Before making such an evaluation, the lawyer must reasonably believe it is *in the client's interest* to do so and the *client must consent.* [Model Rule 2.3(a)]

   c. **Duty of care in making evaluation:** [§527] Because the evaluation is made with the knowledge that a third party will rely on it, the lawyer will be liable *to the third party* for any negligence in determining the facts. [Greycas, Inc. v. Proud, 826 F.2d 1560 (7th Cir. 1987)—lawyer certified client's title to farm equipment without checking records; in fact, all was previously mortgaged]

   d. **Confidentiality of information not required to be disclosed:** [§528] Even though the investigation is for the purpose of making a disclosure, any facts learned by the lawyer that are not required to be disclosed must be treated by the lawyer as confidential and protected by Model Rule 1.6. [Model Rule 2.3(b)]

5. **Cases in Which Lawyer's Opinion Is To Be Widely Disseminated:** [§529] Consistent with the above rules, when a lawyer agrees to certify facts to a large number of persons who can be expected to rely on the lawyer, the lawyer has a special obligation to be complete, accurate, and candid.

   a. **Securities cases:** [§530] This special obligation is most often enforced when the lawyer has prepared an opinion letter to be used in disclosure documents for securities investors. The lawyer may be held liable for *both* misstatements and omissions of material facts. [SEC v. National Student Marketing Corp., 457 F. Supp. 682 (D.D.C. 1978)]

   b. **Due diligence required:** [§531] A lawyer is not a guarantor of every fact in the disclosure materials about the company or the transaction, or even those upon which the lawyer relies in rendering an opinion. However, if disclosures are inconsistent, or the lawyer has any other reason to doubt their accuracy, the lawyer has a *duty to inquire* to determine what the correct facts are. [ABA Opn. 335]

c. **Tax shelter opinions:** [§532]   When a lawyer gives a widely disseminated legal opinion about the tax treatment likely to be afforded an investment, the lawyer must candidly disclose and estimate the degree of risk that the IRS will not allow the tax deductions being sought, even if such disclosure will be contrary to the interest of the lawyer's client in maximum sales of the investment. [ABA Opn. 346]

C. COMMUNICATING DIRECTLY WITH ADVERSE PARTY

1. **Adverse Party Represented by Counsel:** [§533]   A lawyer who *knows* that an adverse party is represented by counsel must not communicate directly with that party on any subject of controversy unless that party's counsel is present or has given prior consent. [Model Rule 4.2; DR 7-104(A)(1); Cal. Rule 2-100(A)]

    a. **Scope of prohibition:** [§534]   Any communication touching on the subject of controversy is prohibited. The purpose of the ban is to prevent *any possibility* of interference with the lawyer-client relationship on the other side. [Mitton v. State Bar, 71 Cal. 2d 525 (1969)]

        (1) **Improper intent not required:** [§535]   Where the lawyer knows that the opposing party has counsel of record in the case, it is improper for the lawyer to contact the opposing party even for the purpose of "confirming" that such party is represented or for the purpose of "checking the facts." [*In re* Schwabe, 408 P.2d 922 (Or. 1965)]

    b. **Indirect contacts also prohibited:** [§536]   The ban on a lawyer's contacting the opposing party without the consent of that party's counsel extends to contacts by any person *affiliated* with the lawyer or acting on the lawyer's behalf (*e.g.*, investigators, secretaries, etc.).

        (1) **Note:** It also applies where a lawyer instigates a meeting with the opposing party *by suggesting to his own client* that the case "could probably be settled if he [opposing party] would come in to see me without that troublemaking lawyer of his." [ABA Opn. 75]

        (2) **But note:** The parties, of course, can always get together in the absence of either lawyer and settle the matter on their own. Even if they do so, however, neither lawyer can deal directly with the opposing party (in procuring signatures on releases or settlement agreement) without the consent of opposing counsel. [Abeles v. State Bar, 9 Cal. 3d 603 (1973)]

    c. **Communicating with nonparty witnesses for opposing party:** [§537]   The ban on communicating directly with the opposing party does *not* apply to communicating with *nonparty witnesses*. The witnesses in a case do not "belong" to anyone; therefore, counsel may properly communicate with persons who are testifying, or who propose to testify, for the opposite side. [*See*

International Business Machines v. United States, 493 F.2d 112 (2d Cir. 1973)—right to interview adversary witnesses without adversary counsel being present]

2. **Adverse Party Unrepresented by Counsel:** [§538]   Where an adverse party is not represented by counsel, the lawyer may be forced to communicate directly with the party.

   a. **Limitations:** In such a case, the lawyer may not *advise* such a party beyond suggesting that the party secure counsel to represent her interests. [Model Rule 4.3; DR 7-104(A)(2)]

   b. **And note:** If the adverse party refuses to employ counsel, and insists upon representing herself (in propria persona), the lawyer will then have to negotiate and deal with the adverse party directly. As a practical matter, however, courts are often very protective of laypersons appearing in propria persona, and do not permit lawyers to take "unfair advantage" of such persons by virtue of their special skills.

3. **Acquisition of Evidence from a Nonclient:** [§539]   The Model Rules also forbid the lawyer to "use methods of obtaining evidence that violate the legal rights" of another person. [Model Rule 4.4]

   a. **Obligation not to secretly record conversations:** [§540]   Ethics opinions hold that a lawyer should not record any conversation by any means without the consent or prior knowledge of *all parties* to the conversation, and this applies to conversations with clients, other lawyers, or any other member of the public (including witnesses and public officials). This is true even though the lawyer is a party to the conversation, and hence, under the laws of most states, the recording is *not illegal.* [ABA Opn. 337]

   b. **Prosecutorial duty to supervise police:** [§541]   It has also sometimes been held that actions of police officers who violate the rights of suspects will be treated as actions of the prosecutor. [United States v. Thomas, 474 F.2d 110 (10th Cir. 1973)]

D. THREATS OF CRIMINAL PROSECUTION

1. **In General:** [§542]   A lawyer may not file or threaten to file criminal charges solely to obtain an advantage for a client in a civil case. For example, a lawyer for an accident victim may not threaten to go to the police and accuse the driver of drunk driving if he does not agree to a settlement. [DR 7-105(A); People *ex rel.* Gallagher v. Hertz, 608 P.2d 335 (Colo. 1979)]

   a. **Rationale:** The civil adjudicative process is designed to settle disputes between parties, whereas the criminal process is designed to protect society as a whole. Threatening to use the criminal process in order to coerce settlement of private civil matters tends to diminish public confidence in the legal system. [EC 7-21]

b. **Not limited to criminal charges:** [§543] It is equally improper for a lawyer to file or threaten to file charges that would expose the other party to *administrative or disciplinary* sanctions—*e.g.*, threatening another lawyer with disbarment. [Cal. Rule 7-104]

c. **Sanctions against lawyer for improper threats of prosecution**

(1) **Professional discipline:** [§544] A lawyer who threatens to file such charges to gain an advantage in a civil proceeding is subject to professional discipline. [*In re* Charles, 618 P.2d 1281 (Or. 1980)]

(2) **Criminal penalties:** [§545] Where, as under many penal codes, the threat of criminal proceedings to obtain a settlement also constitutes the crime of *extortion*, the lawyer can be convicted accordingly.

(3) **Tort damages:** [§546] The threat of filing criminal charges has even been held to constitute the intentional infliction of emotional distress. [Kinnemon v. Staiman & Snyder, 66 Cal. App. 3d 893 (1977)]

2. **Omission of Prohibition in Model Rules:** [§547] When the Model Rules were adopted, coverage of this issue was *omitted*, apparently in the belief that it was primarily a subject of tort and criminal law rather than a matter of legal ethics. The law is not really different in Model Rules states, but for purposes of the Multistate Professional Responsibility Examination, students should note that this is an area where the ABA Code and Model Rules diverge.

E. OBLIGATION TO IMPROVE THE LEGAL SYSTEM

1. **Representing Client Seeking Legislation:** [§548] A lawyer representing a client before a legislative or rulemaking body has duties both to the client and the public body.

a. **Duty of zeal generally:** [§549] A lawyer appearing before an administrative rulemaking body or a legislative committee owes the same obligation of zealous representation of the client's interests as in an adversary proceeding. Thus, a lawyer can properly argue and press a client's claims or viewpoints without disclosing the weaknesses or possible defenses thereto. It is the lawyer's duty to act as an *advocate*; it is the legislature's function to evaluate the merits of the claims presented. [EC 7-15, EC 7-16]

b. **Duty to disclose representative capacity:** [§550] In any such appearance or *communication* with a public body, the lawyer must disclose the fact that she is an attorney representing interests that may be affected by the action or legislation under consideration. Moreover, the lawyer should also disclose the *identity* of the client represented, if this information is not privileged. [Model Rule 3.9; EC 7-15, EC 7-16]

(1) **Exception—obtaining public information:** [§551] A lawyer who is merely seeking information *available to the public generally* (*e.g.*, zoning information) need not identify herself or her client. [EC 7-15]

2. **Support of Legislation in Public Interest:** [§552] The lawyer should participate actively in proposing and supporting legislation and programs to improve the system, rather than leaving needed reforms only to public-spirited laypersons.

   a. **Particular legislation:** [§553] Because of their unique qualifications, lawyers should, wherever possible, encourage *simplification* of laws and improvements in *legal procedures*. [EC 8-2, 8-9]

   b. **Views of clients irrelevant:** [§554] Personal support for legislation may be given without regard to the general interests or desires of clients or former clients. [EC 8-1; *compare* Model Rule 6.4—service in law reform groups]

3. **Service in Public Office:** [§555] Service by lawyers in a public capacity is encouraged as a significant method of improving the legal system. [EC 8-8]

4. **Lawyers in Public Service Generally:** [§556] Lawyers who serve as legislators or other public officials must not engage in activities in which their personal or professional interests are, or *foreseeably may be*, in conflict with their official duties. [EC 8-8]

   a. **Use of public position to advance client's interests:** [§557] Lawyers holding public office owe their primary duty to the public, and therefore may not use public office to obtain special advantages for themselves or a client. [Model Rule 3.5(a); DR 8-101(A)(1), (2)]

      (1) **Accepting gifts:** [§558] Lawyer-public officials must of course refuse to accept anything of value from any source when they know (or it is obvious) that the offer is made to influence their actions as public officials. [DR 8-101(A)(3)]

   b. **Appearances before other public bodies:** [§559] The right of a lawyer holding public office to appear as counsel on behalf of clients before a public body is narrowly limited.

      (1) **Judicial review:** [§560] Appearance before a fact-finding board or other body whose decision is *subject to review in the courts* is sometimes permitted. [*In re* Becker, 158 N.E.2d 753 (Ill. 1959)]

      (2) **Legislative review:** [§561] However, such lawyer (or the lawyer's firm) is *not* permitted to represent clients before an entity whose rulings are reviewable only by the legislative body of which the lawyer is a member. [ABA Opn. 296]

5. **Selecting Judges:** [§562] Lawyers are uniquely capable of evaluating the qualifications of those seeking or being considered for judgeships, and therefore owe a special duty to aid in the selection of qualified persons. A lawyer should protest vigorously against the appointment or election of those who are not qualified, and do everything possible to prevent political considerations from outweighing judicial fitness in the selection process. [EC 8-6]

   a. **Defending the judiciary:** [§563] Judges are not wholly free to defend themselves against unjust criticism. Thus, it is also the responsibility of the organized bar, and of lawyers individually, to defend judges and the judiciary against inaccurate or irresponsible charges. [EC 8-6; Comments to Model Rule 8.2]

   b. **Criticizing the judiciary:** [§564] The duty to defend the judiciary does not mean that lawyers cannot criticize judges in public statements. However, any criticisms must be aimed at improving the legal system. Reckless or knowingly false accusations are grounds for discipline. [Model Rule 8.2; DR 8-102(B); EC 8-6]

      (1) **Rationale:** Unrestrained or intemperate criticism of judges by lawyers tends to lessen public confidence in the legal system and may weaken the impact of *legitimate* complaints about the judiciary. [Kentucky Bar Association v. Heleringer, 602 S.W.2d 165 (Ky. 1980)]

      (2) **Sanctions:** [§565] Charges going to the *integrity* of the courts are particularly dangerous. A lawyer who makes such charges against a judge or the judicial system is subject to serious disciplinary sanctions if the charges prove untrue. (*Example:* A lawyer accused "the judges of the state supreme court" of having accepted a bribe. The lawyer was disbarred, even though the accusation was *partially* true; *i.e.*, *some* of the judges *had* accepted a bribe.) [*In re* Grimes, 364 F.2d 654 (10th Cir. 1966)]

6. **Campaigning For or Against Judicial Candidates:** [§566] Lawyers are subject to special constraints in their activities campaigning for or against candidates for judicial office.

   a. **Contributions calculated to obtain favoritism prohibited:** [§567] A lawyer is prohibited from making any contribution to a judge or candidate for judicial office in an attempt to influence judicial decision making for the personal benefit of the lawyer or the lawyer's clients. [N.Y. Co. Lawyers Ass'n Opn. 304]

   b. **Campaign tactics:** [§568] Lawyers must abstain from excessive statements in campaigning for or against a candidate for judicial office. Making false statements of fact concerning such candidates is a ground for discipline. [Model Rule 8.2; DR 8-102(A)]

7. **Personally Running for Judicial Office:** [§569]   Where the lawyer is seeking election to a judgeship (either against another candidate or in a merit system election), the lawyer must comply with the applicable provisions of the ABA *Code of Judicial Conduct* (CJC) (*see infra*, §§933 *et seq*.). [Model Rule 8.2(b); DR 8-103(A)]

VI. SPECIAL OBLIGATIONS OF LAWYERS IN LITIGATION

chapter approach

As has been discussed, a lawyer has duties to persons other than the client. The last chapter discussed duties that apply regardless of whether the subject of the representation is in litigation. This chapter presents the special duties of lawyers involved in litigation.

Some things to keep in mind for exam purposes are:

1. A lawyer must **reject actions brought merely to harass or injure**, and must not delay proceedings for improper purposes.

2. A lawyer must not try the case in the media; *i.e.*, the lawyer must **restrict his out-of-court comments** about a case, especially in criminal proceedings.

3. A lawyer may **present the client's case in the best possible light**, but there are **limitations**; for example, the lawyer must not suppress evidence when there is a legal duty to reveal or produce it, must not use untruthful testimony or false evidence, must not ignore professional standards or court rules in presenting evidence, etc.

4. A lawyer must **not lend money to the client** except for **litigation expenses**. (Note that the ABA Code requires the client to remain liable for those expenses, but the Model Rules allow repayment to be contingent on the outcome of the case.)

5. A lawyer must **not knowingly make a false statement of material fact** to the court, and **must disclose adverse legal authority.**

6. A lawyer ordinarily must **not act as both an advocate and a witness.**

7. A lawyer must **not take actions that could affect the impartiality of the court**; *i.e.*, the lawyer may not make gifts or loans to court personnel, contact judges without notice to the other party, or contact jurors during the trial.

Recall too that a **public prosecutor or government attorney** has a duty, beyond those above, **to seek justice** in the proceeding, as well as represent the state or government.

A. DUTY TO REJECT ACTIONS BROUGHT MERELY TO HARASS OR INJURE THIRD PARTIES [§570]

A lawyer has a duty to reject baseless lawsuits and a duty not to delay proceedings for improper purposes.

1. **Baseless Lawsuits:** [§571]   A lawyer may not file suit on behalf of a client unless:

   (i) There is a **nonfrivolous** basis for doing so, which includes a **good faith argument** for an **extension, modification, or reversal** of existing law [Model Rule 3.1; DR 7-102(A)(2)]; and

   (ii) The purpose of the suit is **not merely to harass or maliciously injure** the opponent [DR 7-102(A)(1); Model Rule 3.1, Comment].

   a. **Sanctions**

      (1) **Professional discipline:** [§572]   A lawyer is subject to professional discipline for filing a suit or claim that is **obviously** without factual or legal merit. [Gullo v. Hirst, 332 F.2d 178 (4th Cir. 1964)—discipline imposed against lawyer who filed for declaratory relief as to a domestic relations matter that was not only outside federal jurisdiction, but already res judicata]

      (2) **Civil liability for abuse of process:** [§573]   In addition, if the suit or court process was filed for an **ulterior purpose** and has resulted in damage to the opposing party, the lawyer (as well as the client for whom the lawyer was acting) may be subject to tort liability for malicious prosecution or abuse of process. (*See* Torts Summary.)

2. **Abusive Delay in Litigation**

   a. **Deception in setting trial date:** [§574]   A lawyer may be subject to discipline for proposing or agreeing to a trial date that the lawyer **knows** she will not be able to meet; to do so is a deception of the court. [Cal. State Bar Informal Opn. 1972-30]

   b. **Failure to appear:** [§575]   The sanction most frequently imposed against lawyers for failing to appear at a scheduled hearing or trial is a **citation for contempt of court.** [Kandel v. State, 250 A.2d 853 (Md. 1969)]

      (1) **Note:** [§576]   Courts especially insist upon prompt attendance in **criminal proceedings.** At minimum, a lawyer who is unable to appear owes a duty to give notice **in advance,** based on an adequate excuse. [Arthur v. Superior Court, 62 Cal. 2d 404 (1965)]

      (2) **And note:** The fact that the client has refused to pay an agreed fee is **not** an excuse for failure to appear at a hearing, and the lawyer may be held in contempt of court. [People v. Buster, 222 N.E.2d 31 (Ill. 1966)]

   c. **Courts' inherent power to sanction:** [§577]   Courts have been held to have **inherent power** to punish lawyers for using delay to get an advantage in the litigation process. [Chambers v. NASCO, Inc., 111 S. Ct. 2123 (1991)]

(1) **Disobedience of court order:** [§578] Of course, where the court has previously **ordered** the lawyer to perform some act (*e.g.*, to file a particular pleading by a particular date), the lawyer's failure to do so may be punished as a contempt of court. [People v. Endress, 245 N.E.2d 26 (Ill. 1969)]

(2) **Other grounds for discipline:** [§579] In addition, certain statutes and rules authorize discipline against lawyers for specified misconduct.

   (a) **ABA Code:** [§580] The ABA Code prohibits a lawyer from delaying a trial "merely to harass or maliciously injure another." [DR 7-102(A)(1)]

   (b) **Model Rules approach:** [§581] One of the major departures of the Model Rules from the ABA Code is the affirmative requirement of lawyers to "expedite litigation." Benefits to the client from "improper delay" may not be taken into account by a lawyer. [Model Rule 3.2]

   (c) **Federal Rules:** [§582] Federal Rule of Civil Procedure 11 requires that a lawyer **sign every pleading** and stipulates that the lawyer's signature constitutes a **certification** that the pleading "is not being interposed for the purpose of delay." For abuse or violation of this rule, a lawyer or client may be forced to pay attorney's fees and other expenses incurred by the opponent in dealing with a pleading interposed for delay.

d. **Discovery abuse:** [§583] A lawyer is subject to professional discipline and judicially-imposed compensation to the opponent for (i) making a frivolous request in discovery, or (ii) failing to make a diligent effort to comply with a legally proper discovery request by opposing counsel. [Model Rule 3.4(d); 28 U.S.C. §1927; Roadway Express, Inc. v. Piper, 447 U.S. 752 (1980)]

B. LIMITATIONS ON TRIAL PUBLICITY [§584]

The goal of impartial adjudication of disputes could be adversely affected by unlimited public comment by advocates about court proceedings. Thus, certain restrictions are imposed on out-of-court statements in connection with pending criminal and civil proceedings. [Model Rule 3.6; DR 7-107]

1. **General Rule:** [§585] A lawyer may not make an out-of-court statement likely to be reported by the news media if the lawyer reasonably should know that the statement would have a *"substantial likelihood of materially prejudicing an adjudicative proceeding."* [Model Rule 3.6(a)]

2. **Criminal Proceedings**

   a. **Criminal investigations:** [§586] A lawyer associated with the investigation of a criminal matter (*e.g.*, a district attorney) is forbidden to make any out-of-court statement capable of public dissemination that does more than state *without elaboration*: (i) the crime being investigated; (ii) the general scope of the investigation; (iii) a request for assistance in apprehending a suspect or other assistance; (iv) a warning of any danger to the public; or (v) any information in a public record. [Model Rule 3.6(c)(2)-(6); DR 7-107(A)]

(1) **Affirmative obligation:** [§587] When a suspect is charged with a crime, any public statement about the charge must explain that the charge is merely an accusation and that the defendant is presumed innocent. [Model Rule 3.6(b)(6)]

b. **Pretrial criminal proceedings:** [§588] During the pretrial stage of criminal proceedings, a lawyer's out-of-court statements capable of public dissemination must *not* relate to any of the following subjects: (i) the character, reputation, or prior criminal record of the accused; (ii) the possibility of a guilty plea; (iii) the existence or contents of any confession or other statement by the accused, or refusal or failure of the accused to make a statement; (iv) the performance or results of any tests, or refusal or failure to submit to tests; (v) the identity, testimony, or credibility of a prospective witness; or (vi) any opinion on the merits of the case or the evidence. [Model Rule 3.6(b)(1)-(4); DR 7-107(B)]

(1) **Lawyers affected:** [§589] These restrictions apply to any lawyer or firm associated with either the prosecution or defense of the case.

(2) **Permissible statements in pretrial stage:** [§590] The lawyer *may* properly announce the following information during the pretrial period: (i) name, age, address, occupation, and family status of the accused; (ii) information necessary for apprehension or to warn the public of danger; (iii) request for assistance in obtaining evidence; (iv) identity of victim; (v) details of arrest; (vi) identity of investigating officers and length of investigation; (vii) nature of the charge; (viii) quotations from public records in the case; (ix) scheduling or result of judicial proceedings; and (x) any denial of charges by the accused. [Model Rule 3.6(c); DR 7-107(C)]

c. **During trial proceedings in criminal cases:** [§591] During the selection of a jury or the trial of a criminal matter, lawyers or firms associated with the prosecution or defense may *not* make out-of-court statements capable of public dissemination relating to the *trial, parties, issues, or other matters likely to interfere with a fair trial—except* that a lawyer may quote from or refer without comment to *public records* of the court in the case (*e.g.*, pleadings, exhibits in evidence, etc.). [Model Rule 3.6(b)(4)-(6); DR 7-107(D)]

d. **During pre-sentencing period:** [§592] During the period following completion of trial (or other disposition) and prior to the imposition of sentence, the ABA Code prohibits lawyers involved with the case from making any statements capable of public dissemination that are *reasonably likely to affect sentencing.* [DR 7-107(E)]

e. **Professional or juvenile disciplinary proceedings:** [§593] All of the above limitations on statements during criminal actions apply as well to professional disciplinary proceedings or juvenile proceedings, to the extent they are consistent with other rules applicable to such matters. [Model Rule 3.6(a); DR 7-107(F)]

3. **Civil Proceedings:** [§594] During the investigation or litigation of a civil action, it is not proper for a lawyer or firm associated with the action to make any out-of-court statement (other than quotes from, or references to, public records) capable of public dissemination relating to: (i) evidence in the matter; (ii) the character, credibility, or criminal record of a party, witness, or prospective witness; (iii) performance or results of any tests, or the refusal or failure of a party to submit to such tests; (iv) the lawyer's opinion on the merits (except as required by law); or (v) any other matter substantially likely to materially prejudice a fair trial of the action. [Model Rule 3.6(b); DR 7-107(G)]

4. **Administrative Proceedings:** [§595] The restrictions applicable to civil proceedings govern statements made outside the official course of administrative adjudications. [Model Rule 3.6(a); DR 7-107(H)]

5. **Statements in Lawyer's Own Defense:** [§596] None of the restrictions imposed in civil, criminal, or administrative proceedings precludes a lawyer from replying publicly to *charges of misconduct publicly made against that lawyer.* [DR 7-107(I)]

6. **Duty to Prevent Improper Statements by Associates or Employees:** [§597] The restrictions on out-of-court statements by lawyers apply as well to their associates or employees (clerks, secretaries, etc.). Thus, a lawyer has a duty to exercise *reasonable care* to prevent employees or associates from making any statement the attorney is barred from making. [Model Rule 5.3(c); DR 7-107(J)]

7. **Constitutionality of Trial Publicity Rules Upheld:** [§598] The Supreme Court has upheld the constitutionality of the Model Rules' "substantial likelihood of material prejudice" standard as applied to pretrial statements by lawyers. However, it held that permitting lawyers to describe the "general nature" of a defense "without elaboration" was void for vagueness. This decision is expected to cause the ABA to further liberalize its rules on pretrial comments, at least as applied to defense counsel in criminal cases. [Gentile v. Nevada State Bar, 111 S. Ct. 2720 (1991)]

C. CONDUCT IN COURT PROCEEDINGS

1. **Conduct Affecting Witnesses and Evidence**

a. **Suppression of evidence:** [§599] A lawyer may not *suppress* any evidence that the lawyer or the lawyer's client has a legal obligation to reveal or produce (*e.g.*, in response to legitimate discovery requests or examination at trial). [Model Rule 3.4(a); DR 7-109(A); Cal. Rule 5-220]

b. **Inducing favorable testimony:** [§600]   A lawyer should counsel witnesses to testify truthfully and may not seek to influence their testimony by money or any other means. [Model Rule 3.4(b); EC 7-28]

  (1) **Prohibition on excessive payments to witness:** [§601]   Thus, a lawyer may not pay (or guarantee, or allow the client to pay) any amount to witnesses other than *reasonable* reimbursement for their *expenses* and *loss of time.* [DR 7-109(C)]

   (a) **Experts:** [§602]   Of course an expert witness may be paid a reasonable fee for services, both in testifying and pretrial preparation. [DR 7-109(C)]

  (2) **Fees contingent on outcome of case:** [§603]   Under *no* circumstances may the lawyer agree to pay even an expert witness a fee *contingent* upon the content of the witness's testimony and/or the outcome of the proceeding. [DR 7-109(C); Cal. Rule 5-310(B); *and see* Model Rule 3.4, comment]

   (a) **Constitutionality of prohibition upheld:** [§604]   This provision has been held constitutional in spite of the argument that the rule is unfair to litigants who cannot otherwise afford expert testimony. [Person v. Association of the Bar of the City of New York, 554 F.2d 534 (2d Cir. 1977)]

   (b) **Influencing adversary witnesses:** [§605]   Similarly, a lawyer may not make promises to *adversary* witnesses in an attempt to thwart or "soften" damaging testimony. [Model Rule 3.4(f)]

c. **"Coaching" witnesses:** [§606]   Discussions with a witness prior to putting the witness on the stand are normally essential to pretrial preparation and presentation of the evidence. However, such discussions must not turn into "coaching" sessions whereby the witness is improperly influenced to give certain testimony.

  (1) **Application:** It is clearly improper for the lawyer to "bend" the testimony or "put words in the witness's mouth." However, it is not improper for the lawyer to probe the witness's recollection, to point out fallacies or inconsistencies in the witness's version of the facts, and even *to refresh* and *"remind"* the witness of key points in the evidence that the witness has trouble recalling. [People v. McGuirk, 245 N.E.2d 917 (Ill. 1969)— not improper for prosecutor to help nine-year-old rape victim frame her testimony before trial]

  (2) **Note:** Of course, it is very difficult to draw a line between improper "coaching" and proper "reminding" of a witness. All that can be said is that the *essential nature* of the witness's testimony may not be altered or colored by the lawyer's emphasis or suggestions prior to trial.

d. **Perjured testimony or false evidence:** [§607]   A lawyer may not knowingly use perjured testimony or false evidence. Likewise, a lawyer is prohibited from participating in the ***creation or preservation*** of evidence that the lawyer knows (or should know) is false. [Model Rule 3.3(a)(4); DR 7-102(A)(4), (6)]

   (1) **Sanctions:** [§608]   The ***knowing*** use of fraudulent, false, or perjured testimony or evidence may subject the lawyer to ***criminal*** as well as disciplinary sanctions. [EC 7-26]

   (2) **Disclosure requirement:** [§609]   As part of the general obligation to prevent fraud upon the court, a lawyer who learns that a ***witness*** has committed perjury has a duty to urge that person to rectify the matter, and, if the person refuses, to advise the court. [Model Rule 3.3(a)(4)—must take "reasonable remedial measures"; DR 7-102(B)(2)—"promptly reveal the fraud to the tribunal"]

   (3) **Perjury by client:** [§610]   Perjury by one's own client raises the problems discussed *infra*, §§664 *et seq.*

e. **Treatment of adverse witnesses at trial:** [§611]   The rules of evidence give a lawyer considerable leeway in cross-examining a hostile witness, including the right to impeach the witness and undermine the witness's credibility with the jury. Nevertheless, there are certain restraints on the zeal with which such examinations can be conducted.

   (1) **Examining to degrade or harass witness:** [§612]   It is misconduct for a lawyer to use cross-examination simply to degrade or harass a witness, or for the purpose of prejudicing the jury. [DR 7-106(C)(2); *compare* Model Rule 4.4—not "embarrass" a third person]

      (a) **Example:** It is improper to cross-examine by asking a question that the lawyer has ***no reasonable basis*** to believe is relevant to the case and which is intended solely to embarrass the witness or prejudice the jury (*e.g.*, asking a witness to a traffic accident about the witness's sex habits on the day of the accident without any reasonable belief that this is somehow relevant).

   (2) **Expressing personal opinion on witness's credibility:** [§613]   It is likewise improper for a lawyer to express a ***personal opinion*** as to the credibility of the testimony, although the lawyer ***may*** properly ***argue credibility*** of the witness to the jury. [Model Rule 3.4(e); DR 7-106(C)(4)]

2. **Strategy and Tactics in Trial:** [§614]   While the lawyer is expected to be a partisan advocate for the client, there are limits to the tactics the lawyer may employ in the courtroom. Procedural and evidentiary rules are one means of insuring that the proceedings are conducted in the interests of justice; professional standards also impose restrictions on the lawyer. [EC 7-25]

a. **Reference to matters unsubstantiated by evidence:** [§615] In court appearances, a lawyer must not state or allude to any matter that the lawyer has no reasonable basis to believe will be supported by admissible evidence. [Model Rule 3.4(e); DR 7-106(C)(1)]

    (1) **Rationale:** The trier of fact must decide the issues on the basis of admissible evidence. Statements by counsel should aid in this task rather than lead the trier astray.

    (2) **Opening statement by counsel:** [§616] A lawyer should not make references in the opening statement to purported facts in the case without having a *good faith* belief that they will be supported by admissible evidence. [EC 7-25]

    (3) **Unsubstantiated "testimony" from witness:** [§617] It is likewise improper for the lawyer to imply, in the way the lawyer frames questions to a witness, the existence of facts *not in the record or incapable of being proved*.

    (4) **Improper arguments:** [§618] It is *misconduct* for a lawyer to suggest or imply in argument to the jury the existence of *facts not proved*.

        (a) **Example:** A lawyer is not permitted to suggest what a witness *might* have testified to but for the objection of opposing counsel ("Well, we all know what the witness would have said, if defense counsel hadn't objected . . ."). [Jacobson v. National Dairy Products, 176 N.E.2d 551 (Ill. 1961)]

        (b) **Example:** Courts have frequently criticized prosecutors in criminal cases for making personal references to the good qualities of the victim, where no evidence bearing on character has been placed in the record. [People v. Dukes, 146 N.E.2d 14 (Ill. 1958)]

b. **Personal knowledge or opinion of lawyer:** [§619] The lawyer is also prohibited from asserting *personal knowledge* of the facts in issue (except in testifying as a witness). Nor may the lawyer present a *personal opinion* on the justness of a claim, the *credibility* of a witness, the culpability of a civil litigant, or the guilt or innocence of an accused. [Model Rule 3.4(e); DR 7-106(C)(3), (4); Cal. Rule 5-200(E); *and see* Hawk v. Superior Court, 42 Cal. App. 3d 108 (1974)]

    (1) **Rationale:** With respect to factual matters, statements of personal knowledge are improper because all admissible evidence must be presented as *sworn testimony*. As to opinions, such expressions are improper in that (among other things) the *silence* of a lawyer on some particular occasion might be construed unfavorably to the client—thereby *necessitating* expressions of opinion on every issue. [EC 7-24]

(2) **Argument to the jury:** [§620]   The restrictions on expressing personal opinion apply equally when the lawyer is arguing the case to the jury. Of course, the lawyer may, **upon an analysis of the evidence**, attempt to convince the jurors as to any fact or conclusion, including the credibility of witnesses, as long as the lawyer avoids expressing personal opinions or beliefs. [Model Rule 3.4(e); DR 7-106(C)(4); EC 7-24]

    (a) **Example:** It is **improper** for the lawyer to argue: "You heard Witness testify that Defendant appeared to be drunk. I believe what Witness said. I think that Defendant was lying when he denied having anything to drink."

    (b) **Compare:** The lawyer may **properly** argue: "Witness, who has nothing to gain or lose in this case, has told you that Defendant appeared to be drunk. Defendant, who has a lot to lose, has denied drinking. I leave it to you to decide which of them was telling the truth."

c. **Appeals to emotion or prejudice:** [§621]   Some appeal by an advocate to the emotion of jurors is inevitable. However, it is misconduct for a lawyer to arouse the emotions or prejudices of jurors as to matters that are not supported by admissible evidence and hence are legally irrelevant. [Model Rule 3.4(e); DR 7-106(C)(1)]

(1) **Prejudice:** [§622]   Any attempt by counsel to appeal to the racial, social, or even communal prejudices of the jurors is manifestly improper conduct. (*Example:* Comments by local counsel emphasizing fact that opposing party and his lawyer are from a different county and suggesting that this should influence outcome of case are improper.)

(2) **References to poverty of client and wealth of opponent:** [§623]   Unless relevant to the litigation, references by plaintiff's counsel to the plaintiff's poverty or needs and the opponent's wealth or ability to pay are improper. Such references are calculated to arouse the sympathies of jurors on legally irrelevant matters and as such are grounds for discipline. [Green v. Ralston-Purina Co., 376 S.W.2d 119 (Mo. 1964)]

(3) **References to defendant's insurance or lack thereof:** [§624]   In most jurisdictions, it is improper for plaintiff's counsel to make any reference to the fact that the defendant is covered by liability insurance to prove negligence or other wrongdoing. The defendant's insurance coverage is normally irrelevant and its mention is calculated solely to encourage the jury to award a greater sum. And in some jurisdictions, it is equally improper for defense counsel to make reference to the fact that the defendant is **not** insured. [*See* Fed. R. Evid. 411]

(4) **"Golden rule" argument:** [§625]   Jurors are required to act as objective triers of fact and to exclude personal feelings in arriving at their verdict.

Hence, it is *improper* for counsel to ask the jury to "bring back a verdict that you would expect if *you* were the plaintiff." [Miku v. Almen, 193 So. 2d 17 (Fla. 1966)]

d. **Intentional or habitual violation of rules of evidence or procedure:** [§626]   A lawyer must not "intentionally or habitually" violate any established rule of procedure or evidence. [Model Rule 3.5(a); DR 7-106(C)(7)]

  (1) **May test validity of particular rule:** [§627]   It is not improper, however, for a lawyer, acting within the framework of the law, to refuse to comply with a court order or rule of procedure in order to *test the validity* of the order or rule—provided this is done in good faith. [Model Rule 3.1; EC 7-25]

  (2) **Sanctions:** [§628]   The sanctions that may be imposed against lawyers (and/or their clients) for violation of procedural and evidentiary rules depend upon the nature of the violation. Courts may impose *sanctions against the lawyer personally* where it appears that the violations are deliberate. Such intentional conduct may be punished as a *contempt* of court (*i.e.*, by fine or imprisonment), and cause *discipline* to be imposed (*i.e.*, suspension or disbarment).

  (3) **Constitutional limitation:** [§629]   Sanctions may *not* be imposed where the lawyer in good faith advises the client not to comply with an *unconstitutional* court order, when ordinary methods of challenge and review would not sufficiently protect the client's constitutional right. [Maness v. Meyers, 419 U.S. 449 (1975)—client advised not to produce documents where client's privilege against self-incrimination could not otherwise be fully protected; lawyer's contempt conviction set aside]

3. **Requirement of Dignity in Adversary Proceedings:** [§630]   A lawyer's duty to represent the client with zeal must also be balanced against the lawyer's obligation of courtesy and proper behavior toward *all persons* involved in the legal process. [EC 7-10] In handling a case, the lawyer must avoid conduct that is undignified or discourteous to the tribunal. [DR 7-106(C)(6); *compare* Model Rule 3.5(c)—no "disruption" of tribunal]

a. **Conduct toward opposing counsel:** [§631]   A standard of dignity and courtesy is required in all dealings with opposing counsel. Each lawyer must abstain from offensive conduct toward adversaries, and a lawyer who indulges in personal abuse or vilification is subject to discipline. [EC 7-37]

  (1) **Applies to written or oral arguments:** [§632]   The standard of dignity and courtesy applies in *written briefs* as well as oral arguments, although a matter may be the subject of sharp disagreement between counsel.

  (2) **Compliance with local customs and practice:** [§633]   A lawyer must comply with "known local customs of courtesy or practice of the bar

or a particular tribunal," unless the lawyer gives opposing counsel timely notice of his intention not to comply. [Model Rule 3.4(c); DR 7-106(C)(5)]

    (a) **Example:** Where *oral* agreements to extend time to respond to a complaint are an accepted local practice, a lawyer who orally agreed to an extension may not properly seek entry of a default because there is no *written* stipulation in the file.

    (3) **Compliance with reasonable requests:** [§634] Likewise, a lawyer should accede to reasonable requests from opposing counsel regarding court proceedings, settings, continuances, waiver of procedural formalities, or similar matters that do not prejudice the client's rights or interests. [EC 7-38]

  b. **Conduct toward the court:** [§635] As noted above, the ABA recognizes the need for respectful behavior by prohibiting undignified or discourteous conduct degrading to the tribunal. [Model Rule 3.5(c); DR 7-106(C)(6)] In assessing a lawyer's conduct in any given situation, however, the courts must reconcile this obligation with the concomitant duty of "zealous" representation.

    (1) **Objections to questions or comments by the judge:** [§636] It is not improper for a lawyer to *object* to any *questions* the trial judge may ask of a witness (whether the witness was called by the court or by another party).

        (a) **Example:** Where the jury had been deliberating in a murder trial for over three weeks, and the judge interrupted their deliberations with a "dynamite" charge and comment regarding credibility of witnesses which was heavily slanted against accused, defendant's lawyer was held entitled to object. [Cooper v. Superior Court, 55 Cal. 2d 291 (1961)]

        (b) **Compare:** However, most states *permit* a judge to comment to the jury on the credibility of a witness or the significance of evidence (*see* Civil Procedure Summary), and in such states there is no basis to object and it is improper for the lawyer to do so.

    (2) **Respect for court rulings in proceedings:** [§637] Respect for judicial rulings is essential to the proper administration of justice. Thus, a lawyer may not disregard (nor advise the client to disregard) rulings made by the court in the proceeding. [Model Rule 3.4(c); DR 7-106(A)]

        (a) **Right to challenge in proper fashion:** [§638] However, the lawyer *may* properly take appropriate steps in *good faith* to test the correctness of any ruling or action by the court. [Model Rule 3.4(c); DR 7-106(A)]

(b) **Right to advise client to invoke privilege:** [§639] The duty of obedience to court orders does not preclude a lawyer from advising the client *in good faith* to refuse to obey court orders for the production of evidence on grounds of self-incrimination. *Rationale:* Subsequent appellate review of such orders may not be a satisfactory remedy; it cannot always "unring the bell" once damaging information is released. [Maness v. Meyers, *supra*, §629]

(3) **Physical appearance of lawyer in court:** [§640] As part of the lawyer's duty to maintain the dignity of court proceedings, a lawyer should refrain from sensationalism or exhibitionism in personal appearance or attire in court. A trial judge may properly order lawyers to comply with rules of courtroom decorum in their appearance so as to ensure a fair and impartial trial.

(4) **Undue solicitude toward court:** [§641] While the dignity of judicial proceedings is adversely affected by discourteous behavior on the part of counsel, it may also be compromised by flattery or other actions designed to obtain favorable treatment from the court. [EC 7-36]

D. LIMITATIONS ON ADVANCING MONEY TO CLIENT [§642]

A lawyer's financial support of litigation smacks of "champerty and maintenance," and so was traditionally prohibited along with solicitation because of the tendency to "stir up litigation." Today, the concern is that the more financially involved the lawyer becomes, the more difficult it is to exercise independent judgment in handling the case.

1. **ABA Code Standards:** [§643] Where *litigation is pending or contemplated*, the ABA Code *prohibits* the lawyer from lending money (or guaranteeing a loan) to the client, except that the lawyer may lend the client money for litigation expenses, *"provided the client remains ultimately liable for such expenses."* [DR 5-103(B)]

   a. **"Litigation expenses":** [§644] These include such things as court costs, expenses of investigation and discovery, expenses of medical examination in preparation for trial (but not expenses for treatment), and expenses of obtaining and presenting evidence (*e.g.*, expert witness fees).

   b. **Client's obligation to repay loan:** [§645] The client must remain ultimately liable for any expenses advanced by the lawyer. (However, nothing in the ABA Code requires the lawyer to sue if the client fails to repay the funds.)

2. **Model Rules Approach:** [§646] The Model Rules adopt a more permissive attitude toward financial assistance.

   a. **Litigation expenses:** [§647] The Model Rules *permit* a lawyer to advance court costs and other litigation expenses, repayment of which may be *contingent* on the outcome of the case.

    b.   **Indigent client:** [§648] And if the client is indigent, the lawyer need make no provision for repayment of the expenses. [Model Rule 1.8(e)]

3.   **Criticism of ABA Rules:** [§649] Prohibiting the lawyer who is handling the case from lending money to cover the client's living expenses may leave the client without means of support. The client may often be forced to accept an inadequate settlement, thus defeating both the client's interest and that of the lawyer (who is handling the matter on a contingent fee basis).

E. DUTY OF HONESTY [§650]

Although acting as the partisan representative of the client, a lawyer must not "knowingly make a false statement of material fact to a tribunal." [Model Rule 3.3(a)(1); DR 7-101(A)(3), (5)]

1.   **In Pleadings:** [§651] Pleadings prepared by a lawyer are in effect representations to the court and hence must be truthful and accurate. They must not contain allegations the lawyer knows or has reason to know cannot be proved.

    a.   **Federal courts:** [§652] In federal practice and in many states, a lawyer must sign every pleading, and this signature operates as a certification that there are "good grounds" to support it (as well as that it is not being interposed for purpose of delay). [Fed R. Civ. P. 11]

2.   **In Motions, Petitions, and the Like:** [§653] When the court acts on petitions, pretrial motions, and the like, it must rely upon the facts as presented by counsel, usually by affidavit (oral testimony is seldom presented on such occasions). Furthermore, opposing counsel is less likely to be aware of the true facts at the preliminary stages of the case. For these reasons, counsel for the moving party or petitioner has an obligation not to mislead the court by omitting important facts.

    a.   **Preliminary injunctions:** [§654] If a lawyer seeking a preliminary injunction knows of some facts that might be "harmful" (*e.g.,* indicate some defense to injunctive relief), it is up to the lawyer to bring those facts to the attention of the court and then attempt to explain them away. [Model Rule 3.3(d)]

    b.   **Continuances:** [§655] Likewise, where a lawyer seeks or obtains a continuance by evasive or deceptive statements to the court (*e.g.,* "I am already engaged in trial," when this is not so), sanctions may be imposed (including contempt of court, or suspension or disbarment for deceit).

3.   **No Duty To Initiate Factual Disclosures:** [§656] In general, a lawyer is under ***no affirmative duty*** to disclose ***facts*** that would be harmful to the client's case. Such facts are protected by the lawyer's professional duty of confidentiality. [Model Rule 1.6; DR 4-101] Under our adversary system of justice, it is left to opposing counsel to bring such matters to the court's attention.

a. **Exception:** [§657] However, the lawyer ***must*** disclose ***even otherwise confidential information*** when necesary to "avoid assisting a ***criminal or fraudulent act*** by the client." [Model Rule 3.3(a)(2), (b); *but see* DR 7-102(B)(1)—"***except*** when the information is protected as a privileged communication"]

4. **Duty Not To Misstate Law:** [§658]   A lawyer must not seek to ***mislead*** the judge as to the law. The lawyer must not misquote the language of any statute or decision, nor ***knowingly*** cite as authority any decision that has been overruled or statute that has been repealed. [Model Rule 3.3(a)(1); Cal. Rule 5-200(C)]

5. **Duty To Disclose Adverse Legal Authority:** [§659]   As an officer of the court, the lawyer owes an affirmative duty to disclose the ***law*** applicable to the matter at hand—whether such law supports or is adverse to the client's case. *Rationale:* A court's action must always be based upon the law, and any attempt to mislead the court as to the applicable law would undermine the legal system itself. [Model Rule 3.3(a)(3); DR 7-106(B)(1)]

   a. **Any doubts resolved in favor of disclosure:** [§660] Unless the adverse authority is applicable to the issue at hand, there is of course no need to make any mention of it. However, any doubts as to its applicability must be resolved in favor of disclosure.

      (1) **Application:** The adverse decision does not have to be on "all fours." It is sufficient that it be the kind of precedent that a ***reasonable judge might wish to consider*** in dealing with the case at hand. If it is, the lawyer owes a duty to disclose it. [Katris v. Immigration & Naturalization Service, 562 F.2d 866 (2d Cir. 1977)]

   b. **What constitutes "adverse authority":** [§661]   The ABA Code and Model Rules require disclosure only of ***directly contrary authority from the controlling jurisdiction***. Thus, a lawyer could not be ***disciplined*** for failing to disclose a case decided by the courts of a sister jurisdiction or a case that was adverse only by implication or analogy. [Model Rule 3.3(a)(3); DR 7-106(B)(1); EC 7-23]

   c. **Manner of presenting adverse authority:** [§662]   Where the lawyer concludes that adverse authority should be cited, but nevertheless believes that such decisions are distinguishable from or tangential to her basic position, the lawyer need ***not*** diffuse the main point of her argument by dealing with them exhaustively. The use of footnotes, "catchall" paragraphs, or parenthetical asides may be useful ***stylistic*** devices by which a lawyer can fulfill the duty of disclosure while still presenting the client's position in its best light.

   d. **Right to challenge soundness of adverse authority:** [§663]   The lawyer's obligation of candor in disclosing adverse law does not override the duty of zealous representation. Once the adverse authority is disclosed, the lawyer may (and should) attempt to distinguish it or present reasons why it is unsound and should not be followed in the present case. [EC 7-23]

F. DUTY TO DISCLOSE PERJURY [§664]

A lawyer faces a difficult dilemma when it becomes clear that someone has given or plans to give perjured testimony favorable to the lawyer's client. The lawyer has a duty to the court not to rely upon false evidence, but has a corresponding duty to minimize injury to the client.

1. **ABA Code Approach:** [§665]   The ABA Code directs the lawyer to act differently depending on whether the perjury, false document, etc., has come from the lawyer's client or from another witness.

   a. **Witness other than the client:** [§666]   If a lawyer discovers that someone other than the client has made a mistake in testimony or committed perjury, the lawyer *must promptly reveal* that "fraud" to the court. [DR 7-102(B)(2)]

   b. **Perjury by the client:** [§667]   Where the false evidence has come from the lawyer's client, the lawyer must:

      (i)   Promptly call upon the client to correct the record; and if the client does not,

      (ii)   Reveal the fraud to the court, *except where the information is protected as privileged.*

      [DR 7-102(B)(1)] As interpreted by the ABA, the exception in (ii) swallows up the rule; "privileged" here means not only information protected by the attorney-client evidentiary privilege but includes all information that the lawyer is required to hold confidential. [ABA Opn. 341]

2. **Model Rules Position:** [§668]   The text of the Model Rules does not draw a distinction based on who gave the false evidence. In *all* cases, the lawyer is required to *"take reasonable remedial measures."* [Model Rule 3.3(a)(4)]

   a. **Duty supersedes duty of confidentiality:** [§669]   The Model Rules make clear that, contrary to the ABA Code, the lawyer's duty applies "even if compliance requires disclosure of information protected by Rule 1.6," the duty of confidentiality. [Model Rule 3.3(b)]

   b. **Recognition of constitutional issue in criminal cases:** [§670]   The comment to Rule 3.3 recognizes that constitutional rights of *criminal* defendants might supersede the lawyer's duty stated in the rule, but it at least applies in all other cases.

3. **Intention of Client To Commit Perjury:** [§671]   Somewhat different issues are presented when the client or another witness has not yet committed perjury but

has an *intention* to do so. Here, the ABA Code and Model Rules are *consistent*, but not very informative.

  a. **Attempt to dissuade:** [§672]   At minimum, the lawyer must seek to persuade the client or witness not to testify at all or at least not to commit perjury. [Louisiana State Bar Association v. Thierry, 366 So. 2d 1305 (La. 1978)]

   (1) **Example:** In the leading Supreme Court case dealing directly with this problem, the lawyer *coerced* his criminal defendant client into telling the truth by threatening to "impeach" the client's intended lie. Without deciding that this was the best way to handle such a situation, the Court unanimously held that the lawyer's action was not a denial of effective assistance of counsel. [Nix v. Whiteside, 475 U.S. 157 (1986)]

  b. **Attempt to withdraw:** [§673]   Next, the lawyer should attempt to withdraw from the representation. This will often not be permitted, especially if the trial is imminent, and it is likely to make the judge suspicious of the client; indeed, the threat itself may persuade the client not to testify, but these problems do not make a lawyer's attempt improper. [People v. Schultheis, 638 P.2d 8 (Colo. 1981)]

  c. **Use of narrative testimony:** [§674]   Some suggest that if withdrawal is not permitted, the lawyer should let the client take the stand and tell his story in narrative form. Under this approach, the lawyer may not rely on the false testimony in arguing the case. [*But see* Lowery v. Cardwell, 575 F.2d 727 (9th Cir. 1978)—approach may constitute "abandonment of a diligent defense"]

  d. **Prevent client from testifying:** [§675]   Reasoning that a client may have a constitutional right to testify, but not a right to commit perjury, the ABA Ethics Committee has said that if the client cannot be persuaded to tell the truth, the lawyer should prevent the client from testifying at all. If the client objects to the court, the lawyer may explain that the client intends to lie. [ABA Opn. 87-353] Many lawyers would disagree with such an approach, and the question remains unsettled.

G. LAWYER AS WITNESS AND ADVOCATE

1. **Nature of the Problem:** [§676]   When a lawyer representing a client in litigation also desires to appear as a witness on behalf of that client, differing interests arise. The function of the lawyer as advocate is to advance and *argue* the client's case, whereas the function of a witness is to state facts *objectively*. The advocate-witness is forced to argue her own credibility, is more easily impeached, and may therefore be less effective both as counsel and witness. [EC 5-9]

2. **Prohibition on Appearance in Both Capacities:** [§677]   The general rule is that a lawyer may *neither accept nor continue employment* in litigation where the lawyer knows (or it is obvious) that she may be called as a witness *on behalf* of the client during the proceedings. [Model Rule 3.7; DR 5-101(B), 5-102(A); *but see* Cal. Rule 5-210(C)—permits client consent to dual role]

a. **Doubts resolved in favor of lawyer withdrawing from case:** [§678]   If there is even a reasonable *possibility* that the lawyer might be called upon as a witness on behalf of the client, the lawyer should decline the case or, having accepted it, withdraw. Any doubt is resolved in favor of the lawyer's being available as a *witness* rather than as advocate. [EC 5-10; Comden v. Superior Court, 20 Cal. 3d 906 (1978)]

b. **Total withdrawal from proceedings:** [§679]   The testifying lawyer is required to withdraw *completely* from the proceedings. Merely withdrawing as counsel while testifying and then returning to the trial later is not permitted.

3. **Exceptions to General Rule:** [§680]   In certain situations, however, the lawyer may properly appear as a witness on behalf of the client while continuing to serve as advocate.

a. **Testimony is on uncontested matter:** [§681]   A lawyer (or another lawyer in the firm) who intends to testify solely upon *an uncontested matter*, or upon *a matter of formality* where there is no reason to expect substantial evidence in opposition (*e.g.*, as witness to execution of some deed or instrument or to establish receipt of correspondence, etc.), may properly act as both witness and counsel. [Model Rule 3.7(a)(1); DR 5-101(B)(1), (2); Haack v. Great Atlantic & Pacific Tea Co., 603 S.W.2d 645 (Mo. 1980)]

   (1) **Will execution:** [§682]   It is permissible for a lawyer to testify as a witness to the *execution of a decedent's will* and to express an opinion as to the decedent's testamentary capacity, freedom from undue influence, etc.

   (2) **Will contest:** [§683]   However, in the event of a *will contest* in which testamentary intent or capacity is at issue, the lawyer who drafted the will *cannot* appear as an attorney for any party to the will contest. The lawyer is a crucial witness on the issue of testamentary intent or capacity, and therefore appearing as an advocate would be improper.

b. **Testimony is on nature and value of legal services:** [§684]   The lawyer is not barred from representing a client as both counsel and witness when testimony is required about the nature and value of legal services rendered by the lawyer or his law firm (*e.g.*, where client sues third party to recover legal expenses as a result of third party's breach of contract). [Model Rule 3.7(a)(2); DR 5-101(B)(3)]

c. **Preventing hardship to client:** [§685]   The ABA Code also permits the lawyer to testify with respect to *any* matter if failure to do so or withdrawal as counsel would "work as a substantial hardship on his client because of the distinctive value of the lawyer or his firm as counsel in the particular case." [Model Rule 3.7(a)(3); DR 5-101(B)(4)]

   (1) **Relevant factors:** [§686]   In determining whether a "hardship" situation exists, the following factors are relevant: (i) the *personal or financial*

sacrifice caused the client if the lawyer refuses or withdraws from employment; (ii) the *materiality* of the lawyer's testimony; and (iii) the *effect* of such testimony on the lawyer's advocacy in the case. [EC 5-10]

(2) **When testimony necessary:** [§687]   Where the testimony of counsel is needed to prevent a miscarriage of justice, such testimony is proper.

    (a) **Example:** A lawyer may properly take the stand to refute testimony of an opposing witness concerning a *purported conversation between lawyer and client*. *Rationale:* Failure to do so might be construed as a tacit admission of the opposing witness's story. [Schwartz v. Wenger, 124 N.W.2d 489 (Minn. 1963)]

    (b) **Example:** Likewise, a prosecutor may testify to refute the *unexpected denial* by defendant of a prior conversation with the prosecutor. Such testimony is required to rehabilitate the prosecutor's position before the jury. [People v. Stokely, 266 Cal. App. 2d 1009 (1968)]

(3) **Caution—dual role rarely required:** [§688]   However, the ABA Code emphasizes that situations in which a lawyer *must* testify and still remain counsel are few in number. [EC 5-10]

4. **Lawyer Called as Witness by Opposing Party:** [§689]   A lawyer who discovers *after* commencing employment that he may be called as a witness *other than* on behalf of the client (*e.g.*, adverse party calls lawyer as hostile witness to prove date on which notice to the client was received) may continue to represent the client unless or until it appears that such testimony might prejudice the client. [Model Rule 3.7(a); DR 5-102(B)]

    a. **Note:** Among other things, this exception prevents a party from calling the opposing counsel as a witness and then objecting to his continuing as counsel in the trial.

    b. **But note:** Of course, a lawyer who is aware from the beginning of the possibility of being called as a witness by an opposing party on some crucial matter should *decline employment* altogether (unless some other exception to the rule applies). [DR 5-101(B)]

5. **Representation by Another Lawyer in Witness-Lawyer's Firm:** [§690]   While the ABA Code requires disqualification of *all* lawyers in the witness-lawyer's firm [DR 5-105(D)], the Model Rules provide that the disqualification is not imputed; *i.e.*, another lawyer in the witness's firm *may* act as advocate in the trial. [Model Rule 3.7(b)]

    a. **Exception:** [§691]   Of course, some *other* conflict of interest principle might bar the firm's participation (*e.g.*, the opponent is a former client). [Model Rule 3.7(b)]

b. **Testimony contrary to client:** [§692]   And if the lawyer-witness's testimony will "substantially conflict" with that of the client, representation by some other lawyer from the lawyer-witness's firm would be improper. [Comment to Model Rule 3.7]

H. IMPROPER CONTACTS WITH COURT OFFICIALS AND JURORS [§693]

Proper functioning of the adversary system depends on the *impartiality* of judges, court officials, and jurors and on *equal access* of the litigants to the tribunal. [EC 7-34, 7-35]

1. **Gifts or Loans to Court Personnel:** [§694]   Ordinarily, a lawyer should never make a gift or loan to a judge, hearing officer, or other employee of a tribunal. [DR 7-110(A); EC 7-34; Florida Bar v. Saxon, 379 So. 2d 1281 (Fla. 1980); Cal. Rule 5-300—*permits* gifts if there is a "personal or family relationship" such that gifts are customarily exchanged; *and see* Model Rule 3.5(a)—no attempt to influence by means "prohibited by law"]

    a. **Scope of prohibition:** [§695]   This prohibition extends not merely to monetary compensation but to *anything* of value. [DR 7-110(A)]

    b. **Exception for political contributions:** [§696]   However, a lawyer may contribute to the *campaign fund* of a candidate for judicial office—provided the contributions comply with all requirements of the ABA Code of Judicial Conduct. [Model Rule 8.4(f); DR 7-110(A)]

2. **Communication with Judge or Hearing Officer:** [§697]   In an adversary proceeding, the lawyer may communicate with a judge or hearing officer regarding the *merits of the case* only in the course of the proceedings or under certain specified conditions. [Model Rule 3.5(b)]

    a. **Written communication:** [§698]   The lawyer may not communicate with the judge or hearing official in writing without promptly delivering a *copy* of the writing to opposing counsel (or to the adverse party if not represented by counsel). [DR 7-110(B)(2)]

    b. **Oral communications:** [§699]   It is improper for a lawyer to speak to the judge or hearing officer regarding a pending matter, other than in the course of the proceeding, unless adequate *prior notice* has been given to the opposing party. [DR 7-110(B)(3)]

        (a) **Example:** It is improper for a lawyer to ask to see the judge alone in chambers (or elsewhere) regarding a matter currently before the judge, unless the other side is given an opportunity to be present.

    c. **Communications "otherwise authorized by law":** [§700]   Communication with the court is only permitted to the extent authorized by applicable federal or state law. [Model Rule 3.5(b); DR 7-110(B)(4)] The most frequent instance in which such communications are authorized is in connection with ex parte applications to the court.

3. **Contacts with Jurors:** [§701] To safeguard the impartiality of the judicial process, veniremen and jurors must be protected against extraneous influence. Therefore, a lawyer owes a duty to the legal system to avoid improper communications or contacts with jurors, and a duty to disclose to the appropriate court any such conduct by others. [Model Rule 3.5(a); DR 7-108; Cal. Rule 5-320]

   a. **Communications prior to trial:** [§702] Before the trial of a case, lawyers connected with the matter must not communicate (or cause anyone else to communicate) with any person known to be a member of the jury panel from which a jury for the case will be selected.

      (1) **Compare—investigations of prospective jurors:** [§703] On the other hand, it is not improper for a lawyer to *investigate* members of the jury panel to determine their backgrounds and the existence of any factors that would be grounds for a challenge (*e.g.*, bias, relationship to party, etc.). However, any such investigation must be conducted with "circumspection and restraint" so as not to discourage jury service. [EC 7-30; DR 7-108(E)]

   b. **Contacts during trial:** [§704] Other than addressing the jurors as part of the official proceedings (*e.g.*, on voir dire), a lawyer who is connected with the case may not communicate (or cause another to communicate) with a member of the jury during the course of a trial. [DR 7-108(B)(1)]

      (1) **And note:** Even lawyers *not connected* with the case are prohibited from communicating with the jurors during trial about matters *concerning the case*. [DR 7-108(B)(2)]

   c. **Communication with jurors after trial:** [§705] After the conclusion of trial, a lawyer has somewhat more freedom to communicate with jurors regarding the case. [EC 7-29]

      (1) **To determine basis for challenging jury verdict:** [§706] A jury verdict may be subject to challenge for certain kinds of irregularities in the jury deliberations—*e.g.*, improper influence from outsiders, or a verdict arrived at by flipping a coin. (*See* Civil Procedure Summary.) To discover such irregularities, the lawyer must be able to interview the jurors after the trial. [ABA Opn. 319]

      (2) **To improve advocacy skill:** [§707] Another reason for permitting contact with jurors after trial is to inform lawyers of the factors that led to the jury verdict and thus enable the lawyers to improve their skill and efficiency for other clients. [ABA Opn. 319]

(3) **Limitations:** [§708]   However, a lawyer may not interrogate any juror who does not wish to be interviewed. Moreover, in questioning those jurors willing to talk, the lawyer must take great care *to avoid* questions or comments that are calculated to *harass or embarrass* the jurors or to influence their conduct in future jury service. [DR 7-108(D); *compare* Model Rule 4.4—lawyer may not "embarrass, delay, or burden a third person"]

(4) **Judicial attitudes toward post-trial communications:** [§709]   Not all courts are as permissive as the ABA Code. A number of decisions flatly hold that post-trial interrogation of jurors is permissible only when the lawyer possesses some evidence of irregularities in the deliberations *prior* to the interrogation; interviewing jurors for mere "educative" purposes is not proper. [United States v. Driscoll, 276 F. Supp. 333 (S.D.N.Y. 1967)]

d. **Communication with members of juror's family:** [§710]   The same restraints on communications with veniremen or jurors during any particular stage of an adversary proceeding apply as well to contacts with members of their families. [DR 7-108(F); EC 7-31]

e. **Duty to disclose improper conduct of others:** [§711]   As part of their duty to the legal system, lawyers must promptly reveal to the court any improper conduct they know of by or toward veniremen, jurors, or members of their families. [DR 7-108(G); EC 7-32]

I.   SPECIAL OBLIGATIONS OF PUBLIC PROSECUTORS AND GOVERNMENT LAWYERS [§712]

The "client" of the public prosecutor or government lawyer is the state, and the prosecutor's responsibility is to *seek justice* rather than to convict. As a result, the obligations of such lawyers are somewhat different from those of the private advocate.

1. **Special Limitations on Prosecutorial Function:** [§713]   Four basic limitations set the prosecutor apart from a lawyer representing a private client.

a. **Restraint in exercise of governmental power:** [§714]   As a representative of the sovereign, the prosecutor is obliged to use *restraint* in the discretionary exercise of governmental powers, and particularly in the *selection of cases to prosecute.* [EC 7-13]

(1) **Example:** In this connection, a public prosecutor may not institute criminal charges when she knows (or it is obvious) that such charges are *not supported by probable cause.* [Model Rule 3.8(a); DR 7-103(A)]

(2) **Example:** Similarly, a prosecutor may not seek to get an unrepresented accused to *waive important pretrial rights* such as the right to a preliminary hearing. [Model Rule 3.8(c)]

b. **Must help accused obtain counsel:** [§715] The prosecutor must also reasonably assure that the accused knows how to obtain counsel and has had a chance to do so. [Model Rule 3.8(b)]

c. **Dual role during trial:** [§716] At trial, the prosecutor is both an advocate *and* a representative of the broad public interest. Thus the prosecutor's decisions must be fair to all, rather than calculated merely to obtain an expedient result in the pending action. [EC 7-13]

d. **Presumption of innocence for accused:** [§717] The ordinary advocate proceeds on the assumption that the client should prevail, and conducts the case accordingly. But a prosecutor must operate under the standard that the accused is presumed innocent and is entitled to the benefit of all reasonable doubts. [EC 7-13]

2. **Duties Respecting Witnesses and Evidence:** [§718] In light of the special responsibility to see that justice is done, the prosecutor has certain duties with respect to witnesses and evidence in criminal proceedings.

   a. **Obligation to disclose evidence beneficial to defense:** [§719] The prosecutor has a constitutional as well as a professional obligation to make timely disclosure to the defense of any available evidence known to the prosecutor that may negate guilt, mitigate the degree of the offense, or reduce the appropriate punishment. [Model Rule 3.8(d); DR 7-103(B); Brady v. Maryland, 373 U.S. 83 (1963); *and see* Johnson v. Superior Court, 15 Cal. 3d 248 (1975)—prosecutor had duty to call defendant's exculpatory testimony to attention of grand jury]

   b. **Failure to pursue "harmful" evidence:** [§720] Similarly, a prosecutor may not intentionally fail to pursue evidence merely because such evidence may damage the prosecution's case or aid the accused. [EC 7-13]

   c. **Access to government witnesses:** [§721] The public prosecutor must also permit defense counsel to *interview* government witnesses and may not properly counsel such witnesses to refuse to talk to the defense. [Gregory v. United States, 369 F.2d 185 (D.C. Cir. 1966)]

   d. **Use of subpoena to get defense records:** [§722] A relatively new practice of United States Attorneys has been to subpoena defense lawyers' files or call the lawyers before a grand jury to testify about sources of their fees and other information about their clients.

      (1) **Model Rules:** [§723] Model Rule 3.8(f) now prohibits such conduct unless the prosecutor reasonably believes:

         (i) The information is not privileged;

    (ii) The evidence is essential to an ongoing investigation or prosecution; and

    (iii) There is no other feasible way to get the information.

    In addition, the prosecutor must get prior judicial approval after an opportunity for an adversary proceeding. [Model Rule 3.8(f)(1), (2)]

(2) **Note:** It has been held that the Supremacy Clause prevents a state from enforcing this rule against a *federal* prosecutor who is a member of the state's bar. [Baylson v. Pennsylvania Supreme Court, 975 F.2d 102 (3d Cir. 1992)]

3. **Obligations of Government Lawyers Generally:** [§724] Many of the above duties are incumbent upon *all* government lawyers, not merely public prosecutors.

    a. **Terminating actions:** [§725] Thus, a government lawyer with discretionary power relative to civil litigation should not institute or continue actions that are obviously unfair. [EC 7-14; Freeport-McMoRan Oil & Gas Co. v. F.E.R.C., 962 F.2d 45 (D.C. Cir. 1992)]

    b. **Developing full record:** [§726] Even where litigation appears warranted, the government lawyer has a responsibility to develop a full and fair record; the lawyer must not use her position or the economic power of the government to harass parties or to force unjust settlements or results. [EC 7-14]

VII.   THE BUSINESS OF PRACTICING LAW

chapter approach

This chapter covers the rules involving the basic rules of running a modern law office. For exam purposes, you should be familiar with the following:

1. *Forms of law practice*—sole practitioner, law firm, legal services agency, etc. Most of the issues concern the private law firm situation, especially the rules regarding supervision of lawyer and nonlawyer employees, firm names, and fee sharing with nonlawyers.

2. *Advertising and solicitation*—Although the provisions of the ABA Code and Model Rules differ somewhat, lawyer advertising generally is permitted as long as it is **not false and misleading** and is **not solicitation**. Solicitation is the **direct contact** with a **potential client** made by the lawyer or another **for the lawyer's personal gain**. Solicitation is prohibited, except for advice to close friends, relatives, or present or former clients.

3. *Lawyer specialization*—Generally lawyers may not identify themselves as specialists or experts except as to traditional specialities (*e.g.*, patent or admiralty law), state-authorized specialties, or in reporting private certifications of specialty. Note however, that a lawyer may **limit** his practice to certain types of cases, but this is not to be confused with specializing.

4. *Fee sharing with lawyers outside of the firm*—Fee sharing is now permitted as long as the client gives informed consent, the total fee is reasonable, and both lawyers share responsibility for the matter.

A.   ASSOCIATIONS OF LAWYERS FOR THE PRACTICE OF LAW [§727]

Much of the ABA Code was written as though law were practiced primarily by sole practitioners in a general practice. That, of course, is no longer true. The Model Rules better recognize that law firms, legal services agencies, legal clinics, and other groups, corporations, and government agencies are all settings for the practice of law. [Model Rules 5.1-5.3, 7.5; ABA Code DR 2-102]

1. **Private Law Firm**

    a. **Roles in a traditional law firm:** [§728]   Partly as a result of the benefits to be derived from specialization and partly for economic reasons (*e.g.*, sharing overhead), partnerships or other associations of lawyers are common.

        (1) **Partners:** [§729]   Partners are the principals in a traditional firm. Lawyers may not hold themselves out as partners unless they in fact are partners. [Model Rule 7.5(d); DR 2-102(C)]

(a) **Effect of partner relationship:** [§730] Partners normally share the fees generated by the firm. Remember that this financial interest in each other's work affects the conflict of interest rules (*see supra*, §479). Therefore, if one lawyer has a conflict in a case, all lawyers in the firm are barred from serving in the case.

(2) **Associates:** [§731] Reference to a lawyer as an "associate" is proper only where the lawyer has an ongoing relationship with a law firm (or another lawyer) other than as a partner (or shareholder of an incorporated firm). Normally, an "associate" performs legal services for the firm's clients as a salaried employee of the firm (although the term is also sometimes applied to an "independent contractor" of such services). [ABA Opn. 310; *compare* Model Rule 5.2—responsibilities of a subordinate lawyer]

(a) **Rights of associates:** [§732] In the past, little was said about the rights or status of associates. However, associates have been held entitled both to sue their law firms for *discrimination* under Title VII of the Civil Rights Act of 1964 [Lucido v. Cravath, Swaine & Moore, 425 F. Supp. 123 (E.D. Va. 1977)], and *to form a union* to bargain with the law firm under federal labor laws [Foley, Hoag & Eliot, 229 N.L.R.B. 80 (1977)—NLRB jurisdiction where law firm has over $250,000 a year in billings and many clients with activities in interstate commerce].

(b) **Promotion to partner:** [§733] The Supreme Court has also held that a failure to admit a lawyer to partnership in a firm is a decision subject to the Civil Rights Act of 1964. The case involved an "up or out" rule in which the failure to make partner was also a decision that the female associate would no longer be employed by the firm, but the case is not necessarily limited to such a situation. [Hishon v. King & Spalding, 467 U.S. 69 (1984)]

(3) **"Of counsel":** [§734] This terms signifies a lawyer's continuing relationship with a law firm, *other than* as a partner or associate. Often, the title is taken by a lawyer who formerly was a member of the law firm and who has *occasional* client contact or responsibility; the lawyer may or may not continue to maintain an office with the firm. [DR 2-102(A)(4)]

(4) **Paralegals:** [§735] The organized bar expressly authorizes the use of nonlawyer legal assistants ("paralegals"). This benefits the client through more efficient service at reduced cost and the lawyer through increased net income. [Model Rule 5.3; EC 3-6; ABA Opn. 320]

b. **Supervisory relationships in a law firm:** [§736] The Model Rules contain provisions on supervisory responsibilities in a law firm or law office that have no direct counterparts in the ABA Code.

(1) **Responsibility to put measures in place:** [§737]   A law firm partner must make reasonable efforts to assure the firm has measures in place to reasonably assure that all lawyers in the firm will conform to ethical standards. [Model Rule 5.1(a)]

(2) **Direct supervisor of another lawyer:** [§738]   A lawyer who directly supervises another must make reasonable efforts to see that the other lawyer conforms to ethical standards. [Model Rule 5.1(b)]

(3) **Responsibility for another lawyer's ethical violation:** [§739]   A lawyer is responsible for another lawyer's violation of the Model Rules if the lawyer:

  (i)   Ordered or with knowledge ratified the other's conduct, or

  (ii) Is a partner or supervisor of the other and fails to take reasonably available remedial action to avoid or mitigate consequences of the action.

[Model Rule 5.1(c)]

(4) **Responsibility of a subordinate lawyer:** [§740]   A lawyer is bound by the Model Rules even though directed to act contrary to them by another person. [Model Rule 5.2(a)]

  (a) **Exception:** [§741]   If the question of professional duty is arguable, the subordinate lawyer may rely on the reasonable, though incorrect, interpretation of that duty by a supervising lawyer. [Model Rule 5.2(b)]

(5) **Responsibilities concerning nonlawyer assistants:** [§742]   The duties of partners and supervising lawyers are the same with respect to nonlawyers under their supervision as with respect to lawyers. [Model Rule 5.3]

c. **Practice through professional law corporations:** [§743]   In most states today, lawyers may form a corporation to carry on the practice of law by complying with special incorporation requirements. [*See* Cal. Bus. & Prof. Code §§6127.5, 6160-6172]

d. **Firm name:** [§744]   Traditionally, a firm name could not contain names other than those of persons who were, in fact, lawyers in the firm. Thus, neither a lawyer nor a law firm engaged in private practice could do business under a trade name (*e.g.*, "The Winners") or a misleading name ("Associates of Perry Mason"). [DR 2-102(B)]

  (1) **Model Rules more liberal:** [§745]   The Model Rules now permit a trade name if it is *not misleading* and does *not imply connection with a government agency* or a legal services organization (*e.g.*, "City Legal Clinic"). [Model Rule 7.5(a)]

(2) **Names of deceased or retired members:** [§746] A firm name may include the names of deceased or retired members, and a professional corporation or association may (and in some states *must*) include the abbreviation P.C. or P.A. in its name. [Model Rule 7.5, Comment; DR 2-102(B)]

(3) **Multistate firms:** [§747] A firm comprised of lawyers licensed in different jurisdictions may use the same firm name in each jurisdiction. However, the firm's letterhead and other listings must make clear any jurisdictional limitations of the members and associates. [Model Rule 7.5(b); DR 2-102(D)]

(4) **Lawyers on leave from the firm:** [§748] The name of a lawyer who enters public service for a substantial period, and thus is not engaged in firm business, must be removed from the firm name. [Model Rule 7.5(c); DR 2-102(B)]

e. **Association with nonlawyers in practice:** [§749] The restrictions on unauthorized practice of law by nonlawyers have already been discussed (*see supra*, §§85 *et seq.*). These same restrictions also govern the extent to which a lawyer may *associate* himself with nonlawyers.

(1) **Partnerships with nonlawyers prohibited:** [§750] The ABA Code and Model Rules flatly prohibit partnerships between lawyers and nonlawyers where *any* of the partnership activities include the practice of law. [Model Rule 5.4(b); DR 3-103(A)]

(a) **Example:** A lawyer and an accountant may not form a partnership in which legal advice on tax matters is given to clients—and this is true even if the *lawyer alone* furnishes such legal advice. [ABA Opn. 297]

(b) **Law corporations:** [§751] Law corporations are also heavily regulated to exclude nonlawyers from any role in the corporation. All officers, directors, and shareholders must be licensed to practice law and actually employed to render services to the corporation. [*See* Model Rule 5.4(d); DR 5-107(C)]

(c) **Partnerships not involving practice of law:** [§752] A lawyer is free to enter a partnership that confines itself *solely* to *nonlegal* activities (*e.g.*, investments, operation of a business, etc.).

(2) **Sharing fees with nonlawyer prohibited:** [§753] Finally, both the ABA Code and Model Rules prohibit the division of legal fees with a nonlawyer. [Model Rule 5.4(a); DR 3-102; Crawford v. State Bar, 54 Cal. 2d 659 (1960)]

(a) **Example:** Bank included a provision in its consumer loan agreements obligating Borrower to pay attorney's fees in the event Bank had to institute suit against Borrower after default. *Held:* Since Bank used its in-house lawyers to file suit and did not pay the collected fees to a lawyer on a per-case basis, the bank was engaged in the unauthorized practice of law and was aiding and abetting its salaried lawyers to engage in unethical fee splitting. [Thompson v. Chemical Bank, 84 Misc. 2d 721 (1975)]

(b) **Permissible fee sharing:** [§754]   However, the ban on fee sharing does *not* apply to the following:

   1) **Employment on flat salary basis permitted:** [§755]   A lawyer is permitted to *employ* nonlawyers as long as their compensation is not tied to fees collected for legal services. (This applies to clerks, secretaries, investigators, or co-professionals; *e.g.*, a lawyer may properly hire an accountant on a salary basis to perform accounting work related to the lawyer's practice.) [ABA Opn. 297]

   2) **Profit sharing permissible in firm plans:** [§756]   A broad exception to the rule against "fee splitting" with nonlawyers permits salaried employees of a lawyer or law firm to participate in retirement or profit sharing plans, even though the plans inevitably are based upon sharing fee income with the lawyer-employer. [Model Rule 5.4(a)(3); DR 3-102(A)(3)]

(c) **Payments to estate of deceased lawyer permissible:** [§757]   Another exception to the rule against fee sharing with nonlawyers permits the surviving members of a law firm to pay the estate of a deceased lawyer a sum of money for a reasonable period of time after his death. [Model Rule 5.4(a)(1); DR 3-102(A)(1)]

   1) **Computation:** [§758]   As to fees for services performed prior to the deceased lawyer's death, a *fair proportion* of the total compensation ultimately received by the lawyer who assumes the case may be paid to the estate or heirs of the decedent. [Model Rule 5.4(a)(2); DR 3-102(A)(2)]

   2) **Compare—sale of law practice:** [§759]   The ABA has different rules for the sale of a practice by one *living* lawyer to another. (*See infra,* §847.)

f. **Noncompetition agreements:** [§760]   To ensure that lawyers are not bound to their firms forever, both the ABA Code and Model Rules forbid agreements that restrict the right of a lawyer to practice after termination of the relationship, except as a condition for continued payment of retirement benefits. [Model Rule 5.6(a); DR 2-108(A)]

(1) **Same rule applies to settlement of individual cases:** [§761] A lawyer also may not settle an individual case on the condition that the lawyer will restrict his practice (*e.g.*, agree not to represent any more parties in suits against the defendant). [Model Rule 5.6(b); DR 2-108(B)]

g. **Ancillary business activities:** [§762] For many years, some law firms have engaged in activities beyond the traditional practice of law. Services have ranged from investment advice to the sale of title insurance. In 1991, the ABA prohibited most such "ancillary" business activities [Model Rule 5.7], but it then repealed the prohibition in 1992. Debate over whether such ancillary activities are appropriate is likely to continue.

2. **Legal Assistance Agencies**

a. **Organizations serving indigent clients:** [§763] Traditionally, indigent clients were served by private lawyers and firms on a free or low-fee basis. Today, however, public and private legal services agencies exist to address many needs of clients below defined income levels.

(1) **Independence of lawyers required:** [§764] The lawyer assigned to a given matter must be allowed to use independent judgment in making decisions for the client. Hence, although the governing board of a legal services agency may handle the day-to-day operation of the agency (*e.g.*, establish categories of cases the agency will or will not undertake, allocate resources and establish proper priorities), it may not ordinarily direct the actions of the lawyer responsible in a given case. [ABA Opn. 334; *compare* Model Rule 5.4(c); DR 5-107(B)]

b. **Military legal assistance offices:** [§765] Military legal assistance offices provide services to military personnel and their dependents.

(1) **Independence of lawyers:** [§766] As with organizations providing services based on indigency, the ABA has held it improper for a commanding officer to direct a military lawyer's management of a case. (However, a situation in which a military lawyer is ordered by a commanding officer to commit an act that would violate the Code was avoided by the ABA.) [ABA Opn. 343]

3. **Group and Prepaid Legal Services Plans:** [§767] These programs are designed to make legal services easily available to middle-income citizens who are union members or members of other voluntary associations.

a. **Traditional opposition to group legal services plans:** [§768] For many years, it was feared that group plans would interfere with a client's free choice of counsel and would divide the lawyer's loyalty between the group and the individual client. Thus, a lawyer was flatly prohibited from participating in group plans (considered to be "unauthorized practice of law") by the intermediary).

b. **Constitutional right to provide group services:** [§769] On four separate occasions, the United States Supreme Court held that, under certain circumstances, the right to furnish group legal services is protected under the "freedom of expression and association" guaranteed by the First and Fourteenth Amendments to the United States Constitution.

(1) **Services necessary to further group's constitutional objectives:** [§770] In *NAACP v. Button*, 371 U.S. 415 (1963), the Court struck down a Virginia statute that barred the NAACP from retaining lawyers for litigants challenging various forms of racial discrimination. Under the NAACP program, the lawyer (although paid by the NAACP) had complete control over the litigation, and the client could withdraw the case at any time. The Court held that such activity was a "mode of expression and association" which could not be prohibited by state regulation.

(2) **Group legal services for union members:** [§771] Three other Supreme Court decisions upheld labor union plans designed to furnish legal services to members bringing workers' compensation claims. The Court approved the plans on the ground that they were protected by First Amendment guarantees of free speech, assembly, and petition. The right to employ counsel was considered part of the union members' right to band together and express themselves on matters of common interest. [Brotherhood of Railroad Trainmen v. Virginia, 377 U.S. 1 (1964); United Mine Workers v. Illinois State Bar Association, 389 U.S. 217 (1967); United Transportation Union v. State Bar of Michigan, 401 U.S. 576 (1971)]

c. **Present status:** [§772] The above Supreme Court decisions clearly invited the organized bar and state courts to develop and expand group plans to meet the increased need for legal services while still preserving professional standards.

(1) **Types of plans:** [§773] At present, there are two main types of group and prepaid legal services plans.

(a) **Closed panel plans:** [§774] Under a closed panel plan, a group of clients hires a specific lawyer or group of lawyers to handle the clients' legal work—on an annual flat fee basis, or according to an agreed schedule of fees covering various types of work. The client group in a closed panel plan is typically a trade union, professional association, employee association, or nonprofit organization.

(b) **Open panel plans:** [§775] In an open panel plan, a large number of lawyers practicing in a geographic area agree to do legal work for groups of clients. Ordinarily the fees for such work are wholly or partly covered by legal insurance (*i.e.*, the client pays a periodic premium and thereby becomes entitled to a set amount of legal services during the policy period). This type of plan allows the insured client to select a lawyer from the panel of lawyers who have agreed to take work on this basis.

    (2) **ABA Code treatment of such plans:** [§776] In states still following the ABA Code, DR 2-103(D)(4) permits a lawyer to participate in such a plan if it satisfies the following conditions:

        (a) *The sponsoring organization does not make a profit on the rendering of the legal services.* (If the sponsoring organization is a profit-making body in other respects, *e.g.*, an insurance company, the plan may be used only in matters where the organization is ultimately liable on claims against its members or beneficiaries.)

        (b) *The participating lawyers do not initiate or promote the formation of the sponsoring organization for the primary purpose of their own profit.*

        (c) *The plan does not act as a "feeder"* of outside legal business to the participating lawyers.

        (d) *The person to whom the legal services are rendered is recognized as the client* to whom the lawyer owes loyalty.

        (e) *A person who does not want to use the lawyer furnished by the sponsoring organization is free to go to an outside lawyer*, and an *"appropriate procedure for relief" is furnished* by the sponsoring organization to a person who believes that the lawyer designated by the organization cannot handle the matter adequately, properly, or ethically.

        (f) *The plan complies with local laws and rules of court.*

        (g) *The sponsoring organization files an annual report with the state bar detailing its operations.*

    (3) **ABA Model Rules treatment of such plans:** [§777] The Model Rules of Professional Conduct place *no limits* on such plans.

B. REGULATION OF THE MANNER OF LAWYERS SEEKING EMPLOYMENT—SOLICITATION AND ADVERTISING

1. **Traditional Position of Organized Bar—"Passive Acceptance of Employment":** [§778] The organized bar *traditionally* took the position that a lawyer was *not permitted* to publicize his services actively. In effect, every lawyer was presumed to have an established clientele, and it was further presumed that the lawyer's reputation for good work among these (presumed) existing clients would inevitably lead others to seek out the lawyer's services. Under this approach, direct publicity by lawyers was *strictly controlled*. [EC 2-6]

    a. **Criticism of traditional approach:** [§779] The traditional "passive" standard was criticized as appropriate only for lawyers who had established practices and for clients who had the sophistication to recognize their legal problems plus the ability to locate competent lawyers to represent them.

    (1) **Affluent favored:** Thus, it was argued that the standard was totally inappropriate for lawyers without established clientele and for most lower- and middle-income clients who might be unaware of their needs for legal services until "too late," or who might simply have no idea how to locate a competent lawyer to represent them.

    (2) **Competition:** Furthermore, the traditional approach was attacked as anticompetitive and in conflict with the consumer's need to receive information about lawyers and their services.

b. **Beginnings of change:** [§780] The above criticisms developed strength in the mid-1970's as consumer groups, the Antitrust Division of the Justice Department, and some lawyers combined to oppose the restrictions on lawyer advertising.

    (1) **Legal profession not exempt from antitrust laws:** [§781] In *Goldfarb v. Virginia State Bar*, 421 U.S. 773 (1975), a case involving minimum fee schedules (*see supra*, §222), the Supreme Court added momentum to these efforts by *rejecting* the notions that lawyers are exempt from antitrust laws as members of a "learned profession," or that enforcement of minimum fee schedules was exempted state action.

    (2) **Consumers' First Amendment "right to know":** [§782] The critics' position was further strengthened by two subsequent Supreme Court decisions that (although not specifically concerned with advertising by lawyers) held that commercial advertising was entitled to some First Amendment protection. [Bigelow v. Virginia, 421 U.S. 809 (1975); Virginia State Board of Pharmacy v. Virginia Citizens Consumer Council, 425 U.S. 748 (1976)]

2. **Lawyer Advertising and Publicity—Current Status of the Law**

a. **Relaxation of traditional restraints—*Bates*:** [§783] In 1977, the Supreme Court at last squarely confronted the issue of lawyer advertising. In *Bates v. State Bar of Arizona*, 433 U.S. 350 (1977), disciplinary action had been brought against a lawyer for placing a newspaper ad that listed his fees for routine, standardized legal services. In finding the lawyer not subject to discipline, the Supreme Court held that:

    (1) Advertising by licensed lawyers may *not be "subjected to blanket suppression"*;

    (2) Truthful advertising in *newspapers* conveying the "availability and terms" (fees) of "routine legal services" is protected by the First Amendment; but

(3) **Reasonable restrictions** may be imposed on the time, place, and manner of legal advertising; and

(4) Advertising that is **"false, deceptive, or misleading"** is subject to restraint.

b. **ABA reactions to** *Bates*

(1) **ABA Code response:** [§784] During the short time between the *Bates* decision and its annual meeting in August 1977, the ABA hurriedly amended Canon 2. These amendments **accommodated** *Bates*, but took advantage of the permissible **restrictions** left by the Court and **ignored** all related issues not covered by *Bates*.

(a) **Manner of dissemination:** [§785] The ABA Code permitted both (i) **printed** advertising (*e.g.*, in newspapers, magazines, and yellow pages) and (ii) **radio and television** broadcast advertising, but required that both be "presented in a dignified manner." [DR 2-101(B); *and see* Model Rule 7.2]

(b) **Areas of dissemination:** [§786] Under the ABA Code, advertising could be distributed or broadcast only in the geographic area or areas in which the lawyer (i) **resided**, (ii) **maintained offices**, or (iii) in which a "significant part" of her **clients resided**. [DR 2-101(B)] (There is no such limitation under the Model Rules.)

(c) **Information that may be disclosed:** [§787] The ABA Code first stated a general prohibition of any public communication by a lawyer that contained a false, deceptive, self-laudatory, or unfair statement or claim. [DR 2-101(A)] The Code then listed over 20 specific categories of information that **could be included** in advertising. [DR 2-101(B)] These may be conveniently grouped into three types:

1) **Biographical information:** [§788] Such information included specific items such as name; date and place of birth; bar admissions; schools attended; offices held; legal authorships and teaching positions; memberships in bar associations, legal societies, and other professional associations; and foreign language ability.

2) **Office information:** [§789] Advertisements could also include name, address, and telephone number of the law firm and professionals in it; fields of practice or specialization to the extent authorized by state law; names of clients regularly represented (with their consent); prepaid or group legal services programs in which the lawyer participates; whether credit cards or other credit arrangements are accepted; and office and telephone answering service hours.

3) **Fee information:** [§790] This included the fee for an initial consultation; availability upon request of a written schedule of fees and/or an estimate of the fee to be charged for specific services; contingent fee rates; range of fees for services; hourly rates; and fixed fees for specific legal services.

    a) **Additional disclosures required:** [§791] In advertising any of the above types of fee information, the lawyer generally had to make additional disclosures. For example, in advertising a contingent fee rate, the ad had to state whether percentages are computed before or after deduction of costs; in advertising fee ranges, hourly rates, and fixed fees, the lawyer had to disclose that the client was entitled without obligation to an estimate of the actual fee likely to be charged.

    b) **Duration of fee information:** [§792] A lawyer who advertised a particular fee for a legal service had to provide the service for no more than that fee during the period specified in the ad. If no period was specified, the lawyer was bound by broadcast fee information for at least 30 days, and by published fee information until publication of the succeeding issue (but at least 30 days if the publication is issued more than once a month, and at least one year if no succeeding issue is scheduled). [DR 2-101(E)-(G)]

(d) **No amendment of ABA Code since *Bates*:** [§793] Because the Model Rules were under consideration in the years following *Bates*, the ABA never amended the Code to conform to later cases. Thus, today, the ABA Code is *not a reliable guide* to the law of lawyer advertising and solicitation.

(2) **Model Rules approach to advertising:** [§794] By the adoption of the Model Rules, the ABA had time to reflect on the best approach to advertising.

(a) **Only false and misleading advertising prohibited:** [§795] The Model Rules *permit all advertising except* that which is *"false and misleading,"* which is defined as:

    (i) *Containing a material misrepresentation* of fact or law, or omitting a fact necessary to make the statement not materially misleading;

    (ii) *Likely to create an unjustified expectation* about the results the lawyer can achieve, or implying that the lawyer can achieve results *by improper means*;

(iii) ***Unfairly comparing the lawyer's services*** with those of other lawyers—*i.e.*, in ways that cannot be factually substantiated.

[Model Rule 7.1]

(b) **Manner of dissemination:** [§796] Under the Model Rules, advertising may be done through any public media, or through any written communication not involving "solicitation" (*see infra*). [Model Rule 7.2(a)]

(c) **Requirements—copy, lawyer's name:** [§797] A copy or recording of an advertisement must be kept at least two years and must include the name of at least one lawyer responsible for its content. [Model Rule 7.2(b), (d)]

c. **Law according to *Zauderer*:** [§798] The Supreme Court appeared to confirm the Model Rules approach to lawyer advertising in *Zauderer v. Office of Disciplinary Counsel*, 471 U.S. 626 (1985). It specifically held both that illustrations in lawyer advertising are as protected as text, and that appeals may be made in an advertisement encouraging persons with a particular kind of injury to consult the lawyer.

(1) **Permissible state regulation:** [§799] More specifically, *Zauderer* held that a state ***may***:

(a) ***Prohibit*** lawyer advertising that is ***false, deceptive, or misleading,*** or that proposes an ***illegal transaction***; and

(b) ***Require a lawyer to include a reasonable disclaimer*** or other information in order to help assure that potential clients can make an informed choice among lawyers.

(2) **Limitations on state regulation:** [§800] However, a state ***may not***:

(a) ***Require*** that lawyer advertising ***be "dignified"***; or

(b) ***Limit*** lawyer advertising ***except*** "in the service of a ***substantial government interest***," and even then, "only through means that ***directly affect that interest***."

3. **Solicitation:** [§801] The term "solicitation" by itself refers to any conduct on behalf of a lawyer that has as one of its purposes obtaining new clients. It thus traditionally included advertising. However, when *Bates* came down permitting advertising, the term "solicitation" came to mean ***direct contact with a potential client*** that was ***not protected as advertising***. [Model Rule 7.3; EC 2-3, 2-4]

a. **Scope of prohibition:** [§802] The ABA Code and Model Rules differ in the form of their prohibitions:

(1) **ABA Code:** [§803]   The Code's prohibition is two-fold:

    (a)   A lawyer must not recommend her own employment unless consulted in reference thereto. [DR 2-103(A)]

    (b)   A lawyer who gives unsolicited advice to a layperson that he should seek legal counsel may not accept employment resulting from that advice.

(2) **Model Rules:** [§804]   The Model Rules speak more generally, prohibiting all "in-person or live telephone contact" with potential clients whom the lawyer has not theretofore served where a "significant motive" for the contact is the "lawyer's personal gain." [Model Rule 7.3(a)]

    (a)   **Duress prohibited:** [§805]   The Model Rules also prohibit contact with a prospective client if (i) the person has made known to the lawyer a desire not to be solicited, or (ii) the solicitation involves coercion, duress, or harassment. [Model Rule 7.3(b)]

    (b)   **Warning to be affixed:** [§806]   All written or recorded communications with such a prospective client known to be in need of legal services in a particular matter must also say "Advertising Material" on the envelope or the recording. [Model Rule 7.3(c)]

b.   **Constitutionality:** [§807]   The United States Supreme Court has confirmed the validity of prohibiting in-person solicitation of clients for cases in which a fee will be charged, at least where the solicitation "in fact is misleading, overbearing, or involves other features of deception or improper influence." [Ohralik v. Ohio State Bar Association, 436 U.S. 447 (1978)]

c.   **Prohibited forms of solicitation**

(1) **Solicitation by lawyer:** [§808]   The most obvious form of in-person solicitation by a lawyer is "ambulance chasing"—*i.e.*, the lawyer approaches a potential client offering to represent him.

(2) **Solicitation by employees of lawyer:** [§809]   The use of "cappers," "runners," investigators, or other persons employed by a lawyer to solicit prospective clients on the lawyer's or law firm's behalf also constitutes "solicitation" by the lawyer. It is the lawyer's responsibility to instruct employees about the rule against solicitation and to see that they comply with it. [*See* DR 2-103(A), (B); Geffen v. State Bar, 14 Cal. 3d 843 (1975)]

(3) **Payment for referrals:** [§810]   It is likewise "solicitation" for a lawyer to provide compensation, or make **gifts or loans** to **any** person (lawyer or layperson) **in return** for the referral of a case or client. This is true even though there was no request by the lawyer to refer cases, no agreement

to pay any compensation, and no correlation between such payments and the fee earned from the referral. [DR 2-103(B)]

    (a) **Rationale:** A person who receives compensation in return for referring a case or client may refer potential clients to the lawyer who pays the most, rather than to the lawyer who is most competent. [*In re* Krasner, 204 N.E.2d 10 (Ill. 1965)]

    (b) **Form of compensation immaterial:** [§811] The ban on "payment" extends to any form of compensation that is in fact attributable to the referral of cases.

d. **Exceptions to general prohibition on solicitation:** [§812] There are certain situations in which conduct otherwise prohibited as solicitation is allowed by the Code. (Although nothing explicit is mentioned on these points in the text of the Model Rules, they would also likely be recognized.)

    (1) **Advice to close friend, relative, or present client:** [§813] Generally, a lawyer who volunteers legal advice to a layperson should not accept employment arising from that advice. However, a lawyer who gives unsolicited advice to a person who is a close friend, relative, or **present** client of the lawyer, may accept employment resulting therefrom. [Model Rule 7.3(a); DR 2-104(A)(1)]

    (2) **Advice to former client:** [§814] Similarly, it is not improper for a lawyer to volunteer legal advice to a person who was formerly a client, and to accept any employment resulting therefrom as long as the advice is germane to the former employment. [Model Rule 7.3(a); DR 2-104(A)(1)]

        (a) **Example:** Lawyer may send letters to persons for whom she has previously drafted wills, advising of changes in tax laws affecting the tax treatment of the will provisions, and may accept employment to revise wills accordingly. [ABA Opn. 213 (1941); *In re* Madsen, 370 N.E.2d 199 (Ill. 1977)]

    (3) **Request for referrals from lawyer referral service or legal aid organization:** [§815] A lawyer may properly request referrals from a **lawyer referral service** in the lawyer's locality, and from **legal aid organizations**. [Model Rule 7.3(d); DR 2-103(C)]

    (4) **Services offered to persons in need:** [§816] Traditionally, courts have refused to discipline lawyers who have offered their services **free of charge** to persons in need thereof. [*In re* Primus, 436 U.S. 412 (1978)]

        (a) **Rationale:** Here the solicitation is used as a vehicle for "political expression and association," within the protection of the First Amendment. Furthermore, unlike solicitation of fee-generating business, the potential for overreaching is too slight. [*In re* Primus, *supra; and see* NAACP v. Button, *supra*, §770]

(5) **Organizing prospective litigants—class action:** [§817] It was also traditionally improper for lawyers to *initiate* the organization of prospective litigants as a means of providing employment for themselves. [DR 2-104(A)(5)]

   (a) **Compare:** However, the Supreme Court has held it is improper for a court to set excessive limits on a lawyer's contact with prospective class members. [Gulf Oil v. Bernard, 450 U.S. 907 (1981)]

   (b) **But note:** A court can constitutionally impose severe sanctions on a *defense lawyer* who counsels or personally tries to persuade class action plaintiffs to opt out of the class. [Kleiner v. First National Bank of Atlanta, 751 F.2d 1193 (11th Cir. 1985)]

4. **Other Types of Permitted Personal Publicity:** [§818] Forms of lawyer publicity other than advertising of legal services were not considered in *Bates*, and in these areas the ABA Code provisions remain largely unchanged. The Model Rules, on the other hand, leave all of the following matters *unregulated*, except for the general *prohibition against "misleading" communications* in Model Rule 7.1.

   a. **Professional cards:** [§819] A lawyer's cards may properly state the lawyer's name, address, and telephone number, the law firm's name, the names of the lawyer's partners and associates, and any information about the lawyer's practice permitted under DR 2-105 (*see infra*, §§829-835). [DR 2-102(A)(1)]

   b. **Letterheads:** [§820] Letterheads may give the lawyer's name, address, telephone, firm name, names of partners and associates, and any permitted information about the nature of the practice. They may also include names of deceased and retired firm members and names under which the firm has previously been known. Designations such as "Of counsel" may be included on letterheads if otherwise proper (*see supra*, §734). [DR 2-102(A)(4)]

   c. **Office signs:** [§821] The location of a lawyer's office may be identified by a dignified sign on or near the lawyer's office *door*, and in the building directory. [DR 2-102(A)(3)]

   d. **Announcements regarding change of practice:** [§822] It is proper for a lawyer to mail "brief" and "dignified" announcements of changes pertaining to the lawyer's practice, such as the opening of an office; change of office address; joining, changing, or withdrawing from a firm or partnership; retiring from practice; entry or discharge from military service; etc. [DR 2-102(A)(2)]

   e. **Publications:** [§823] Lawyers may identify themselves by profession in connection with any book or other publication they author if their profession is *germane* to the publication. *Example:* Identification of the author as a lawyer is certainly proper on legal texts or books about the legal system, but it might not be on a novel or cookbook totally unrelated to the law. [DR 2-101(H)(5)]

f. **Political campaign materials:** [§824]   A lawyer may properly permit her name and profession to be used in political advertisements and campaign materials if these are germane to the campaign. Such information serves the legitimate function of *identifying* the lawyer. [DR 2-101(H)(1)]

g. **Routine reports of organizations:** [§825]   A lawyer may allow her name and profession to be used in "routine reports and announcements of a bona fide business, civic, professional, or political organization" in which she serves as a director or officer. [DR 2-101(H)(3)]

h. **Legal documents:** [§826]   A lawyer may also permit publication of her name and profession in connection with all legal documents prepared or reviewed by the lawyer. Again, such publication serves a proper identification purpose. [DR 2-101(H)(4)]

i. **Public service organizations:** [§827]   Organizations such as legal aid offices, lawyer referral services, and other *nonprofit* legal service organizations may properly publicize the nature and availability of their legal services or benefits. In addition, individual lawyers may assist such organizations in publicizing their legal services to laypersons. [DR 2-103]

C.   REGULATION OF LAWYER SPECIALIZATION

1. **Introduction:** [§828]   In today's complicated legal structure, no lawyer can be thoroughly competent in every field of law. Large firms have traditionally been able to provide expert legal services in many fields of law by de facto specialization, but present rules tend to make it difficult for the individual lawyer to tell potential clients of the kinds of work she is qualified to do.

2. **General Rule—No Designation of Specialty:** [§829]   As a general rule, it is *not* proper for lawyers to identify themselves as specialists or experts in any particular field of law in their advertising, on their cards, letterheads, or office signs. [Model Rule 7.4; DR 2-105]

3. **Exceptions:** [§830]   There are exceptions to the general rule:

a. **Patent lawyers:** [§831]   As a matter or custom, lawyers engaged in patent practice are permitted to indicate this fact on their *letterheads and office signs*. [DR 2-105(A)(1)] This privilege now extends to their formal advertising. [Model Rule 7.4(a); DR 2-101(B)(2)]

b. **Admiralty practice:** [§832]   Under the Model Rules, a lawyer engaged in admiralty practice may so designate. [Model Rule 7.4(b)]

c. **State-certified specialists:** [§833]   In addition, the ABA Code permits lawyers to hold themselves out as specialists *if* so certified by the appropriate *state* authority. [Model Rule 7.4(c); DR 2-105(A)(3)]

   (1) **Requirements for certification:** [§834]   A number of states now have programs to certify lawyer specialists (*e.g.*, California certifies specialists in taxation, criminal law, family law, and workers' compensation). Such programs typically require proof of qualifying experience in the specialty field (such as five years practice, more than 50% of which is devoted to the specialty), and/or passage of a written examination.

   (2) **Criticism of certification:** [§835]   If lawyers do specialize, requiring certification may tend to reduce the number of lawyers available to handle certain kinds of cases. Some argue that this will not only cause inconvenience, but will also lead to excessive fees. [61 A.B.A. J. 42 (1975)]

4. **Limitation of Practice:** [§836]   Both the ABA Code and Model Rules recognize a concept of "limiting practice." This is distinguished from specialization, in that it is said to carry no implication of special skill.

   a. **ABA Code approach:** [§837]   Under the ABA Code, the right to describe the categories in which one practices is limited to designations and definitions prescribed in state law. [DR 2-105(A)(2)]

      (1) **Constitutional limits on such designations:** [§838]   The Supreme Court has struck down a state rule prescribing categories very narrowly (*e.g.*, "property law" was acceptable but "real estate law" was prohibited). Categories may only be as narrow as "furthers the state's substantial interest." [Matter of R.M.J., 455 U.S. 191 (1982)]

   b. **Model Rules approach:** [§839]   The Model Rules, on the other hand, *do not limit* or prescribe the fields of law by which a lawyer may describe her practice. [Model Rule 7.4]

5. **Certification by Private Organizations:** [§840]   The Supreme Court has held that a lawyer may not be disciplined for noting on her letterhead that she has been "certified" by a private organization if the claim is *both verifiable* and *true.*

   a. **Confusion with specialization not sufficient to justify prohibition:** [§841]   The state's fear that potential clients would believe the statement was a claim of special skill was found insufficient to justify prohibiting it. [Peel v. Attorney Registration & Disciplinary Commission, 496 U.S. 91 (1990)]

   b. **Reflection in Model Rules:** [§842]   The ABA has amended the Model Rules to recognize private certification, but if the certifying organization does not have official sanction, the lawyer must so indicate. [Model Rule 7.4]

D. DIVISION OF FEES WITH LAWYERS OUTSIDE ONE'S FIRM [§843]

In some areas, it has been common for lawyers to share a fee with the lawyer who referred or "forwarded" the client. The ABA has traditionally viewed the practice as suspect.

1. **Fee Sharing under ABA Code:** [§844] The general rule under the ABA Code is that fee splitting with lawyers who are not one's partners or associates is **prohibited**, unless three tests are met:

   (i) The client gives **informed consent**;

   (ii) The total fee is **reasonable**; and

   (iii) The division corresponds to the **services performed and responsibilities assumed** by each lawyer.

   [DR 2-107(A)]

2. **Model Rules Approach:** [§845] The Model Rules have liberalized the standard. Now, assuming client consent and a reasonable total fee, lawyers who assume **"joint responsibility"** for a matter may share the fee in whatever proportions they agree, regardless of how much work each did. [Model Rule 1.5(e)]

3. **Fee Sharing with Former Partners and Associates:** [§846] An exception to the general rules on fee splitting permits making payments to a former **partner or associate** pursuant to a separation or retirement agreement. [DR 2-107(B); *compare* Model Rule 5.4(a)(1)—payments to estate of deceased lawyer]

4. **Purchase of Lawyer's Practice:** [§847] A lawyer who retires or otherwise leaves practice may wish to sell that practice to a **nonpartner or associate** for a price that reflects "goodwill," *i.e.*, future fees the new lawyer will earn from present clients. Such sales of goodwill were once prohibited, but the Model Rules now permit them, and the implicit fee splitting involved in them, *if*:

   (i) *The selling lawyer entirely ceases practice* in the jurisdiction;

   (ii) *The practice is sold in its entirety* to another lawyer or firm;

   (iii) *Notice is given to each client* that the client may retain other counsel and need not continue with the lawyer buying the practice; and

   (iv) *The fees are not increased to the clients*, except that the buying lawyer may announce that he will not undertake to represent the clients except at a fee level he charged previous clients before the purchase.

   [Model Rule 1.17]

VIII. ENFORCEMENT OF LAWYERS' PROFESSIONAL OBLIGATIONS

chapter approach

The previous chapters have discussed the obligations a lawyer has to clients, the court, and others. This chapter considers what may happen to a lawyer who fails to meet those obligations.

In considering this issue, keep in mind that lawyer conduct can result in:

(i) *Discipline* by the state (*e.g.*, disbarment, suspension, and reprimand or censure);

(ii) *Malpractice liability* (*i.e.*, damages); and/or

(iii) *Contempt sanctions* (*i.e.*, fine or imprisonment).

Be sure you understand the difference between discipline and malpractice: Discipline is available to *protect the public* from "bad" lawyers—*i.e.*, those who violate the disciplinary rules, commit crimes involving moral turpitude, or engage in dishonest, fraudulent, or deceitful conduct. A malpractice action, on the other hand, seeks to *compensate a victim* of the lawyer's negligence. Thus, to recover in a malpractice action, the client must show that the lawyer breached the standard of care, and in doing so caused the client to suffer some harm. If the lawyer was merely wrong (but not negligent), or if the client wasn't harmed by the lawyer's negligence, there is no recovery. Contempt sanctions in turn, enforce proper standards of litigation conduct.

A. THE FORMAL DISCIPLINARY PROCESS

1. **General Grounds for Discipline:** [§848]   A lawyer may be disciplined on any of the following grounds:

   a. **Violation of a Disciplinary Rule:** [§849]   The violation of an ABA Code Disciplinary Rule, a Model Rule, or the equivalent in states that have not adopted the ABA provisions is grounds for discipline. [Model Rule 8.4(a); DR 1-102(A)(1), (2)]

      (1) **Comment:** It is on this general ground that the courts punish most conduct by which lawyers take advantage of their clients. [Schullman v. State Bar, 10 Cal. 3d 526 (1973)]

      (2) **Note:** Mistake or ignorance of the rules is no defense. A lawyer is charged with knowledge of the ethical rules. [Abeles v. State Bar, *supra*, §536]

   b. **Conviction of a crime involving moral turpitude:** [§850]   A lawyer convicted of any crime involving moral turpitude is subject to discipline. The crime need not have been connected with the lawyer's professional activities; criminal acts wholly unrelated thereto are still proper grounds for discipline. [DR 1-102(A)(3)]

(1) **Moral turpitude defined:** [§851]   Moral turpitude has been defined as conduct that "offends the generally accepted moral code of mankind." [*In re* Colson, 412 A.2d 1160 (D.C. 1979)] *Examples:*

(a) *Convictions of "murder, forgery, extortion, bribery, perjury, robbery, embezzlement and other forms of theft"* are per se grounds for professional discipline. [*In re* Rothrock, 16 Cal. 2d 449 (1940)]

(b) *Conviction of possession of large quantities of marijuana with the intent to distribute* it for financial gain, and with awareness of the illegality thereof, likewise involves moral turpitude. [*In re* Kreamer, 14 Cal. 3d 524 (1975)]

(c) *Tax fraud* has been held to involve moral turpitude, but *failure to file* tax returns has been held not to involve moral turpitude. [*In re* Fahey, 8 Cal. 3d 842 (1973)]

(2) **Model Rules provision:** [§852]   The Model Rules better address the same issues by focusing on the relation of the crime to traits needed to be a lawyer. They impose discipline for commission of a "criminal act that reflects adversely on the lawyer's honesty, trustworthiness, or fitness as a lawyer in other respects." [Model Rule 8.4(b)]

(3) **Effect of appeal:** [§853]   Normally, disciplinary proceedings are deferred until criminal proceedings are final, giving the lawyer the opportunity to appeal the conviction. But this is discretionary with the court before which the disciplinary proceedings are brought, and it has the power to order an immediate suspension. [Cal. Bus. & Prof. Code §6102(a)—providing for immediate suspension upon conviction of any crime in which there is "probable cause to believe" that moral turpitude was involved]

(4) **Effect of reversal of conviction or pardon:** [§854]   The fact that the conviction has been reversed on appeal, or even pardoned, does *not* affect the power of the court to proceed with the disciplinary hearing. The standards of proof are different; thus, a lawyer may even be disciplined for conduct as to which he was *acquitted* in the criminal proceedings (*see* below).

c.   **Engaging in conduct involving dishonesty, fraud, deceit, or misrepresentation:** [§855]   A lawyer may be disciplined for her involvement in conduct involving dishonesty, fraud, deceit, or misrepresentation. Note that these acts do *not require a conviction*; indeed, they may not even be crimes, but they can result in the lawyer's disbarment. [Model Rule 8.4(c); DR 1-102(A)(4)]

(1) **Example:** A lawyer who impersonated her husband and took the bar exam for him was disbarred. [*In re* Lamb, 49 Cal. 3d 286 (1976)]

(2) **Example:** Plagiarism in preparation of an LL.M thesis also merited professional discipline. [*In re* Lamberis, 443 N.W.2d 549 (Ill. 1982)]

d. **Engaging in conduct prejudicial to administration of justice:** [§856]   This is grounds for discipline under both the ABA Code and Model Rules, but it is less often cited as a basis for discipline in actual cases. [Model Rule 8.4(d); DR 1-102(A)(5)]

e. **Specific statutory grounds for discipline:** [§857]   A number of state statutes also define specific acts that will subject a lawyer to discipline. For example, a lawyer in *California* may be disbarred or suspended from practice for:

(1) *Violating the Attorney's Oath* [Cal. Bus. & Prof. Code §§6068, 6103];

(2) *Appearing for another as attorney without authority therefor* [*Id.*, §6104];

(3) *Advocating the violent overthrow of government* [*Id.*, §6106.1]; or

(4) *Switching from the prosecution to the defense in a criminal case* [*Id.*, §6131].

2. **Types of Sanctions:** [§858]   The following types of formal sanctions can be imposed upon lawyers who are guilty of misconduct:

a. **Disbarment:** [§859]   This is a *permanent* revocation of the lawyer's license to practice. In some states, a disbarred lawyer who has been rehabilitated may apply to the state bar for readmission (*see infra*, §886).

b. **Suspension from practice:** [§860]   This is a *temporary* revocation of the right to practice. After the period of suspension has passed, the lawyer can return to practice. [*See In re* Mackay, 416 P.2d 823 (Alaska 1964)]

c. **Reprimand or censure:** [§861]   The state bar may impose reprimands or censure either *publicly or privately*.

d. **Mitigating or aggravating circumstances:** [§862]   The sanctions imposed in a given case depend upon all of the circumstances. Aside from the seriousness of the offense itself, factors that might affect the appropriate penalty include the following: (i) previous record (if any) and general reputation of the lawyer; (ii) the lawyer's personal problems (such as inexperience, emotional difficulties, etc.); (iii) reparation to injured parties; (iv) motive or intent, both of the lawyer and of the complaining party; (v) attitude of the lawyer during the disciplinary proceeding (*i.e.*, frankness, remorse, etc.); (vi) extent of rehabilitation; and (vii) *present* moral character. [Doyle v. State Bar, 15 Cal. 3d 973 (1976)]

(1) **Mental illness or chronic alcoholism:** [§863]   This is usually recognized as affecting the culpability of a lawyer. Sanctions in such cases are often limited to *suspending* the lawyer from practice pending proof of recovery. [Petition of Johnson, 322 N.W.2d 616 (Minn. 1982); Newton v. State Bar, 658 P.2d 735 (Cal. 1983)]

   (a) **Note:** Alcoholism and mental illness are not only mitigating factors in discipline cases, but may also be a basis for suspension of a lawyer *before* wrongdoing. Although such a sanction has serious consequences, in that it denies the lawyer a right to make a living, many states use summary procedures to suspend impaired lawyers before too many clients' cases have been neglected or their interests damaged. [*See* ABA Model Rule for Lawyer Disciplinary Enforcement 23]

(2) **Financial misfortune or economic necessity:** [§864]   A lawyer's financial problems are *not* by themselves generally regarded as a mitigating factor in disciplinary proceedings. [*In re* Park, 274 P.2d 1006 (Wash. 1954)]

   (a) **But note:** Financial pressures can be given some consideration along with other factors. [*See In re* Kreamer, *supra*, §851—lawyer engaged in illegal drug dealings because of need to raise funds for medical care of fiancee]

(3) **Any other punishment:** [§865]   Other punishment suffered by the lawyer for the same conduct (*e.g.*, imprisonment) may also properly be considered by the court. [*In re* Kreamer, *supra*]

   (a) **But note:** Restitution made only under pressure of a state bar investigation is entitled to no weight. [Sevin v. State Bar, 8 Cal. 3d 641 (1973)]

3. **Stages in Disciplinary Proceedings**

   a. **Complaint to state bar:** [§866]   Disciplinary proceedings against a lawyer are initiated by lodging a complaint with the state disciplinary authorities—most often the state bar. While most complaints come from aggrieved clients, they may also be made by fellow lawyers, judges, or any other person with knowledge of the alleged misconduct.

   (1) **Privilege recognized:** [§867]   Courts have stressed that the ability to complain about misconduct is a "safety valve" for the public and is vital to public assurance that the bar does not shelter lawyers engaging in such activities. For this reason, the filing of a complaint with the state bar is considered *privileged* as a matter of public policy. [Chronicle Publishing Co. v. Superior Court, 54 Cal. 2d 548 (1960); 77 A.L.R. 2d 493 (1961)]

(a) **Rationale:** This prevents any subsequent action by the lawyer against the complainant for defamation or malicious prosecution. [Toft v. Ketchum, 113 A.2d 671 (N.J. 1955)]

(2) **Federal civil rights action to enjoin proceedings:** [§868] However, in a few cases lawyers have been allowed to file suit under section 1983 of the Federal Civil Rights Act (which allows suit to enjoin a deprivation of federal constitutional rights by state or local officials) where the lawyer alleges that the disciplinary action was instituted in bad faith to harass and punish the lawyer because of his controversial clients, unpopular positions, etc. [Taylor v. Kentucky State Bar, 424 F.2d 478 (6th Cir. 1970); 9 A.L.R. Fed. 422 (1971)]

b. **Screening of complaint by state bar:** [§869] As a general rule, complaints are referred initially to a local grievance or administrative committee of the state bar. Where the charges result from lawyer-client misunderstandings, an appropriate discussion with the client at this point usually resolves the matter—often without involving the lawyer at all.

(1) **Explanation by lawyer:** [§870] If the charge presents a prima facie case of misconduct, however, the lawyer may be asked to submit an explanation to the committee (either personally or in writing). After further investigation, the grievance committee may again find the charges unwarranted and dismiss the complaint.

(2) **Dismissal not reviewable:** [§871] Since disciplinary proceedings are a matter of internal regulation within the bar, the complaining party has *no right of review* once a charge is dismissed by the committee—nor may the party subsequently reinstitute a complaint on the same facts.

c. **Hearing before grievance committee:** [§872] Complaints not disposed of by a preliminary investigation are generally scheduled for nonpublic hearing before the local committee.

(1) **Complainant represented by "examiner":** [§873] To preserve the independence of the grievance committee or hearing panel as an *adjudicative* body, an "examining attorney" is usually appointed by the committee to prepare the evidence against the lawyer and present it at the hearing.

(2) **Lawyer's resignation generally not permitted:** [§874] A lawyer under disciplinary charges will generally *not* be permitted to resign, at least not without admitting the offenses in detail. Otherwise, if the lawyer later files a petition for reinstatement (*see infra*, §886), there would be no clear findings as to what the lawyer had done.

(3) **Lawyer's right to procedural due process:** [§875] The accused lawyer is entitled to procedural due process at the hearing. To this end, *proper*

notice, a right to be heard and to introduce evidence, a right to counsel, and a right to cross-examine adverse witnesses are usually guaranteed by statute. [*See, e.g.,* Cal. Bus. & Prof. Code §6085; Giddens v. State Bar, 28 Cal. 3d 730 (1980)]

(a) **Note:** Due process also requires that the hearing be *limited to charges made in the complaint.* [*In re* Ruffalo, 390 U.S. 544 (1968)]

(b) **Compare:** The exclusionary rules of criminal law are *not* part of the due process required in disciplinary proceedings. Thus, for example, evidence obtained by wiretap or even by unlawful search and seizure *may* be used against a lawyer in disbarment proceedings. [Emslie v. State Bar, 11 Cal. 3d 210 (1974); Kelly v. Greason, 23 N.Y.2d 368 (1969)]

　　1) **Rationale:** The essential purpose of the disciplinary proceedings is to preserve the integrity of the bar, not to "punish" the lawyer. Hence, they are not "criminal" (or quasi-criminal) proceedings to which the Fourth Amendment applies.

(4) **Privilege against self-incrimination applies:** [§876] The lawyer has a constitutional privilege under the Fifth Amendment (*see* Evidence Summary) to refuse to answer questions in disciplinary proceedings concerning the lawyer's professional conduct, *and no disciplinary action can be taken against the lawyer based solely on such claim of privilege.* [Spevack v. Klein, 385 U.S. 511 (1967)]

(a) **Note:** If a lawyer *admits* misconduct pursuant to an order granting *immunity* from criminal prosecution, the admission *may* be used against the lawyer in a professional discipline case. [*In re* Schwarz, 282 N.E.2d 689 (Ill. 1972)]

(b) **And note:** A grant of immunity from state disciplinary enforcement cannot be granted by a federal prosecutor. [*In re* Daley, 549 F.2d 469 (7th Cir. 1977)]

(5) **No jury right:** [§877] There is *no right* to a jury trial in a disciplinary proceeding. [*In re* Willcher, 447 A.2d 1198 (D.C. 1982)]

(6) **Discovery procedures:** [§878] Many states make their usual discovery procedures—including depositions, interrogatories, requests for admission and production of documents—available to the lawyer in preparing for the disciplinary hearing. [Brotsky v. State Bar, 57 Cal. 2d 287 (1962)]

(7) **Burden of proof:** [§879] The burden of proof is on those presenting the charge. Most states permit only *legally sufficient evidence* to be considered (*i.e.,* inadmissible hearsay is excluded), and require proof *exceeding a preponderance of the evidence* (though allowing something

less than proof beyond a reasonable doubt). [State v. Neilssen, 136 N.W.2d 355 (Neb. 1966)]

d. **Decision by grievance committee:** [§880] After the hearing, the grievance committee (or hearing panel) enters its decision—either dismissing the charges against the lawyer or recommending appropriate sanctions.

e. **Further review before state bar:** [§881] In many states, the decision of the grievance committee has the effect only of a **recommendation** to the state bar; *i.e.*, the decision is referred to a reviewing authority within the state bar which may act upon the recommendations of the grievance committee, take additional evidence, or set aside the decision of the grievance committee and hear the whole case *de novo*.

f. **Review and determination by highest state court:** [§882] Any disciplinary action or recommendation by the state bar is subject to review before the state's highest court.

(1) **Procedure:** [§883] A lawyer who wishes to challenge the action or recommendations of the state bar must file a timely petition for review before the court. The burden is on the lawyer to show that the state bar's action or recommendation is not supported by the record or is otherwise unlawful. [*In re* Bogart, 9 Cal. 3d 743 (1973); Cal. Bus. & Prof. Code §6083]

   (a) **Authority of court:** Whether or not such a petition for review is filed, the court typically has authority to alter or modify the disciplinary action or recommendations made by the state bar. [*But see* Cal. Bus. & Prof. Code §6084—if no appeal, order final]

   (b) **Scope of review:** The court's review is limited to the record below, but the court is **not** bound by the state bar's findings of fact: The court may independently assess the evidence and pass on its sufficiency. Furthermore, the court may impose a greater or lesser sanction than that proposed by the state bar. [Selznick v. State Bar, 16 Cal. 3d 704 (1976)]

      1) **Comment:** As a practical matter, however, the findings of fact of the state bar are usually given great weight by the reviewing court. [*See* Himmell v. State Bar, 4 Cal. 3d 786 (1971)—court will be reluctant to reverse state bar findings, especially where they rest on testimonial evidence]

g. **Original proceeding before state's highest court:** [§884] The state's highest court ordinarily has the power to hear disciplinary charges against any lawyer without any prior proceedings before the state bar—either on its own motion, or upon the accusation of any interested party.

(1) **Criminal convictions:** [§885]   The one instance in which the court often acts directly is when a lawyer has been convicted of a crime that may involve moral turpitude. The record of the lawyer's conviction is often filed directly with the court. The court may then determine from the transcript (or it may order a hearing) whether the lawyer was guilty of "moral turpitude," and sanctions may be imposed directly. [*See* Cal. Bus. & Prof. Code §§6101, 6102]

h.   **Reinstatement:** [§886]   Where a lawyer has been disbarred or suspended from practice for an *indefinite* period, the court may subsequently reinstate the lawyer by an appropriate order. The lawyer must petition the court for reinstatement and must present *supporting evidence* to convince the court of present fitness to practice law. [*In re* Hiss, 333 N.E.2d 429 (Mass. 1975)]

(1) **Definite suspension:** [§887]   A lawyer suspended for a fixed period is deemed reinstated at the expiration of the period without any formal petition or order. [Friday v. State Bar, 3 Cal. 2d 501 (1943)]

4.   **Obligation to Disclose Misconduct by Other Lawyers:** [§888]   The legal profession is largely self-policing, and the enforcement of professional responsibilities requires assistance from its members. Thus, a lawyer is under an affirmative duty to disclose conduct by other lawyers that the lawyer believes to be a violation of any of the rules of professional conduct. Such disclosure must be made to the tribunal or authority empowered to act upon such violation. [EC 1-4; DR 1-103]

a.   **Scope of obligation:** [§889]   Under the ABA Code, a lawyer must disclose not only acts of illegality or "moral turpitude," but any other conduct prejudicial to the administration of justice or reflecting adversely on the other lawyer's *fitness to practice*. [DR 1-103]

(1) **Must be willing to testify:** [§890]   Furthermore, upon proper request, a lawyer is obliged to reveal such information in testimony before a court or disciplinary tribunal. [DR 1-103(B)]

(2) **Model Rules obligation narrower:** [§891]   The Code obligation was so broad that lawyers did not seem to take it seriously; thus, under the Model Rules, a lawyer is required to report only misconduct that "raises a substantial question" as to the other lawyer's "honesty, trustworthiness, or fitness as a lawyer." [Model Rule 8.3(a)]

b.   **Exception for "privileged" knowledge:** [§892]   A lawyer may not disclose knowledge of misconduct by fellow lawyers where knowledge of such conduct is privileged. [Model Rule 8.3(c)] (The scope of "privilege" is discussed *supra*, §§337 *et seq.*) For present purposes, "privilege" refers to any right to confidentiality a *client* may have.

(1) **Compare:** A lawyer is required to disclose misconduct by other lawyers who are not clients "unstintingly." *Example:* The fact that the lawyers

are partners or associates does **not** create any privilege between them which would excuse either from the duty to disclose misconduct by the other. [Attorney Grievance Commission v. Kahn, 431 A.2d 1336 (Md. 1981)]

 c. **Sanctions for failure to disclose:** [§893] Failure of a lawyer to disclose the misconduct of other lawyers *itself* subjects the lawyer to appropriate sanctions. [Model Rule 8.3(a); DR 1-103(A); *In re* Himmel, 533 N.W.2d 790 (Ill. 1988)]

5. **Effect of Disbarment or Suspension in Other Jurisdictions:** [§894] Disbarment or suspension in one state does **not** automatically affect a lawyer's standing in other jurisdictions.

 a. **Federal courts:** [§895] A federal court in the same state is not obliged to disbar a lawyer simply because of state court disbarment. The federal court system is entirely separate and **each** federal court in which the lawyer has been admitted to practice must therefore make an **independent evaluation** of the lawyer's conduct. [Theard v. United States, 354 U.S. 278 (1957)]

  (1) **State disbarment:** [§896] However, the fact that a lawyer has been disbarred by the state is competent evidence in the federal proceedings, and it may be enough to convince the federal court that a similar sanction is warranted. [*In re* Rhodes, 370 F.2d 411 (8th Cir. 1967)]

  (2) **State suspension:** [§897] But note that one decision has held that it was improper for a federal court to **disbar** a lawyer who was **suspended** by the state for one year—at least where the state suspension involved mitigating circumstances. [*In re* Abrams, 521 F.2d 1094 (3d Cir. 1975)]

 b. **Other states:** [§898] An order imposing discipline in one state is not necessarily binding in a sister state, the preferred view being that disciplinary action by the bar of a sister state will be accepted as conclusive proof of the **misconduct** alleged, but not of the **sanctions** warranted by such misconduct. *Rationale:* The standards of conduct imposed on lawyers may differ among the various states. Hence, each state should be free to determine the appropriate discipline for particular acts in light of its own standards. [Florida Bar v. Wilkes, 179 So. 2d 193 (Fla. 1965); *In re* Weaver, 399 N.E.2d 748 (Ind. 1980)]

B. PERSONAL FINANCIAL LIABILITY (MALPRACTICE) [§899]

Most states in which the issue has arisen have held that disciplinary proceedings may not grant **private remedies** and that an injured client who wishes to seek recovery must do so in a separate action. [*Re* Ackerman, 330 N.E.2d 322 (Ind. 1975); *but see* Yokozeki v. State Bar, 11 Cal. 3d 436 (1974)]

1. **General Standard—"Skill and Knowledge in Community":** [§900] The level of competency demanded of a lawyer in malpractice cases is the "skill, prudence, and diligence" possessed by lawyers of ordinary skill and capacity who perform

similar services in the same or similar locality. [Lucas v. Hamm, 56 Cal. 2d 583 (1961)]

a. **Standard is minimum of duty owed:** [§901]   Thus, *at a minimum* the lawyer is held to the standard of care exercised by other lawyers in the community—regardless of whether the lawyer personally possesses such skills.

b. **Higher standard of care owed by specialists:** [§902]   If a lawyer *has* greater competence, she is bound to exercise it; *i.e.*, lawyers who hold themselves out as specialists in a particular field (tax, litigation, probate, etc.) will be held to the standard of care customarily exercised by *fellow specialists*, rather than merely that required of other members of the legal community generally. [Wright v. Williams, 47 Cal. App. 3d 802 (1975)]

c. **Appointed counsel:** [§903]   Even appointed counsel may be held liable to a client for malpractice. [Spring v. Constantino, 362 A.2d 871 (Conn. 1975); Ferry v. Ackerman, 444 U.S. 193 (1979)]

2. **Application**

a. **Knowledge and research ability:** [§904]   As part of the general standard of care, a lawyer is expected *to possess* knowledge of those "plain and elementary principles of law which are commonly known by well-informed attorneys" *and to discover* those additional rules of law which, even though not commonly known, may readily be found *by standard research techniques*. [Smith v. Lewis, 13 Cal. 3d 349 (1975)]

(1) **Ignorance of new laws:** [§905]   Thus, it is *no* defense to a malpractice suit that the lawyer was *unaware* of recent changes in statutes or case law which affected the correctness of her advice. [Theobold v. Byers, 193 Cal. App. 2d 147 (1961)]

(a) **Note:** The lawyer is obliged to make a reasonable investigation of the facts of the case. [Woodruff v. Tomlin, 616 F.2d 924 (6th Cir. 1980)]

(b) **And note:** A lawyer has an *affirmative duty to investigate* upon receiving information that should reasonably put the lawyer on notice that further research or action is required. [Owen v. Neely, 471 S.W.2d 705 (Ky. 1971)—notice of defect in title]

(2) **Foreign law:** [§906]   Normally, lawyers are expected to be familiar with rules of law and procedure *in their own states*. However, where in the exercise of reasonable care they should realize that the case involves an issue that must be decided under the law of some other state or country, lawyers may be under a duty to become familiar with appropriate foreign law (or associate competent counsel with such familiarity). [Rekeweg v. Federal Mutual Insurance Co., 27 F.R.D. 431 (N.D. Ind. 1961)]

b. **No liability for errors in judgment:** [§907] Lawyers are not, however, liable for every mistake they make in practice. They do not guarantee the soundness of their opinions or the validity of instruments they are engaged to draft. If the action or decision involved is one as to which there is **reasonable doubt** by well-informed lawyers, judgmental errors by a lawyer are not malpractice.

(1) **Trial tactics:** [§908] This is especially true as to errors made in the course of **litigation**, where the decision made is often a matter of judgment or tactics (*e.g.*, whether or not to call a certain witness, demand a jury trial, etc.). [Kirsch v. Duryea, 21 Cal. 3d 303 (1978)]

(2) **Law uncertain:** [§909] Likewise, where the area of law in question is **unsettled or unclear**, the fact that the lawyer's advice or interpretation of the law ultimately proves wrong is not enough by itself to establish malpractice. [Lucas v. Hamm, *supra*]

(a) **Example:** Misinterpreting a complicated Rule Against Perpetuities problem in drafting a will has been held **not** to constitute malpractice. [Lucas v. Hamm, *supra*]

(b) **But note:** Even with respect to an unsettled area of the law, it is the lawyer's obligation **to undertake reasonable research** "in an effort to ascertain relevant legal principles and to make an informed decision as to a course of conduct based upon **an intelligent assessment** of the problem." One case has even held a lawyer liable for malpractice for giving **correct advice** about the law where another position was arguable and where asserting it might have helped the client in negotiating a divorce settlement. [Aloy v. Marsh, 38 Cal. 3d 425 (1985)]

3. **Harm to Client Must Usually Be Shown:** [§910] Failure to meet the general standard of care constitutes negligence, but traditionally there is **no malpractice liability unless harm** to the client has proximately resulted therefrom. Thus, the client must show that **"but for"** the lawyer's errors or omissions, the client would have avoided the complained of loss. [Campbell v. Magana, 184 Cal. App. 2d 751 (1960)]

a. **Burden of proof:** [§911] In litigation matters, this has meant that the client **must in effect prove two cases:** (i) that the lawyer was **negligent** in handling the matter; and (ii) that the client would **otherwise have won the lawsuit**.

(1) **Note:** This has often been a very difficult burden for the client—particularly where the lawsuit was a personal injury action or involved disputed facts or close liability questions.

(2) **Example:** Lawyer is hired to defend Client in contract action, but Lawyer fails to appear and the action is lost, resulting in a judgment against Client. Whether Client can recover damages against Lawyer for

malpractice depends on whether Client had a **valid defense** to the action (*i.e.*, whether Client would have prevailed "but for" Lawyer's negligence; *see* above).

(3) **But note:** *Disciplinary* sanctions can be invoked regardless of the "but for" test. Thus, technically, a lawyer could be disciplined for incompetence that does not constitute malpractice.

b. **Modern trend:** [§912]   The California Supreme Court has now effectively eliminated this "but for" test or "suit within a suit" requirement, a development that seems long overdue. [Smith v. Lewis, *supra*, §904]

4. **Liability for Acts of Others:** [§913]   The general standard of care above may render lawyers liable not only for their own acts, but also for the acts of others:

a. **Co-counsel:** [§914]   Where several lawyers have been employed to represent a client concurrently, **each** owes the duty of care stated above. **No delegation or division of responsibility** between counsel excuses one from malpractice liability for errors or omissions of the other, unless the client **expressly** agreed otherwise.

b. **Partners:** [§915]   Malpractice by a partner in a law firm generally renders all other partners equally liable, unless the negligent partner had no actual or apparent authority to act on behalf of the firm in the matter. [Cook v. Lyon, 522 S.W.2d 740 (Tex. 1975)—no liability for partner's faulty investment advice to client where investment was unrelated to matter firm was handling]

c. **Employees:** [§916]   A lawyer is generally liable on a theory of respondeat superior for losses caused to a client by negligent acts of the lawyer's employees or subordinates (*e.g.*, secretary carelessly loses a file, throws out a will, or destroys crucial evidence without which client loses the case).

d. **Referral lawyer:** [§917]   In addition, a lawyer who refers a client to another lawyer whose negligence causes the client loss may be held liable for the other lawyer's negligence **if** the first lawyer made the referral **without reasonable care** (*i.e.*, without checking into the lawyer's reputation and skill). [Tormo v. Yormark, 398 F. Supp. 1159 (D.N.J. 1975)—client's funds embezzled by lawyer to whom referred]

5. **Negligence Liability to Third Parties:** [§918]   Where the lawyer is employed by the client to render **services intended to benefit some third person**, the lawyer's duty of care extends to such persons as well as to the actual client. [Heyer v. Flaig, 70 Cal. 2d 223 (1969)]

a. **Example:** A lawyer who is hired by a testator to draft a will owes a duty of care not only to the testator, but also to the **intended beneficiaries** under the will. Consequently, if the intended gift fails and goes intestate to someone else through the lawyer's negligence, the lawyer is civilly liable to the intended beneficiary for the loss. [Lucas v. Hamm, *supra*]

    b.   **Foreseeability:** [§919] The scope of liability here extends to those third persons as to whom a risk of harm was *foreseeable.*

        (1) **Example:** A lawyer who made negligent misrepresentations in an opinion concerning his client's title to property was liable to third party who relied on opinion to loan money to client, since harm to lender was clearly foreseeable. [Greycas, Inc. v. Proud, 826 F.2d 1560 (7th Cir. 1987)]

  6. **Statute of Limitations in Malpractice Suits**

    a.   **Where the employment contract is in writing:** [§920] Where there is a formal agreement between the lawyer and client, the client's suit can be framed as a breach of contract and can be brought within the generally longer statutory period (*e.g.*, four years) applicable to suits for breach of written contracts. [Bernard v. Walkup, 272 Cal. App. 2d 595 (1969)]

    b.   **Where there is no written contract:** [§921] Where there is no clear agreement, the malpractice action is sometimes subject to a shorter limitations period (*e.g.*, two years in many states).

    c.   **Statutory period:** [§922] In either case, the statutory period does not begin to run until the client actually or constructively *discovers* the negligent act *and* has actually suffered *damages* therefrom. [Neel v. Magana, 6 Cal. 3d 176 (1971)]

  7. **Limitations on Liability Prohibited:** [§923] The ABA Code expressly prohibits any attempt by lawyers to exculpate themselves or otherwise limit their liability to clients for malpractice. [DR 6-102]

    a.   **Contractual waiver:** [§924] A lawyer may *not* enforce a contractual waiver of malpractice liability obtained in advance from a client. [DR 6-102; EC 6-6; *but see* Model Rule 1.8(h)—agreement enforceable if client was separately represented in making it]

    b.   **Insurance:** [§925] Of course, most lawyers carry *malpractice insurance* against liability flowing from their own errors and omissions.

C. CONTEMPT SANCTION [§926]

Although not often thought of as a device for keeping lawyers "ethical," the power of a court to punish a lawyer for contempt is one of the most direct and effective techniques for enforcing professional standards. Indeed, the contempt sanction may be the only practical way to enforce proper standards of courtroom conduct.

1. **Direct Criminal Contempt:** [§927] Direct criminal contempt consists of any conduct *within the personal knowledge* of the judge that tends to obstruct the court in the administration of justice or to bring the administration of justice into disrepute. [People v. Sherwin, 166 N.E. 513 (Ill. 1929)]

   a. **Examples:** A lawyer's willful disruption of a trial [*In re* Isserman, 345 U.S. 927 (1953)] or filing of briefs filled with scandalous language falsely accusing the court of improprieties [People v. Miller, 264 N.E.2d 45 (Ill. 1970)] resulted in direct criminal contempt.

   b. **Summary enforcement:** [§928] Upon commission of a direct contempt in open court, the trial judge may act upon personal knowledge of the facts and punish the offender *summarily*, without a hearing. [*Ex parte* Terry, 128 U.S. 289 (1888)]

   (1) **Delay in acting:** [§929] A judge who does not act summarily must refer the case to another judge (who will presumably be less personally involved) for a hearing. [Mayberry v. Pennsylvania, 400 U.S. 455 (1971)]

   (2) **Right to jury trial:** [§930] If the judge, prior to hearing, proposes to sentence the contemnor to more than a six-month jail term, the accused is entitled to a jury trial. [Bloom v. Illinois, 391 U.S. 194 (1968)]

2. **Indirect Criminal Contempt:** [§931] When the relevant facts regarding the lawyer's alleged contempt are *not within the personal knowledge* of the judge, the contempt is said to be indirect.

   a. **Example:** An alleged violation of an order of the bailiff, not in the presence of the judge, would be indirect contempt. [Johnson v. Mississippi, 403 U.S. 212 (1971)]

   b. **Hearing required:** [§932] Because the trial judge does not personally know the facts, a hearing must be held. If the regular judge is so personally involved with the case that the judge's impartiality might be questioned, the contempt should be referred to another judge.

IX. THE SPECIAL RESPONSIBILITIES OF JUDGES

chapter approach

Judges are lawyers first and thus subject to the rules of ethical conduct for lawyers. On assuming the bench, they become subject to additional ethical norms. This chapter discusses those additional obligations of judges and limitations on their activities both on and off the bench.

A. INTRODUCTION [§933]

The ABA Code of Judicial Conduct ("CJC") establishes the specific rules pertaining to judges. The CJC as amended in 1990 has five Canons. Like the ABA Model Rules of Professional Conduct, it follows a Restatement-type format, which does not distinguish between Disciplinary Rules and Ethical Considerations.

B. GENERAL NORMS

1. **Maintain High Standards of Conduct:** [§934]   A judge must establish, maintain, enforce, and observe high standards of personal conduct. [CJC Canon 1]

2. **Promote Public Confidence in Judiciary:** [§935]   A judge must obey the law and behave in a manner that promotes public confidence in the integrity and impartiality of the judiciary. [CJC Canon 2A]

3. **Avoid Using Influence or Being Influenced:** [§936]   A judge must not let family, social, or other relationships influence judicial acts, or let it appear that they could. [CJC Canon 2B]

    a. **May not advance others' interests:** [§937]   The judge may not use the prestige of the office to advance the private (usually business) interests of others. [CJC Canon 2B]

    b. **May not act as witness:** [§938]   The judge may testify as a character witness only *if subpoenaed*; he may not testify "voluntarily." [CJC Canon 2B]

4. **Avoid Membership in Discriminatory Organizations:** [§939]   A judge may not belong to an organization that "practices invidious discrimination on the basis of race, sex, religion, or national origin." [CJC Canon 2C]

C. JUDGE'S OFFICIAL ACTIONS

1. **Priority of Judicial Duties:** [§940]   A judge is to put her judicial duties ahead of all other activities. [CJC Canon 3A]

2. **Behavior on the Bench:** [§941]   The judge is admonished to be faithful to the law, remain competent, and be unswayed by outside pressures. [CJC Canon 3B(2)]

    a. **Hear all cases:** [§942]   The judge must hear and decide all assigned cases unless disqualified therein. [CJC Canon 3B(1)]

    b. **Order in court:** [§943]   The judge is to maintain order and decorum in the courtroom. [CJC Canon 3B(3)]

    c. **Relations with others:** [§944]   The judge, other court officials, and lawyers are to be patient, dignified, and courteous to lawyers, jurors, witnesses, and others with whom they deal. [CJC Canon 3B(4)]

    d. **Perform duties without bias or prejudice:** [§945]   The judge and other court officials must not exhibit bias or prejudice based on race, sex, religion, national origin, disability, age, sexual orientation, or socioeconomic status. [CJC Canon 3B(5)]

    e. **Not allow lawyers to manifest bias:** [§946]   A judge must not permit lawyers to manifest prohibited bias either, but the judge may not forbid legitimate advocacy when the above factors are at issue in contested proceedings. [CJC Canon 3B(6)]

3. **Ex Parte Contacts:** [§947]   The judge may not initiate or consider ex parte contacts, except as authorized by law. [CJC Canon 3B(7)]

    a. **Scheduling matters:** [§948]   The judge may speak with parties ex parte where necessary to schedule matters or deal with emergency situations that do not affect the merits of a matter, provided that the judge (i) reasonably believes that no party will be advantaged thereby, and (ii) notifies the other parties of the substance of the communication and gives them a chance to respond. [CJC Canon 3B(7)(a)]

    b. **Consultation with disinterested expert on the law:** [§949]   The judge may, without prior notice to the parties, consult with a disinterested expert on the law applicable to a case before the court. But the judge must later tell the parties the name of the person consulted and the substance of the advice obtained, and must give the parties an opportunity to respond. [CJC Canon 3B(7)(b)]

    c. **Consultation with clerks or other judges:** [§950]   The judge may, of course, talk about a case with the judge's law clerk and fellow judges. [CJC Canon 3B(7)(c)]

4. **Disposition of Matters:** [§951]   The judge must dispose of matters promptly, efficiently, and fairly. [CJC Canon 3B(8)]

5. **Relations with News Media:** [§952]   The judge and other court personnel may not comment to the news media on a pending or impending matter. [CJC Canon 3B(9)]

   a. **Rules pertaining to lawyers:** [§953]   The Code of Judicial Conduct only governs the judge's comments; lawyers are covered by DR 7-107 of the Model Code and Rule 3.6 of the Model Rules.

6. **Comments about Jurors:** [§954]   A judge may not commend or criticize jurors for their verdict other than in a court order or opinion, but the judge may thank them for their service. [CJC Canon 3B(10)]

7. **Nonpublic Information:** [§955]   A judge may not use or disclose nonpublic information learned in a judicial capacity. [CJC Canon 3B(11)]

8. **Administrative Duties of the Judge:** [§956]   The judge must diligently discharge the management responsibilities of running the court and insist that court staff do so. [CJC Canon 3C(1)]

   a. **No unnecessary appointments:** [§957]   A judge appointing receivers, trustees, and the like must not do so unnecessarily or with regard to politics or nepotism. Also, compensation must not be excessive. [CJC Canon 3C(4)]

   b. **Reporting lawyer misconduct:** [§958]   The judge is required to take or initiate appropriate disciplinary action against a judge or lawyer for misconduct about which the judge knows. [CJC Canon 3D(1), (2)]

D.   DISQUALIFICATION OF THE JUDGE

1. **Bases for Disqualification:** [§959]   A judge is disqualified to act in any proceeding in which her impartiality might reasonably be questioned. The CJC lists several such situations, but says there may be others. [CJC Canon 3E]

   a. **Personal bias concerning a party:** [§960]   The judge is disqualified if she is biased for or against a party to the case. [CJC Canon 3E(1)(a)]

      (1) **But note:** The judge is not necessarily disqualified where the bias is with respect to a *policy issue.* Thus, a black judge is not normally disqualified to sit in a civil rights case, and either a male or female judge may hear a sex discrimination case.

   b. **Knowledge of disputed evidentiary facts:** [§961]   The judge may take judicial notice of some facts, of course, but if the judge has knowledge as to the facts in dispute, she is disqualified. [CJC Canon 3E(1)(a)]

   c. **Served as a lawyer in the matter:** [§962]   A judge may not hear a case in which she served as a lawyer before coming on the bench, or which someone with whom the judge practiced law handled while the judge was still in practice. [CJC Canon 3E(1)(b)]

d. **Judge or former associate a material witness:** [§963] The judge may not hear a case in which she, or a lawyer with whom the judge practiced, is a material witness. [CJC Canon 3E(1)(b)]

e. **Financial interest in party or subject matter of litigation:** [§964] A judge is disqualified if she has any more than a de minimis economic interest, known to the judge, in a party or in the subject matter of the proceeding. [CJC Canon 3E(1)(c)]

   (1) **Disqualifying interest:** [§965] The disqualifying interest may be that of the judge's *spouse, parent, or child*—or any other *family member residing in the household*—or the judge acting as a *fiduciary* (*i.e.*, an executor, administrator, trustee, or guardian).

   (2) **Economic interest defined:** [§966] An economic interest is a more than de minimis legal or equitable interest, or a relationship as director, advisor, or active participant in the affairs of a party. [CJC: "Terminology"]

       (a) **Exceptions:** [§967] The following are *not* disqualifying interests:

           1) **Mutual fund:** [§968] Ownership of a mutual fund does not constitute a financial interest in the firms whose securities are held by the fund, unless the judge is a manager of the fund.

           2) **Nonprofit organization:** [§969] An office in an educational, charitable, fraternal, or civic organization does not constitute an interest in the securities held by the organization.

           3) **Policyholder or depositor:** [§970] The judge's interest as a policyholder in a mutual insurance company or depositor in a mutual savings association is not disqualifying unless it could be "substantially affected" by the case.

           4) **Government securities:** [§971] The judge who holds government securities is not disqualified from hearing cases involving the government unless the value of the securities could be "substantially affected."

f. **Any other interest that could be substantially affected:** [§972] Any interest although not in a party or the subject matter that could be substantially affected by the outcome of the case is also disqualifying. [CJC Canon 3E(1)(c)]

g. **Cases in which judge's relatives involved:** [§973] The judge is also disqualified by the roles or interests of the judge's *spouse*, or someone within the *third* *degree of relationship* to either of them, or the ***spouse of such a relative***. Disqualification arises when such a person is:

(i) A ***party***, or officer, director, or trustee of a party;

(ii) Acting as a ***lawyer*** in the proceeding;

(iii) Known by the judge to have an ***interest*** that could be substantially affected by the outcome of the case; or

(iv) Known by the judge to likely be a ***material witness***.

[CJC Canon 3E(1)(d)]

(1) **"Third degree of relationship":** [§974] The "third degree of relationship" is calculated according to the civil law system and includes parents, grandparents, greatgrandparents, siblings, aunts and uncles, nieces and nephews, children, grandchildren, and greatgrandchildren. [CJC: "Terminology"]

(2) **Scope of obligation:** [§975] The judge must make ***reasonable efforts*** to be informed about financial interests of her spouse and minor children, but not about the other relatives. [CJC Canon 3E(2)]

2. **Remittal of Disqualification:** [§976] If the judge is disqualified for one of the financial reasons (*see supra*, §§964-975), the parties may decide whether to ***waive*** the judge's disqualification. [CJC Canon 3F]

   a. **Procedure:** [§977] The judge, instead of immediately withdrawing, states on the record the basis of the disqualification. If, outside the presence of the judge, all of the parties agree the problem is insubstantial and wish to waive the disqualification, each of the ***parties and each lawyer*** must so indicate in writing. The writing is then incorporated in the record. [CJC Canon 3F] By implication, if all do not agree to waive the disqualification, the judge may not be told who held out.

E. EXTRAJUDICIAL ACTIVITIES OF THE JUDGE

1. **In General:** [§978] A judge may engage in a number of nonjudicial activities, some associated with law and some not. However, ***all*** such activities are subject to the qualification that the judge may not detract from the ***dignity*** of the office, ***interfere with the performance*** of judicial duties, or ***increase the likelihood*** the judge will have to be ***disqualified*** in cases. [CJC Canon 4A]

2. **Speak, Write, Lecture, and Teach:** [§979] The judge may speak, write, lecture, and teach on both legal and nonlegal subjects. [CJC Canon 4B]

3. **Consult with Legislature and Executive:** [§980]   The judge may appear in a public hearing or otherwise consult with legislators and executive officials, but only on matters concerning the law, the legal system, and the administration of justice, or when appearing pro se on the judge's own behalf. [CJC Canon 4C(1)]

4. **Not Serve on Government Commissions:** [§981]   A judge may **not** serve on a government commission concerned with factual or legal issues other than the law, the legal system, or the administration of justice, but a judge may serve as an official representative at ceremonies or historical, educational, or cultural activities. [CJC Canon 4C(2)]

5. **Officer of Organizations:** [§982]   The judge may be a member and serve as an officer, director, trustee, or nonlegal advisor to nonprofit agencies or educational, religious, charitable, fraternal, or civic organizations not conducted for the economic and political advantage of their members. This includes the board of a law school. [CJC Canon 4C(3)]

    a. **Organization that often litigates:** [§983]   The judge may not serve as an **officer, director, trustee, or advisor** of an organization (i) engaged in litigation that would ordinarily come before the judge, or (ii) engaged frequently in litigation in the court on which the judge serves or a court subject to the judge's appellate jurisdiction. [CJC Canon 4C(3)(a)]

    b. **May not raise money:** [§984]   The judge may not personally raise money for such organizations or permit the prestige of the office to be so used. The judge should **not** be **speaker** or **guest of honor** at a fund raising event, although he may attend such events. [CJC Canon 4C(3)(b)]

    c. **May participate in investment decisions:** [§985]   The judge may participate on boards that make investment decisions for such organizations. [CJC Canon 4C(3)(b)(i)]

F.   MONEY MAKING ACTIVITIES OF THE JUDGE

1. **In General:** [§986]   As with other "outside" activities of the judge, all financial activities are subject to the requirements that they not reflect on the judge's impartiality, interfere with judicial duties, exploit the office, or involve the judge in dealings with persons likely to come before the court. [CJC Canon 4D(1)]

2. **Investments:** [§987]   With the above qualification, the judge may hold and manage investments, including real estate. [CJC Canon 4D(2)]

3. **Not Manage a Business:** [§988]   The judge may not serve as officer, director, manager, advisor, or employee of any business except a closely-held family business or investment trust. [CJC Canon 4D(3)]

4. **Divestiture of Interests Likely to Disqualify:** [§989]   A judge must manage investments so as to minimize circumstances in which the judge will be disqualified

and divest himself of investments that might require frequent disqualification. [CJC Canon 4D(4)]

5. **Gifts, Bequests, Favors, or Loans:** [§990]   The judge **and** members of his family residing in the household must be very careful about accepting gifts, bequests, favors, or loans, but there are some that may be accepted:

(i)   *A gift incident to a public testimonial* to the judge or books from a publisher for official use. [CJC Canon 4D(5)(a)]

(ii)   *Complimentary tickets to a bar-related function.* [CJC Canon 4D(5)(a)]

(iii)   *A gift to the judge's spouse or relative that could not reasonably be perceived to influence* the judge. [CJC Canon 4D(5)(b)]

(iv)   *Ordinary social hospitality.* [CJC Canon 4D(5)(c)]

(v)   *A gift from a relative or friend* fairly commensurate with the occasion and the relationship. [CJC Canon 4D(5)(d)]

(vi)   *A gift from someone whose relationship with the judge would already require disqualification.* [CJC Canon 4D(5)(e)]

(vii)   *A loan from a lending institution* in the ordinary course of business. [CJC Canon 4D(5)(f)]

(viii) *A scholarship* awarded on the same terms as for others. [CJC Canon 4D(5)(g)]

(ix)   *A gift from someone unlikely to come before the court*, provided the gift is reported as if it were compensation if it is over $100. [CJC Canon 4D(5)(h)]

6. **Fiduciary Activities:** [§991]   A judge may not act as executor, administrator, trustee, guardian, or other fiduciary except for a member of the family. [CJC Canon 4E(1)]

   a.   **"Member of the family":** [§992]   A member of the family includes any person related to the judge by blood or marriage or who is treated by the judge as a member of the family and resides in the judge's household. [CJC: "Terminology"]

   b.   **Limitation—not in own court:** [§993]   The judge may not act if it is likely that proceedings in the matter would come before the court on which the judge serves or under its appellate jurisdiction. [CJC Canon 4E(2)]

7. **Arbitrator:** [§994]   A judge may not act as an arbitrator or mediator unless expressly authorized by law. [CJC Canon 4F]

8. **Practice Law:** [§995] A judge may not practice law, but may act pro se and give legal advice to family members without compensation. [CJC Canon 4G]

9. **Receiving and Reporting Compensation:** [§996] All judges are required to report compensation and reimbursement of expenses as required by law. [CJC Canon 4H(1)]

   a. **Compensation reasonable in amount:** [§997] A judge may not accept compensation for services in excess of that which would be paid someone not a judge for the same activity. [CJC Canon 4H(1)(a)]

   b. **Expense reimbursement:** [§998] Expenses are to be limited to actual expenses of the judge and, where appropriate, the judge's spouse or guest. Any excess reimbursement is compensation. [CJC Canon 4H(1)(b)]

   c. **Public reporting:** [§999] The CJC requires public reporting of compensation and expenses at least annually. [CJC Canon 4H(2)]

      (1) **Community property states:** [§1000] Income earned by the judge's spouse but attributed to the judge in community property states need not be reported. [CJC Canon 4H(2)]

   d. **Disclosure of other assets and debts:** [§1001] Other disclosure of a judge's assets and debts need only be made as required by law or other specific portions of the Code of Judicial Conduct. [CJC Canon 4I]

G. JUDGE'S INVOLVEMENT IN POLITICAL ACTIVITY

1. **In General:** [§1002] A judge is basically required to stay out of political activity except as necessary to run for judicial office. [CJC Canon 5D, E] The same rules apply to lawyers running for judicial office as apply to sitting judges. [Model Rule 8.2(b); DR 8-103]

   a. **No office in political organization:** [§1003] A judge may not hold office in a political party or organization. [CJC Canon 5A(1)(a)]

   b. **No speeches for political candidates:** [§1004] A judge may not speak for or publicly endorse a political candidate. [CJC Canon 5A(1)(b), (c)]

   c. **No political fund raising:** [§1005] The judge may not only not raise money for others, but except when the judge is subject to public election, the judge may ***not contribute*** to a political organization, buy tickets to political dinners, and the like. [CJC Canon 5A(1)(d), (e); *but see* Canon 5C(1)—judge who is subject to public election]

      (1) **Note:** The constitutionality of this provision might be subject to challenge, but no judge is likely to do it. In effect, this is a rule that ***protects*** judges when the party solicitor comes to the door.

d. **No running for nonjudicial office:** [§1006] The judge is required to resign as judge when seeking any nonjudicial office other than delegate to a state constitutional convention. [CJC Canon 5A(2)]

2. **Judge's Own Campaign**

a. **Dignified campaign:** [§1007] A candidate for judicial office must see that the campaign is conducted in a dignified manner. [CJC Canon 5A(3)(a)-(c)]

b. **No publication of views:** [§1008] Likewise, a candidate for judicial office should not misrepresent his own or his opponent's qualifications to hold office, make "campaign promises" (other than to do a good job as judge), or publicly announce personal views on disputed legal or political issues. [CJC Canon 5A(3)(d)]

c. **Other campaign activities:** [§1009] In addition, a candidate for judicial office *may*:

   (1) *Speak* to gatherings on his own behalf;

   (2) *Appear in media advertising and distribute promotional literature* supporting his candidacy;

   (3) *Publicly endorse or oppose other candidates* for the same judicial office [CJC Canon 5C(1)(b)]; and

   (4) *Have his name shown on promotional materials for the entire party ticket* unless prohibited by law [CJC Canon 5C(3)].

3. **Solicitation of Campaign Contributions:** [§1010] It is improper for a candidate for judicial office *personally* to solicit campaign contributions or endorsements. Such solicitation is considered demeaning to the judiciary. [CJC Canon 5C(2)]

a. **Committees to raise campaign money:** [§1011] Properly constituted committees may solicit financial contributions and public statements of support on behalf of the candidate. But committee fund-raising activities *are limited* under the CJC *to the period 90 days before and after the election* in which the candidate is campaigning. [CJC Canon 5C(2)]

4. **Person Seeking Appointment to Judicial Office**

a. **No personal solicitation of funds:** [§1012] A person seeking appointment to judicial office may not solicit or accept funds, whether personally or through a committee, to support that candidacy. [CJC Canon 5B(1)]

b. **Other political activity:** [§1013] Neither may such a person engage in political activity to secure the appointment, except that the person *may*:

      (i)   ***Communicate with the nominating authority*** or committee designated to screen candidates;

      (ii)   ***Seek endorsement from organizations*** that ***regularly make recommendations*** for such appointments; and

      (iii) ***If the candidate is not currently a judge***, continue to attend political gatherings, make political contributions, and hold office in a political party.

[CJC Canon 5B(2)]

c.   **Judge seeking other government office:** [§1014] The same rules apply to a sitting judge who is seeking another government office. [CJC Canon 5B]

REVIEW QUESTIONS

1. Indicate whether the following statements are true or false:

   a. While the courts generally administer regulations governing the legal profession, the inherent power of regulation lies with the legislative branch. _____

   b. Under an "integrated" bar system, membership in the state bar association is voluntary but all local bar groups are members of the state association. _____

   c. The ABA Model Rules of Professional Conduct directly regulate the conduct of all practicing lawyers. _____

   d. A lawyer can be disciplined for violating either an ABA Code Ethical Consideration or a Disciplinary Rule, provided these have been adopted by the state bar in question. _____

2. State X requires that applicants for admission to practice law be residents of the state in which they are applying at least six months prior to admission. Is the requirement constitutional? _____

   a. May State X insist upon graduation from an accredited law school as a condition for practicing law? _____

3. If a question is raised regarding an applicant's moral character, the burden of establishing good character rests with the applicant. True or false? _____

4. An adverse determination on moral character by the state bar is final and may not be reviewed by the courts. True or false? _____

5. Wylie applies for admission to practice in State Y. On his application, Wylie notes that he was once arrested for shoplifting but was subsequently acquitted. May the State Y Bar Association consider these charges in assessing Wylie's moral fitness? _____

6. Zelda likewise applies for admission in State Y and notes that she was convicted of petty theft at age 14. Could this be enough to bar Zelda's admission to practice? _____

7. Stanley, an applicant for admission in State Y, was once arrested for indecent exposure, but the charges were immediately dropped when the complaining party was adjudged mentally disturbed. Stanley's record is otherwise impeccable, and he is embarrassed to raise the exposure incident on his application. May he properly omit it? _____

8. Carol seeks admission in State A. She is a member of the Communist Party and acknowledges this fact. Is this enough to bar her admission? _____

9. State X admits lawyers from State W without a bar examination, but requires an examination for State Y lawyers seeking to practice within State X. Does the State X policy have constitutional defects? _____

10. State A requires that any out-of-state lawyer seeking admission pro hac vice associate local counsel and have at least two years of trial experience in her home state. Are these requirements enforceable?

          _____

11. Admission to the bar of a state entitles a lawyer to practice in the federal courts of that state. True or false?

          _____

12. Smith, a lawyer licensed to practice in State X, opens an office in State Y for the purpose of advising clients solely on matters of federal tax law. Can State Y prevent Smith from practicing in the state?

          _____

    a. Would the result be different if Smith were practicing patent law in State Y?

          _____

13. Professor Canon tells his students that "the ABA Code places great reliance on history and custom in determining what constitutes the practice of law." Is he correct?

          _____

14. Harry, a local grocer, is sued by a patron allegedly injured by a protruding nail on a display shelf. Can Harry appear personally to defend himself in court?

          _____

    a. Would the result be different if Harry were appearing as president of his grocery?

          _____

15. Scam-O Title Company, without assistance from a lawyer, completes a standardized mortgage form for the sale of a house to Arthur (who is also unrepresented by counsel). Is this permissible?

          _____

16. Samantha, an enterprising local businesswoman and recent divorcee, opens a "divorce clinic" in which she advises spouses considering divorce on their property rights and obligations. Is Samantha guilty of the unauthorized practice of law?

          _____

    a. Might the result be different if Samantha instead had written a book on the subject and advertised it for sale?

          _____

17. Lawyer Jones is appointed to the federal district court bench. Thereafter, Jones continues to appear in state court from time to time on behalf of clients. Is Jones's conduct proper?

          _____

    a. Might the result be different if Jones were a law student rather than a federal judge?

          _____

18. Acme Agency takes claims for collection under an agreement whereby the holder assigns his claim to Acme in return for 60% of the amount ultimately collected by the Agency. When it is unsuccessful in persuading the debtor to pay, Acme typically sues in its own name to collect on the claim. Is Acme engaged in the unauthorized practice of law?

          _____

19. Lawyer Carol is asked to represent Zeke, an itinerant worker charged with the rape-slayings of six women in the local community. If Carol has strong feelings on the subject of rape, can she properly refuse to represent Zeke?

          _____

a. Would Carol's obligation be different if several of her clients had threatened to find other counsel should she agree to defend Zeke? _____

20. Professor Canon admonishes his ethics class that "while the obligation to represent unpopular causes is a moral one, the duty to reject illegal actions carries the threat of disciplinary sanctions as well." Is he correct? _____

21. Orville files a lawsuit for his client, Wilbur. Shortly thereafter, defense counsel asks that the case be dismissed. May Orville proceed to execute the necessary documents without Wilbur's authorization? _____

22. In discussing a pending lawsuit with opposing counsel, Lawyer admits that her client was "partially at fault" in the matter at issue. Can opposing counsel introduce this admission at trial? _____

a. Would the result be different if the response were made by Lawyer in written answers to interrogatories propounded by opposing counsel? _____

23. Indicate whether the following statements are true or false:

a. When a lawyer is retained by parents to represent their minor child in juvenile court proceedings, the lawyer has a client responsibility to both the minor and the parents and so should honor the parents' decisions about the case. _____

b. To insure zealous representation, it is recommended that a lawyer personally share the viewpoints of her client. _____

24. Client asks Lawyer to represent her in a tax dispute with the I.R.S. Lawyer has never handled tax matters but is presently enrolled in a continuing education course in the subject. May he properly take the case? _____

25. Lawyer Winston is assigned to represent Zach, an indigent accused of manslaughter. At trial, the prosecution seeks to introduce evidence obtained in a search of Zach's hotel room. Winston objects but fails to cite a recent case which would have supported exclusion. If the evidence is admitted and a conviction results, should it be set aside? _____

26. Lawyer's failure to answer a civil complaint results in a default judgment against her client. If the failure was due to Lawyer's inexcusable negligence, should the default be set aside? _____

27. Able is appointed to represent indigent defendant Baker on an appeal requested by Baker. Able examines the record and all the facts, and concludes that the appeal is frivolous. May Able withdraw by advising the client that he finds no merit in the appeal? _____

28. Lawyer A represents her client B in negotiating the purchase of an apartment complex. B gives A $50,000 to be applied toward purchase of the property. Can A deposit the funds in her personal bank account? _____

29. David hires Ted to represent him as a plaintiff in a products liability case at the rate of $100 per hour. After a brief review of the facts and one phone call to defendant, Ted

realizes he can settle the case immediately for a substantial sum. May Ted properly change his arrangement with David to a contingent fee? _____

a. Assume instead that the original agreement called for a flat fee of $10,000. Ted settles the case with 10 hours of work, and David refuses to pay the full fee. Can Ted successfully sue for the $10,000? _____

b. If the court finds the $10,000 fee to be unreasonable and clearly excessive, is Ted subject to disciplinary action? _____

30. The State A Bar Association publishes a minimum fee schedule, which lists $300 as the minimum charge for incorporating a new business. Celia, a new lawyer in State A, wishes to charge her client only $50 for these services. May she ethically do so? _____

31. Elwood agrees to handle the probate of an estate in State X, which imposes a maximum statutory attorney's fee of 3% of the estate assets. During the probate, Elwood handles a number of tax problems for the estate and arranges the sale of certain assets therein. May he properly bill the estate for a fee in excess of the statutory maximum? _____

32. Amore, a leading divorce lawyer, is asked by Stella to represent her in a proceeding for increased alimony from her husband. Amore agrees to do so for 20% of the increase obtained for the following two years. Is this an enforceable fee arrangement? _____

33. Bob represents Ted in a State Y breach of contract suit, obtaining a judgment in Ted's favor. Ted subsequently refuses to pay the agreed fee for Bob's services. State Y recognizes charging liens but not retaining liens. May Bob enforce a lien on the judgment to satisfy his fees in the matter? _____

a. Can Bob foreclose on the judgment for unpaid fees on a business reorganization he previously performed for Ted? _____

34. Client asks Lawyer to file suit against Client's neighbor, X, for breach of contract. After reviewing the facts, Lawyer decides that the case has no merit and is being brought solely to pressure X regarding a boundary dispute. Despite Lawyer's advice, Client refuses to drop the matter. May Lawyer continue to represent Client in the lawsuit? _____

a. If Lawyer wishes to withdraw from employment, must she obtain court permission to do so? _____

35. Client retains Lawyer to represent him in a trademark lawsuit, and subsequently associates Lawyer Z, an expert on trademarks, as co-counsel. Y finds that Z's theories on the case are at odds with his own. If Y is unable to work compatibly with Z, may he withdraw as Client's lawyer? _____

a. If Client consents to Y's withdrawal, must Y return any unearned portion of Client's original retainer fee? _____

36. Lawyer Jones is retained by Smith to represent him in a contract dispute with Williams. The retainer agreement specifies that Jones will be paid $2,000 for her work and will have Smith's authority to conduct the matter as Jones sees fit. Shortly thereafter, Smith decides that he wants another lawyer.

a. May Smith discharge Jones if there is no cause shown therefor? _____

b. If Jones is discharged without cause, can she represent Williams in the dispute? _____

c. Suppose that Jones and Smith had agreed to a 30% contingency fee on Smith's recovery, whereupon Jones is discharged without cause. Smith retains Lawyer Brown, who ultimately obtains $30,000 for Smith. Is Jones entitled to $9,000 from Smith? _____

37. Colleen consults Lawyer Able regarding a potential lawsuit against Baker. In the initial interview, Colleen gives Able sensitive information regarding her business strategies and sales; Colleen then decides to employ David as her lawyer in the matter.

a. The Better Business Bureau subsequently contacts Able regarding Colleen's business operations. May Able disclose the information presented in the prior interview? _____

b. Able's secretary, Rosemary, types up notes on the Able-Colleen discussion. Thereafter, she tells her boyfriend Tom about Colleen's operations. If Tom is one of Baker's employees, is Able subject to discipline? _____

c. Suppose there are friends of Colleen present when her business operations are discussed. Does this permit Able to disclose such discussions at a later time? _____

38. Max is the lawyer for Blimpo Corporation. Blimpo's president asks Max to prepare a memorandum discussing the business and legal ramifications of a proposed merger. Can Max be compelled to disclose the memorandum in a subsequent lawsuit against Blimpo? _____

39. Lawyer George is retained by Stanley to defend him on an indictment for income tax evasion. While reviewing the facts, Stanley admits to George that he previously lied under oath in a civil case regarding his income and disbursements. Is this information privileged? _____

a. At Stanley's trial, the court asks George whether he has any information regarding prior crimes committed by the client. George asserts the attorney-client privilege, whereupon the court orders him to respond. May George reveal his previous discussions with Stanley? _____

40. W contacts his lawyer, X, by telephone and tells him that he is fleeing to another state to avoid prosecution for embezzlement. X cannot persuade W to change his mind. Is X under a duty to disclose this information if sought by the proper authorities? _____

41. Arthur asks his lawyer, Roger, to represent him in negotiating for the lease of an office complex. After contacting the present owners of the building but without telling Arthur, Roger decides to purchase a 10% ownership interest in the property as a personal investment. Thereafter, Roger consummates a lease on office space for Arthur. Has Roger engaged in improper conduct? _____

a. Suppose instead that Arthur owns the office building and asks Roger to represent him in litigation with certain of his tenants. While the matter is in progress, Roger offers to purchase a 10% interest in the building. Arthur agrees and signs the contract drawn up by Roger. Has Roger breached his professional duties? _____

42. X asks her lawyer, Y, to draft a will leaving one-half of her total estate to Y. May Y proceed to prepare the document? _____

    a.   Might the result be different if Y were X's grandson and sole heir? _____

43. Professor Canon tells his class that "a lawyer may properly represent clients with potentially different interests in a nonlitigation matter as long as the lawyer is satisfied that no actual conflict exists." Is the professor correct? _____

44. A and B are indicted for armed robbery, and Lawyer C is appointed to defend them at trial. Although A is a convicted felon and B is not, C believes she can properly represent both and the two defendants acquiesce. Should the court nevertheless appoint separate counsel for each? _____

    a.   Would the result be different if A and B jointly retained C to represent them? _____

45. Sergio represents Acme Finance, a secured creditor of Fido Corporation. Fido institutes bankruptcy proceedings, and one of its other creditors asks Sergio to handle its claim against Fido. Should he do so? _____

46. Edgar represents Charlie in a breach of contract suit against Candice. While the matter is pending, Candice asks Edgar to handle her alimony claim against David. If the two matters are unsettled, may Edgar take the alimony case? _____

47. Jorge is asked to negotiate a lease for client X. May he also represent landlord Y in the matter if both X and Y consent to dual representation? _____

    a.   Would the result be different if the matter involved a dispute between X and Y over the terms of an existing lease? _____

    b.   Suppose Jorge represents X in the lease negotiations. Y is represented by his own lawyer, but after execution of the lease he sends Jorge a check for $500 "in appreciation of your efforts in bringing the parties together." May Jorge properly cash the check? _____

48. X is general counsel for Flim-Flam Brokerage Co., which is under investigation for securities fraud. The president of Flim-Flam is subpoenaed to testify before a grand jury about his knowledge of the matter and asks X to advise and represent him. Should X do so? _____

49. Lawyer Willis is retained by Tightwad Insurance to represent its insured, Baker, in a personal injury suit brought by Able. Prior to trial, Able offers to settle the case for $10,000. Realizing that Baker's policy limit is $12,000, Willis adamantly refuses to discuss any settlement. At trial, Able receives a judgment of $75,000. Is Willis subject to discipline? _____

50. Lawyer Ellen formerly served as general counsel for Widget Corp. As a member of a new law firm, she is now asked to represent the plaintiff in an antitrust case against Widget. May she do so? _____

    a.   Would the result be different if another lawyer in the firm was then asked to represent plaintiff and Ellen took no part whatever in the case? _____

51. Lawyer T files a lawsuit for client P against D, who is represented by lawyer R. Shortly thereafter, T calls D to discuss D's willingness to settle the case at the onset. Is T subject to discipline?

52. Lawyer calls her opposing counsel in a case and tells him that she will institute disbarment proceedings for misappropriation of funds unless he agrees to a settlement with Lawyer's client. If the settlement terms are fair to both parties, is Lawyer subject to discipline?

53. Blimpo Corporation retains Lawyer Helen to appear before a Food and Drug Administration hearing in support of new drugs that Blimpo wants to place on the market. As a public relations matter, Blimpo asks Helen not to reveal that she is representing the corporation. Must Helen nevertheless disclose her capacity at the hearing?

54. Lawyer X is elected to the state senate but continues to maintain a private part-time law practice. May X properly represent a client before a state administrative board?

55. Following a trial in which judgment was entered against his client, Lawyer Mason is asked to analyze the case for news reporters. Mason replies that "the case was clear to most people—but apparently it was a little too complicated for the court." Is Mason subject to discipline for his remarks?

56. A files a lawsuit for her client, B. The opposing party fails to respond to the complaint or request additional time to answer. Is A obligated to seek a default judgment in favor of her client?

   a. Assume instead that the defendant answers and the case proceeds. The court orders both parties to appear for a pretrial conference at a specific time and date. A fails to appear and later notifies the court that her absence was caused by B's refusal to pay outstanding fees and costs. Is A subject to sanctions?

   b. Would the result be different if A's absence was caused by her overcommitted schedule?

57. Lawyer Clark knows that if she can prolong a case for six more months her opponent will be so damaged economically that he will settle for much less. She files a motion in the appellate court for mandamus to have the trial judge recuse himself in the case. She knows there is no basis for the motion but she also knows it will take six months for the court to act. Has she done anything that would subject her to discipline?

58. F. Lee Quickly, a noted trial lawyer, is retained to represent the defendant in a political bribery indictment. Shortly before trial, Quickly sends a letter to the *New York Times* alleging that government witnesses are being paid to give false testimony against his client. Is Quickly subject to discipline for this action?

59. During the bribery trial, the local newspaper publishes an editorial attacking Quickly as "a known opportunist who would say anything to gain publicity for himself and his client." Quickly appears on a television show and refers to the editorial as "totally false and an obvious attempt to injure my reputation." Is Quickly subject to discipline for his statement?

60. Perry Prosecutor has filed multiple murder charges against Barry Bumm. Perry calls a press conference and announces the fact of the charges and the name and address of the accused. Has the prosecutor acted properly? _____

61. Albert, the lawyer for plaintiff in a products liability case, hires X as an expert witness on the defects in defendant's product. Albert tells X that his client is presently short of funds but will pay X 5% of any recovery he obtains in the case. Is this arrangement improper? _____

62. Roscoe, a flamboyant trial lawyer, comments in his closing statement to the jury that "the defendant's chief witness, Smith, is just as crooked as the defendant himself—and his perjury on the stand proves it. I think his testimony is preposterous." Is this proper? _____

63. In commenting to the jury on defendant's own testimony, Roscoe states that "Fifteen witnesses for plaintiff, with no interest in the case, testified that defendant struck plaintiff's car. Defendant, who will suffer a loss if he loses this case, tells you he didn't hit the car. I think you jurors can decide who is telling the truth." Are these comments proper? _____

64. In her closing statement, Lawyer Jones tells the jury that "my client is poor and an innocent victim in this case—treat him as you would want to be treated if you were in his shoes." Is this improper? _____

65. Lawyer Dan is contacted by opposing counsel, who requests an extension of time to answer the complaint filed by Dan's client. Dan orally agrees to the extension, but no written stipulation is entered. Thereafter, Dan notices the defendant's default for failure to answer within the statutory period. Is Dan subject to discipline? _____

66. During the trial of his client's personal injury claim, Attorney Smith attempts to introduce certain evidence helpful to the claim. Defense counsel objects, and the court refuses to admit the evidence. Smith asks the court to reconsider its ruling "because Your Honor is totally wrong." Is Smith subject to discipline? _____

67. Irving is asked by Clyde to handle his securities fraud claim on a contingency arrangement. May Irving properly advance the costs of litigation to Clyde while the case is in progress? _____

68. X files an antitrust case for his client Y against Z Corp., alleging damages due to Z's price-fixing and market restraints. Subsequently, Y tells X that his real injuries resulted from ineffective sales personnel during the period in question. Should X disclose this information to Z's attorney? _____

69. X files an antitrust suit for his client Y against Z Corp. Z Corp. files a motion for summary judgment. In preparing an opposing brief, X discovers that there are several cases adverse to Y's position. By construing the facts favorably to Y, X believes the cases are distinguishable from the present action. Should X disclose the cases in his brief? _____

70. Lawyer W is appointed to defend Z on a charge of selling narcotics. On the stand at trial, Z testifies that he has never used narcotics in his life. During a recess, Z admits to W that he has used cocaine for several years. Should W disclose this to the court? _____

71. Helen is a lawyer for Baker Corporation, which is sued in a products liability case. By chance, Helen was present when the accident in question occurred. Can she properly represent Baker in the litigation? _____

72. Lawyer X anticipates that she may be called as a witness concerning a minor dispute involving service of process in a lawsuit she has filed. This fact becomes known after X has already done substantial work on the case (for which she has been paid). May she continue to represent the client in the litigation? _____

73. During a trial, Judge Hangem calls opposing counsel A and B into chambers for a conference. As they are leaving, B decides to ask the judge about expediting discovery in another case B has before the court. Is this proper? _____

74. Lawyer Marvin represents the defendant in a personal injury lawsuit. Prior to the trial in his case, Marvin encounters a member of the jury panel outside the courthouse and asks him if he has ever been a plaintiff in a personal injury case. If Marvin does not otherwise discuss the case, is his communication proper? _____

   a. Could Marvin properly put the same question to a member of the panelist's family? _____

75. Shortly after a verdict for plaintiff is returned, Marvin decides to call several of the jurors and discuss the factors they found significant in the case. May he properly do so? _____

76. Prosecutor Allen is preparing to try an accused for first degree murder. While interviewing a prospective witness, Allen learns that the accused may not have been present at the scene of the crime. Is he obligated to disclose this information to defense counsel? _____

   a. Allen decides that Charlie will be his chief witness. Can Allen properly instruct Charlie not to discuss the case with defense counsel unless Allen is present? _____

77. Felix and Oscar are lawyers sharing offices and secretarial help. Occasionally, Oscar refers tax matters to Felix. May the two use a letterhead reading "Law Offices of Felix and Oscar"? _____

78. Civil rights legislation and the federal labor laws do not apply to the relationship between an associate and her law firm. True or false? _____

79. May the governing board of a legal services agency direct a lawyer in the agency to concentrate generally on litigation rather than legislative change? _____

80. Indicate whether the following statements are true or false:

   a. The original opposition to group services plans was based on the fact that the intermediary obtained a profit from the provision of legal services. _____

   b. "Open panel" group plans are now permissible, but "closed panel" plans are still prohibited. _____

c.   The ABA Code and Model Rules permit partnerships between lawyers and non-lawyers as long as the practice of law is merely incidental to the primary partnership activities.   _____

d.   In certain situations, it may be permissible for a lawyer to share legal fees with a nonlawyer.   _____

81. X wants to list certain biographical information including her educational background and publications in a local directory. Does it matter whether X chooses the city directory or a bar association directory of lawyers for this purpose?   _____

82. Lawyer Smackum contributes $5,000 to the local civic theatre and in return therefor is allowed to place a statement in theatre programs with his name, occupation, business address, and credit card policy. Has Smackum engaged in improper advertising?   _____

83. Lawyer Eager files an antitrust class action with two named plaintiffs. Thereafter, Eager sends a letter to a trade association of similar business entities, informing them of the lawsuit and his willingness to "discuss the case" with any interested party. Is Eager guilty of solicitation?   _____

84. X is a lawyer state-certified as a tax specialist. May she properly list this tax specialty on her business cards?   _____

85. May a lawyer leaving one law firm to join a new one inform the clients for whom he has done work that the clients may follow the lawyer to the new firm?   _____

86. Nancy, a tax lawyer in River City, systematically refers all personal injury matters involving her clients to Alice, a trial lawyer. Alice then pays Nancy 30% of whatever fee she collects in each such case. Is this arrangement proper?   _____

a.   Would the result be different if Nancy were a physician rather than a tax lawyer?   _____

87. Lawyer Jones informs the state bar that she suspects her partner, Smith, of misappropriating certain funds of his clients. Does Jones have an obligation to testify in formal proceedings against Smith?   _____

a.   At the disciplinary hearing, Smith pleads that he was faced with enormous medical expenses incurred by his sick child and would not otherwise have borrowed the money. Should the state bar consider this plea in assessing sanctions against Smith?   _____

b.   Would the fact that Smith had already paid punitive damages to the clients in question be relevant to the disciplinary proceedings?   _____

c.   During the hearing, the examining lawyer seeks to introduce a taped telephone conversation between Smith and a friend, made via a wiretap set by Jones. Should this evidence be admitted?   _____

d.   Assuming the state supreme court imposes a one-year suspension on Smith, can the local federal court disbar Smith?   _____

88. X asks his lawyer, Y, for an opinion on the tax effects of a complicated leasing transaction. X follows Y's opinion and is later held to have violated certain regulations applicable thereto. Can X hold Y liable for malpractice? _____

89. Lawyer Smith agrees to represent Jones, the defendant in a personal injury lawsuit. In responding to plaintiff's motion for summary judgment, Smith fails to note a recent case favorable to Jones. If summary judgment is entered against Jones, is Smith liable for the amount thereof? _____

90. Lawyer fails to appear for the trial of his client's case and judgment is entered for the defendant. Defendant had a valid defense to the action and would have prevailed at trial in any case. Is Lawyer subject to disciplinary sanctions? _____

91. Arthur asks Lawyer Leonard to defend him in a large lawsuit. Leonard explains that the legal issues are extremely complicated, and that he must have Arthur's agreement not to sue for malpractice before he will take the case. In return, Leonard agrees to charge only 80% of his normal hourly fee. Provided Arthur consents after full disclosure, is the agreement enforceable? _____

92. During the trial of her client's case, Lawyer Jones blurts out to the judge, "You are the stupidest judge I've ever known. This trial is a charade." The judge says nothing but the next morning announces that she is sentencing Jones to 10 days in jail for contempt. Does the judge have authority to act in this way? _____

93. Judge Quashem, a candidate for reelection to the bench, agrees to appear at a fund raising dinner to exchange endorsements with other party candidates. Is this improper? _____

ANSWERS TO REVIEW QUESTIONS

1.a. **FALSE**   Ultimate regulatory power lies with the judicial branch, since the practice of law is intimately connected with the administration of justice. [§2]

   b. **FALSE**   An integrated bar system involves **compulsory** membership by all lawyers in the state bar association. [§9]

   c. **FALSE**   The Model Rules are not directly binding on lawyers. However, over 30 states have adopted the Rules and so they form an indirect basis for regulation of much of the legal profession. [§§24-25]

   d. **FALSE**   Only Disciplinary Rules are mandatory and carry disciplinary sanctions for their violation. The Ethical Considerations are aspirational and constitute guides to proper conduct. [§§21-22]

2. **NO**   The Supreme Court has held that residency requirements for admission to the bar violate the Privileges and Immunities Clause. [§31]

   a. **YES**   Such a requirement has been deemed to meet the test of a "rational relationship" to fitness to practice law. [§33]

3. **TRUE**   The reasoning is that the applicant is in the best position to supply the facts about himself. [§43]

4. **FALSE**   An applicant is entitled to judicial review, usually by the highest state court. [§45]

5. **YES**   **Any** past conduct—including charges on which there is a subsequent acquittal or dismissal—may be deemed relevant to a character investigation. [§47]

6. **YES**   Theft is often considered conduct that reflects upon the ability to practice law. However, it could be argued that (due to Zelda's age at the time) this was mere "adolescent misbehavior," and hence not sufficient per se to block her admission. [§§48, 50]

7. **DEPENDS**   Stanley was not convicted of a crime, and the conduct did not involve dishonesty, but if he is asked about arrests, this must be disclosed—and failure to do so **would** be sufficient to bar Stanley's admission. [§52]

8. **NO**   Membership in the Communist Party is not sufficient per se to exclude an applicant from practicing law. [§56]

9. **NOT NECESSARILY**   If the State X policy is based on **reciprocity** (*i.e.*, State W automatically admits State X lawyers, but State Y does not), the policy does not violate equal protection. [§§62-64]

10. **YES**   Limitations on admission pro hac vice are generally valid, unless applied to block adequate representation in civil rights cases. [§§68-69]

11.	**FALSE**	While no separate examination is required, admission to practice in the federal courts is **distinct** and a separate application must be made. (A few federal courts also require completion of certain courses prior to admission.) [§§72-74]
12.	**YES**	A state may prevent an out-of-state lawyer from maintaining a **continuous** practice of federal law in the state, if there are no specific federal regulations concerning the practice in question. [§80]
a.	**YES**	Here, federal regulations govern Smith's practice, and State Y cannot prevent her from maintaining an office for that purpose. [§77]
13.	**NO**	While some courts still follow the "history and custom" test, the ABA Code has emphasized the **need for professional judgment** as the relevant criterion. [§§89-91]
14.	**YES**	Representation "in propria persona" is always available to an individual in court proceedings. [§§85-86]
a.	**YES**	A corporation **cannot** appear for itself in court (through its nonlawyer officers or directors). [§117]
15.	**SPLIT OF AUTHORITY**	Most courts permit title companies to complete standardized mortgage or deed forms according to information furnished by the parties. Others, however, find this impermissible, on the ground that this is "drafting"—requiring a lawyer's expertise on choice of forms—rather than "scrivening." [§§95-98]
16.	**YES**	Moreover, the sale of such advice may also represent an unlawful interference with family relations. [§104]
a.	**YES**	Some courts have held that publication of such a book by a layperson is not the practice of law (on the theory that the purchaser is "representing himself"). Other courts, however, are contra. [§105]
17.	**NO**	The Code of Judicial Conduct prohibits judges from practicing law, whether or not they are also licensed attorneys. [§109]
a.	**YES**	Ordinarily, law students are also prohibited from appearing in court for clients. However, an exception is made where the student does so in connection with an **authorized law school training program.** [§§111-114]
18.	**PROBABLY NOT**	Most courts permit an agent **by assignment** to sue in its own name on such claims. [§118]
19.	**YES**	Although she has a moral obligation to accept the case unless there is a valid **professional reason** not to do so, a lawyer is not **obliged** to take any case. [§§127-128]
a.	**NO**	The moral obligation exists irrespective of the effects of representation on the lawyer's "good will" in the community. [§128]

20.	**YES**	While there are no sanctions for failure to take a case, discipline *can* be imposed where the lawyer fails to reject an illegal or sham lawsuit or representation. [§§135-137]
21.	**DEPENDS**	If the dismissal is with prejudice, it must be authorized by Wilbur. However, Orville probably has implied authority to execute a dismissal *without prejudice* if he considers it to be in Wilbur's interests. [§162]
22.	**DEPENDS**	If Lawyer was *authorized* to make the statement, it would be admissible; otherwise, it is not admissible. In either event, it is probably not conclusive on the issue. [§168]
a.	**YES**	This is a *judicial* admission, which is binding upon the client unless the court permits an amendment or withdrawal. [§167]
23.a.	**FALSE**	The client responsibility is owed solely to the *child*, regardless of who pays the lawyer's fees. The lawyer should consult with the child and let the child make most of the decisions. [§§170-172, 448]
b.	**FALSE**	A lawyer has no obligation to approve or adopt a client's viewpoints, though she *is* obliged to be circumspect in expressing an opposing position. [§198]
24.	**YES**	A lawyer may accept employment where he expects in good faith to become qualified to perform the necessary services. However, Lawyer should not accept the retainer if there will be unnecessary expense or delay to Client in gaining such competence. [§175]
25.	**PROBABLY NOT**	Unless failure to cite the case would amount to shocking incompetence, there is no basis for setting aside the conviction. A mere mistake is not enough. [§§182-185]
26.	**SPLIT OF AUTHORITY**	Many courts require a reasonable excuse for the failure to answer in order to set aside a default. Others, however, will not charge a client with his lawyer's gross negligence if doing so denies justice in the particular case. [§§188-189]
27.	**NO**	The lawyer must seek permission to withdraw, accompanied by a written brief to the court and counsel citing any *arguable* grounds for an appeal. [§204]
28.	**NO**	The funds must be deposited in a *separately identified* trust (or other bank) account. [§211]
29.	**PROBABLY NOT**	Certainly the change would be improper if Ted did not inform David of the prospects for a quick settlement. And even with disclosure, Ted would have the burden of proving that the new agreement was a reasonable one. [§§227-231]
a.	**DEPENDS**	Courts will review a fee agreement to determine its reasonableness. Whether Ted can collect the full $10,000 depends on *all the circumstances* (*i.e.*, skill, experience, etc.). [§§229-232]

b.	**YES**	The charging of unreasonable and clearly excessive fees may subject a lawyer to discipline. [§229]
30.	**YES**	Fee schedules are at best "advisory"; if used to coerce the charging of minimum fees (through disciplinary sanctions), they would violate the federal antitrust laws. [§§221-223]
31.	**PROBABLY**	Elwood has apparently performed extraordinary services for the estate, and is therefore entitled to an additional reasonable fee for that work. [§240]
32.	**PROBABLY NOT**	Some courts permit contingent fees in domestic relations matters *after* a divorce has been granted. However, the ABA frowns on such arrangements in this area, and some courts might refuse to enforce it. [§§252-254]
33.	**YES**	A charging lien can be affirmatively enforced against a judgment awarded to the client for fees in that matter. [§272]
a.	**NO**	Charging liens are limited to fees and costs incurred in the particular matter in which recovery is obtained. [§278] Note that if State Y recognized retaining liens, Bob could withhold documents or other items he received as lawyer for the reorganization—and use this as "leverage" in obtaining *any* fees unpaid by Ted. [§268]
34.	**NO**	Lawyer has an obligation to withdraw under these circumstances; and she is subject to disciplinary action if she continues with the lawsuit. [§292]
a.	**DEPENDS**	If the matter is *pending* before the court (*i.e.*, a complaint on file), permission of the court must be obtained for withdrawal. [§§297, 307]
35.	**YES**	Inability to work effectively with co-counsel is a recognized ground for permissive withdrawal; hence, Y may properly withdraw. [§299]
a.	**YES**	Whatever the basis for withdrawal, Y is not entitled to retain any unearned portion of fees paid in advance—unless paid solely to insure Y's availability for the case. [§305]
36.a.	**YES**	A client has the unilateral right to discharge his lawyer at any time, without cause and despite any agreement for an "irrevocable" retainer. [§§309-310]
b.	**NO**	Despite the discharge without cause, Jones's fiduciary duties to Smith continue—including the duty not to represent conflicting interests. [§312]
c.	**SPLIT OF AUTHORITY**	Some courts would allow Jones the full 30% contingency (*i.e.*, $9,000) while others would limit recovery to the reasonable value of services rendered by her (quantum meruit). [§§316-321]
37.a.	**NO**	The attorney-client privilege and the professional duty of nondisclosure apply to information obtained from a *potential* client, even though the lawyer is not subsequently employed. [§327]
b.	**PERHAPS**	Able may disclose such information to his office staff, but he has a duty to prevent such employees from disseminating it to others. If Able has not

exercised reasonable care in this regard (*e.g.*, by careful hiring and proper warnings), he is subject to sanctions. [§§333, 335]

c. **NO**   The presence of others may waive the "confidentiality" requirement so that the attorney-client privilege would not apply. However, Able's professional duty of nondisclosure is broader, and is *not* affected by the fact that strangers were present at the interview. [§362]

38. **NO**   "Mixed" communications between a corporation and its counsel are within the attorney-client privilege. [§§348-349]

39. **YES**   A client's confidential admission to counsel that he perjured himself in a prior proceeding is privileged information. [§355]

a. **SPLIT OF AUTHORITY**   Some courts hold that a lawyer must refuse to disclose privileged information whatever the personal consequences to him may be (*e.g.*, citation for contempt). However, the ABA Code allows disclosure of such information in response to a *court order*, and the Comments to the Model Rules state that a lawyer must comply with a final order of court requiring such information. [§357]

40. **DEPENDS**   As a general matter, the whereabouts of a client is privileged information. Note, however, that if the violation of a court order is involved (*e.g.*, W was previously released on bail upon X's motion), X *must* advise the court of his client's whereabouts. [§§372-374]

41. **YES**   It is improper for a lawyer to acquire an adverse interest in the subject matter of his employment, since there is at least the potential for a conflict of interest (*e.g.*, Roger's interest as part owner may conflict with his negotiating the most favorable lease terms for Arthur). [§387]

a. **DEPENDS**   Because of the opportunities for overreachng by counsel, such transactions with a client are subject to a *presumption of undue influence* by the lawyer and are examined very closely by the court. Hence, under the Model Rules the terms of the purchase must be objectively fair to Arthur, he must have had a chance to consult with outside counsel in the matter, and he must have consented in writing. [§§391-394]

42. **NO**   Y should urge X to obtain the assistance of another lawyer in drafting the will, since he is named as a beneficiary. Also, Y should urge X to obtain the disinterested advice of a competent third person. [§§395-397]

a. **YES**   Most courts permit a lawyer to prepare wills for relatives, provided that any bequest therein to the lawyer is "reasonable under the circumstances" and that there is no hint of overreaching. Here, X's bequest appears to be less than Y's intestate share and hence a reasonable gift. [§399]

43. **NO**   A lawyer may undertake such representation only after he has the *consent* of all the clients concerned, upon *full disclosure* of the risks and advantages of joint representation to them. And the client's refusal to consent is binding, regardless of the lawyer's conclusions on the propriety of multiple representation. [§§408-414]

44.	**YES**	The court has a duty to see whether differing interests appear and to appoint separate counsel if they do. Here, A's previous record may indicate differences in the strength of the case against each defendant, and if so, separate counsel should be appointed. [§§416-418]
a.	**YES**	In this situation, the duty is on C (as retained counsel) to consider and disclose any potential conflicts. [§419]
45.	**DEPENDS**	The propriety of representing both creditors depends on whether there are conflicts of interest involved. If the second client is not a secured creditor, and/or if Fido's assets cannot satisfy the claims of both, dual representation would be improper. [§§429-432]
46.	**NO**	Even though Candice's success on her alimony claim might benefit Charlie, it is a conflict of interest to represent opposing clients in unrelated matters. [§§433-435]
47.	**DEPENDS**	Jorge must *fully disclose* to X and Y the possible conflicts in representing both parties to the lease negotiations. If this done, and an informed consent is given by the parties, dual representation is probably permissible. [§§439-444]
a.	**YES**	Here, the conflicts between adversaries are inescapable and may result in litigation. Jorge has a duty to refuse dual representation even if the parties consent to same. [§§405, 410, 444]
b.	**NO**	Compensation from a third party for representing the client gives the appearance of divided interests. Thus Jorge should return the payment unless X is fully informed and consents thereto. [§§390, 449]
48.	**NO**	As general counsel, X owes his loyalty to Flim-Flam. Since the company may have a potential action against the president in this matter, he should retain independent counsel for the grand jury appearance. [§§446-447]
49.	**YES**	A lawyer who rejects a settlement proposal without letting the client make the final decision may be guilty of both unethical conduct and civil malpractice. The lawyer must inform the insurer of its duty to the insured regarding settlement, and must use her best efforts to see that the interests of the insured are protected. Willis's adamant refusal to discuss any settlement was improper. [§§456-459]
50.	**PROBABLY NOT**	A lawyer is prohibited from representing someone where the lawyer would be taking a position materially adverse to a former client in a matter closely related factually or legally to the prior one, or where there is some other substantial risk that the lawyer will use confidential information obtained in the prior representation against the former client. Unless it can be shown that the antitrust case here is unrelated to any matter handled by Ellen at Widget and that the case does not involve confidential information she received while employed by the company, Ellen should probably not take the case. [§§471-474]
a.	**NO**	The prohibitions applicable to Ellen apply as well to any lawyer affiliated with her—*i.e.,* if there is a conflict as to her representation, it applies to the firm as well. [§§479-480]

51. **YES** Where a lawyer knows the opposing party is represented by counsel, the lawyer may not communicate directly with that party on any controverted matter absent the consent of opposing counsel. [§§533-535]

52. **DEPENDS** Zealous representation does not permit the threat of criminal or other charges including disbarment) to gain advantages for a lawyer's client. This is an improper use of the legal process regardless of whether the final results are reasonable, but the ABA Code's explicit prohibition of it was left out of the Model Rules. [§§542-547]

53. **YES** Unless the identity of the client is privileged information (which is not the case here), Helen has a duty to reveal her representative capacity at administrative proceedings. [§550]

54. **DEPENDS** X must avoid any foreseeable conflict between his private interests and his public duties as legislator. If the board's decisions are reviewable by the state senate, X must *not* appear as a private attorney. However, such an appearance (if otherwise proper) is often permitted if review by the *courts* is available. [§§556-561]

55. **POSSIBLY** Such snide or petty comments disparaging the court are unwarranted. Criticism should be expressed in a respectful manner and aimed at improving the judicial system. [§564]

56. **NO** A may feel it is in B's best interest *not* to seek a default; and A would not be disciplined or held liable for civil malpractice for failing to do so. [§§163-164]

  a. **YES** Failure to appear at a court-ordered hearing, particularly without advance notice to the court, is punishable as contempt of court and possibly as neglect of the client's case. [§575]

  b. **NO** Unless there was a purely fortuitous conflict (*i.e.*, hearings in two cases scheduled at the same time), A is liable for overcommitting herself. And, in any case, A should have given advance notice of any conflict. [§650]

57. **YES** The ABA Code prohibits a lawyer from delaying a trial merely to harass or maliciously injure another, and the Model Rules impose a requirement to expedite litigation. Benefits to the client from improper delay may not be taken into account by a lawyer. Here, Clark has filed a motion solely to delay the case and injure her opponent. Thus, she has run afoul of applicable disciplinary precepts. [§§579-580]

58. **YES** Out-of-court pretrial statements by counsel on the credibility of witnesses, where such statements are capable of public dissemination, are prohibited. [§558]

59. **NO** The restrictions on publicity regarding criminal proceedings do not preclude a lawyer from replying publicly to charges of misconduct publicly made against him. [§596]

60. **YES** Each of these items of information is permitted under the ABA Code and Model Rules. [§590]

61. **YES**   Contingent fees for any witness are flatly prohibited. [§603]

62. **NO**   Expressions of a lawyer's personal opinion on testimony by witnesses are improper. [§613]

63. **YES**   These comments argue credibility upon the facts and probably do not constitute a personal opinion on defendant's testimony. [§620]

64. **YES**   Jurors are expected to decide the case as objective triers of fact; and appeals to personal feelings or sympathy are improper (but common). [§§621-625]

65. **DEPENDS**   Dan is obligated to follow local customs on extensions of time unless he notifies opposing counsel to the contrary. If oral agreements to extend time *are* accepted local practice, Dan could be subject to sanctions for attempting to take a default. [§633]

66. **NO**   A lawyer may properly challenge a court ruling by asking for reconsideration. While Smith's statement is a little strong, it is not disrespectful toward the court. [§638]

67. **YES**   Where litigation is pending or contemplated, the ABA Code permits a lawyer to lend the client money for litigation expenses, provided the client remains ultimately liable for such expenses. Under the Model Rules, a lawyer may make the obligation to repay contingent on the outcome of the case, or may make no provision for repayment where the client is indigent. Thus, if Irving complies with the applicable provisions of the Code or the Model Rules, he may properly advance litigation costs to Clyde. [§§642-649]

68. **PROBABLY**   In a matter pending before a tribunal, a lawyer must, under the Model Rules, volunteer a harmful material fact if necessary to avoid assisting the client in a crime or fraud. This duty continues up to the conclusion of the proceedings, and it applies even to otherwise protected confidential information. Here, the client has supplied the lawyer with a false material fact that the lawyer has inadvertently represented to the court in the pleadings. Unless the client agrees to rectify the situation himself, the lawyer must reveal the deceit to either the court or the other party. [§§656-657]

69. **YES**   Doubts involving the applicability of "adverse" decisions should be resolved in favor of disclosure. [§§659-660]

70. **YES (Model Rules); NO (ABA Code)**   Assuming this is a material fact, W must, under the Model Rules, attempt to persuade Z to recant. If Z refuses, W should seek to withdraw. If the court will not permit withdrawal, W must disclose the perjury to the court. The opposite result is reached under the ABA Code, which prohibits the lawyer from revealing the perjury because of the duty of confidentiality. [§§664-670]

71. **NO**   A lawyer may not handle litigation in which it is apparent that she may be called as a witness during the proceedings. [§677]

72. **PROBABLY**   Since the matter for testimony appears to be an insubstantial one, and since there may be hardship to the client in substituting new counsel at this juncture, X probably may remain as counsel. [§§685-686]

73. **PROBABLY NOT**   It is improper for B to communicate with the court ex parte on a pending matter without notifying opposing counsel so that she could be present. However, since this is a mere administrative matter not going to the merits, it may be allowed. [§699]

74. **NO**   Such out-of-court communications are *not* permitted, although Marvin might try to obtain such information by means of a proper investigation. (The question itself *is* a proper one for voir dire examination in open court.) [§§702-703]

a. **NO**   The same restrictions on communications with veniremen or jurors apply as well to members of their families. [§710]

75. **SPLIT OF AUTHORITY**   Many courts would permit such communications (*e.g.*, as a means of improving the lawyer's advocacy skills), as long as there is no harassment of jurors. Others, however, permit post-trial communication *only* if a lawyer has independent evidence or irregularities in jury deliberations. [§§705-709]

76. **YES**   Government prosecutors are required to make timely disclosure to the defense of any available evidence that might negate guilt or otherwise bear upon the accused's position (*e.g.*, mitigation of offense). [§719]

a. **NO**   A prosecutor must permit defense counsel to interview government witnesses and may not properly advise government witnesses not to talk to the defense. [§721]

77. **PROBABLY NOT**   This designation implies that Felix and Oscar are partners. Lawyers may not hold themselves out as partners unless they in fact are partners. [§729]

78. **FALSE**   Recent cases have held that both sets of laws protect law firm associates. [§732]

79. **YES**   The governing board may establish priorities generally and set budgets, but it may not direct the conduct of a staff lawyer in a particular case. [§764]

80.a. **FALSE**   Nonprofit intermediaries were also prohibited from providing such services on the ground that the necessary relationship of trust and confidence between lawyer and client was lacking. [§768]

b. **FALSE**   "Closed panel" plans are constitutionally protected in at least some situations (*e.g.*, union retaining counsel for its members in workers' compensation disputes). And the ABA now imposes the same requirements on both open and closed panel plans. [§§770-777]

c. **FALSE**   Such partnerships are prohibited where *any* of the activities include the practice of law. [§§750, 752]

d. **TRUE**   However, these situations are limited to profit-sharing retirement plans or payment of accrued fees to the estate of a deceased attorney The general rule prohibits fee sharing with nonlawyers. [§§753-758]

81. **NO**   Under the ABA Code and Model Rules, material of this kind may be published for the public generally, not simply lawyers. [§§783-797]

82. **NO**   Under the ABA Code and Model Rules, both the content and manner of dissemination of this ad are proper. [§§785-790, 795-796]

83. **PROBABLY NOT**   Under both the ABA Code and the Model Rules, Eager's conduct could be considered as prohibited direct contact with a potential client. However, with regard to class action litigation, the Supreme Court has held that it is improper for a court to set excessive limits on a lawyer's contact with prospective class members. Under this line of reasoning, it is not likely that Eager's conduct will be deemed to be prohibited solicitation. [§§801-806, 817]

84. **YES**   Under the ABA Code and Model Rules, state-certified specialties may be noted on professional cards if permitted by state rules. [§§819, 833]

85. **PROBABLY**   It has been held improper for former associates to *encourage* clients to follow them to their new firm. However, simple announcements merely *informing* former clients of the change of practice are proper. [§822]

86. **DEPENDS**   Fee sharing with lawyers is permitted but only where the client knows and consents and the total fee is reasonable, and (under the ABA Code) the division (here 70-30) corresponds to the *services performed*. Under the Model Rules, lawyers who *assume joint responsibility* for a matter may share the fee in whatever proportions they agree. If these conditions are met, the Nancy-Alice fee arrangement is permissible. [§§844-845]

   a. **YES**   Fee sharing with nonlawyers is completely prohibited. [§753]

87. **YES**   A lawyer is bound not only to disclose any acts of moral turpitude, but also to testify on the subject before a court or disciplinary board. And the fact that Smith and Jones are partners does not create a privilege not to testify. [§§888-892]

   a. **POSSIBLY**   The factor of his child's illness probably warrants consideration of the unusual pressure Smith was under in this case. [§§862, 864]

   b. **YES**   Any other penalty imposed for the same conduct may be considered with respect to appropriate disciplinary sanctions. [§865]

   c. **YES**   The normal exclusionary rules of criminal procedure (*e.g.,* as to illegal wiretaps) do not apply to disciplinary hearings. [§875]

   d. **YES**   The federal court is not bound by the state proceedings but will often follow a state's decision in such a case. [§§894-897]

88. **PROBABLY**   Y owes X a duty to exercise the skill and knowledge normally possessed by lawyers in the area. If Y is a tax specialist, the duty is to exercise the care of other such specialists; if he is not, the duty is to associate such a specialist (with the client's consent), develop the necessary expertise, or decline the matter. If Y has breached the applicable duty, he can be held liable for malpractice. [§§174-176, 900-902]

89. **DEPENDS** Smith owes a duty to discover recent developments in the law available through standard research techniques. Before civil malpractice can be proved, however, Jones must usually show that summary judgment would have been avoided had Smith cited the case in question. [§§904, 910]

90. **YES** Professional duties of competency are more stringent than the legal standard for civil malpractice. Thus, the mere fact that the defendant had a valid defense (which might bar malpractice liability) will not prevent the imposition of disciplinary sanctions. [§§910-911]

91. **NO** A lawyer cannot exculpate himself in advance from liability for malpractice, regardless of the "consideration" (*i.e.,* lesser fee) paid therefor. (*Note:* Under Model Rule 1.8(h), the agreement could be enforceable if Arthur was separately represented in making the agreement.) [§§923-924]

92. **NO** If the judge had acted immediately, the summary procedure would have been proper. But since she waited until the next day, the case must be sent to another judge to hold a hearing. [§§928-929]

93. **NO** A judge may not contribute to a political organization, buy tickets to political dinners, and the like, except when the judge is subject to public election. Also, a candidate for judicial office may publicly endorse or oppose other candidates for the same office. Thus, the conduct of Judge Quashem is not improper. [§§1005, 1009]

SAMPLE EXAM QUESTION I

Sarah Smart has just graduated from law school and wants to go into practice on her own.

1. Sarah's first potential client is an inventor who wants to issue stock in a company he has formed. Sarah talks to him for two hours and takes good notes, but she realizes she is not competent to handle a public issue of securities. She calls a friend in a well-regarded securities firm in the city and sends the client, plus a written summary of their discussion, to that firm. A week later, Sarah receives a check for $1,000 from the firm as "a down payment on your one-third of our fee in this matter." What should she do with the check? Discuss.

2. A local television station invites Sarah to appear on a talk show about "women's issues in the law." She expects to be asked questions by the host and telephone callers about child support, abortion, rape, etc. Do you have any advice as to the way she should respond to questions? May she offer to have viewers come to her office for further advice? Explain.

SAMPLE EXAM QUESTION II

Harry Johnson was an associate at Black & White in New York. He worked on prospectuses for securities issues, one of which was for G & E, a national manufacturer of electrical items. After three years in the firm, he took a position as Assistant U.S. Attorney for the Southern District of New York. One of his first assignments was to help prosecute G & E for tax fraud. In the middle of that case, he left the U.S. Attorney's office to become a partner in a Philadelphia firm. That firm was defending the G & E tax fraud case, but Harry was assigned to work on other cases exclusively.

Does anyone have a right to complain about Harry's career path? What relief could they obtain, if any? Explain.

SAMPLE EXAM QUESTION III

"Mister Tax" is the newest addition to the tax advisory firms springing up around the country. It has one difference; it purports to do tax planning as well as fill out tax returns. Mary Adams has been hired as general counsel and has been made a full partner in the firm. The other partners are accountants and financial analysts. Her job will be to write booklets explaining tax planning to clients. She will also give seminars for the CPAs who will actually fill in the blanks on the clients' preprinted wills. If "Mister Tax" can get itself named executor of clients' estates, Mary will act as counsel for the executor.

Mary describes this plan to you. After you recover your composure, what would you tell her about the propriety of the plan and her role in it? Explain.

SAMPLE EXAM QUESTION IV

Bob Brilliant became a busy barrister. He had plenty of time to talk to prospective clients and obtain retainers but little time to follow up his cases. One day an inventor brought a great invention to Bob's office and asked him to apply for a patent. Bob did not know anything about patent law but accepted a $500 retainer and agreed to do the necessary work. He put the file in his "IN" basket, where it stayed until nine months later, when the inventor stormed into Bob's office. A competitor had applied for a patent on the same idea so that the inventor's claim was now worthless.

Does Bob have reason to be worried? What options does the inventor have? Explain.

SAMPLE EXAM QUESTION V

Jones and Yates have been partners for 12 years. They have a personal injury and probate practice and each has worked on issues brought into the office by the other. Now they have decided to split up, although they will both remain in the same city. Each is concerned about keeping "his" cases.

1. Describe what they should tell their clients and in what way.

2. What are the rights and duties of each partner with respect to firm files?

SAMPLE EXAM QUESTION VI

Mary and Bill have come to you and say they want a divorce. They have two children but little money and want a "clean break." Neither one wants the children, but Mary says she will take them. Mary tells you privately that she will inherit a large sum of money soon. Publicly, Mary is asking for one-third of Bill's salary as alimony and another one-third as child support.

1. Can you take this case? *After* Mary has confided in you, are your obligations any different?

2. May you charge one month's child support as your fee in this case? Explain.

SAMPLE EXAM QUESTION VII

Mark Russell represented Pat Novak in a divorce. Pat was ordered to pay child support. He has fallen behind. Mark is subpoenaed and asked Pat's address. He refuses to give it, citing both the evidentiary privilege and his professional obligation. The court overrules both grounds and orders Mark to answer.

1. What should Mark do? How will the issue arise? Explain.

2. The court asks Mark, "Is Novak a drug addict?" Mark believes the answer is yes because while handling Pat's case Mark had overheard Pat and a friend discussing Pat's use of narcotics. What should Mark's answer be? Explain.

SAMPLE EXAM QUESTION VIII

Doris Dash represents Mavis Martin, a local building contractor. Mavis asserts that she has not been paid for materials used on a job she is doing for a larger firm. Doris has filed suit on Mavis's behalf. As Doris investigates, however, she hears that Mavis may actually have sold the materials to another contractor and may be trying to recover twice. She looks at Mavis's files more closely and sees a letter from the other contractor thanking Mavis for her help. Doris obliquely asks Mavis what is going on and Mavis tells her to mind her own business.

What should Doris do? Explain.

SAMPLE EXAM QUESTION IX

Claudia Carns has finished law school and seeks admission to the bar. She was a member of the radical Weatherspoon group in the 1960's. Arrested for 21 counts of arson, she pleaded guilty to three counts of malicious damage to property and spent four months in jail. She was also charged with perjury for her testimony in a friend's trial on the same charges, but the perjury charges were later dropped in order to reduce the prosecutor's backlog of cases. She has refused to "on principle" to fill out the required character and fitness committee form.

Will Claudia be denied admission to the bar for any of this? Explain.

SAMPLE EXAM QUESTION X

Former Governor Don Runner has filed a lawsuit accusing the current secretary of state of illegally overcharging for automobile license plates. Don called a press conference to charge the secretary with mismanagement and the present governor with lax supervision. Don issued a general call for citizens to send $10 and join his class action. During his press conference and later TV interviews, Don posed under a large sign reading "Don (The People's Lawyer) Runner: Law for the Little Guy."

Is there any basis for subjecting Don to professional discipline? Explain.

ANSWER TO SAMPLE EXAM QUESTION I

1. Sarah should return the check.

    Sarah has behaved properly in this case. She listened to the client's story, understood the limits of her own ability, and put the client in touch with a firm that would be able to serve his needs. She prepared a basic memorandum of the facts and is entitled to be paid for that effort. However, the check she received is greatly in excess of a reasonable sum for two hours work. The issue then is whether the check plus a share of the second firm's fee is proper.

    Under the Model Rules, if the client consents and the total fee is reasonable, lawyers who assume joint responsibility for a matter may share the fee in whatever proportions they agree, regardless of how much work each did. Thus, if Sarah and the firm have assumed joint responsibility for this matter (and the client has consented and the total fee is reasonable), Sarah would not be required to return the check. However, Sarah may not wish to assume joint responsibility since she could be liable if the firm does not handle the matter properly; therefore, she should probably return the check.

    Note that under the ABA Code, Sarah should return the check. The Code requires the division of fees to correspond to the services performed and responsibilities assumed by each lawyer. The value of Sarah's services would not amount to $1,000 or more.

2. Sarah may appear on the program and provide general information about the law. However, she should not try to solve individual problems of viewers over the telephone, and she should not offer to have viewers come into her office for further advice.

    The public needs information about legal issues and lawyers are often in the best position to provide that information. Sarah should certainly try to do a good job of communicating valuable information on the issues that viewers raise. However, each actual case is unique, and a lawyer should not try to solve an actual case without a detailed and careful understanding of the facts. This would violate the lawyer's duty of competence (*i.e.,* handling the client's problem with care). Also, the public nature of a television talk show interferes with the confidentiality of the lawyer-client relationship, which is designed to give clients a chance to provide the facts candidly and fully. Thus, Sarah should refuse to give advice in specific cases.

    Sarah should not offer to have viewers come to her office. While a lawyer may advertise her services generally on television, direct contact with a potential client would not be proper. Under the Model Rules, all "in-person or live telephone contact" with potential clients whom the lawyer has not previously served is prohibited where a "significant motive" for the contact is the lawyer's personal gain. Thus, Sarah may not suggest that viewers come to her office for further help, although she may (and sometimes should) recommend that they seek advice of a lawyer. If a viewer later turns up at her office seeking personal advice, Sarah is not forbidden to deal with the client's problem, but she cannot solicit the person's business on the television show.

ANSWER TO SAMPLE EXAM QUESTION II

G & E could object to Harry's work while in government, and the Justice Department can complain about Harry's firm's participation in the tax fraud case.

The problem here is that of representation contrary to the interest of a former client. The first such problem arose when Harry went to work for the government and was assigned a case prosecuting a firm he had formerly represented. This was potentially a serious conflict of interest and G & E might have filed a motion to have Harry reassigned to another matter. However, the kind of information Harry received in his work on the securities cases was probably not the kind of information involved in this alleged tax fraud; indeed, it may have been made public in the prospectuses anyway, so that G & E's interest in confidentiality would probably not have been great enough to cause Harry to be ineligible to prosecute the later tax case. Even if Harry were ineligible, other U.S. Attorneys could prosecute the case, as a court would be reluctant to attribute the knowledge of one Assistant U.S. Attorney to the whole office.

After Harry left government, he clearly could not defend the case he formerly prosecuted. That would constitute participation in both sides of the same case and would run directly afoul of Model Rule 1.11(a), which prohibits a former government lawyer from representing a private client in a matter in which the lawyer participated personally and substantially while in government, and ABA Code DR 9-101(B), which forbids a lawyer to work on a matter for which he had "substantial responsibility" as a government lawyer. However, Harry's assignment by his new firm to work exclusively on other cases would effectively screen him from any participation in the tax fraud case. Under Model Rule 1.11(a)(1) and case law, a former government lawyer's *firm* is not necessarily disqualified if the lawyer is screened and he shares no fees earned from the case. Thus, it is probable that the government could not have Harry's firm disqualified as defense counsel for G & E.

ANSWER TO SAMPLE EXAM QUESTION III

Mary's new venture has a series of problems, the most basic of which is that she is practicing law with nonlawyers and helping persons engage in the unauthorized practice of law.

No problem is presented by Mary's writing booklets explaining tax planning to clients. Some activities of lay firms (*e.g.*, divorce clinics) have been held to be unauthorized practice, but the writing of booklets has generally not been held to constitute unauthorized practice, even in areas traditionally reserved to lawyers.

Giving seminars for CPAs is likewise not a problem, but having the CPAs fill in blanks on pre-printed wills is almost certainly the unauthorized practice of law. There are case holdings that allow real estate agents to fill in blanks for routine items on certain standard contracts. However, wills are sufficiently diverse and involve such a high degree of judgment and individual tailoring that it is almost certain that CPAs would not be permitted to supply missing terms. Mary's assisting in this process would cause her to be in violation of Model Rule 5.5(b) and DR 3-101(A), which forbid aiding others in the unauthorized practice of law.

Furthermore, Model Rule 5.4(a) and DR 3-103 prohibit a lawyer from forming a partnership with nonlawyers where any of the activities involve the practice of law. Mary's involvement in the "Mister Tax" partnership would violate these rules. The nature of the tax planning activities is such that Mary, if not the entire company, would be deemed to be engaging in the practice of law, and thus Mary's role as a partner is improper. Many persons believe that this is an uncalled for ethical prohibition because the work of firms such as this may well be of value to the public, but the Model Rules and the ABA Code clearly prohibit this type of arrangement.

Finally, Mary's acting as counsel when her company is named executor of clients' estates would probably constitute a violation of the duty of loyalty to the clients as well as involve

Mary in assisting in the practice of law by a corporation. Whenever a lawyer seeks to encourage or require a client to name her executor or counsel to the executor, there is a potential problem of overreaching. "Mister Tax" seems to be heavily involved in that here.

ANSWER TO SAMPLE EXAM QUESTION IV

Neglect by busy lawyers is an all too common situation and Bob should indeed be worried. The inventor may file a complaint with the state's discipline commission and almost certainly has a viable malpractice claim against Bob.

Although Bob was not familiar with patent law, it was not improper for him to take the inventor's case. However, upon doing so, Bob had an obligation to promptly become familiar with the area of law and to proceed to prosecute the patent claim. Alternatively, Bob had an obligation to involve a more experienced firm in the process and require them to get the patent on file. The failure to do either one of these things constituted neglect on Bob's part, and the inventor could file a complaint with the state's discipline commission.

The inventor could also file a malpractice claim against Bob for this neglect. To succeed, the inventor would have to demonstrate that Bob breached a duty to him and that he was harmed thereby. As explained above, Bob clearly breached his duty to the inventor. If the inventor could show that he would have received the patent claim if Bob had proceeded expeditiously, he can successfully sue Bob. The damages would be the royalties the inventor would have received from the patent.

The fact that Bob had received a retainer for his services is not decisive of any issue, but it is a factor that courts frequently look to in making the penalty for the neglect more severe.

ANSWER TO SAMPLE EXAM QUESTION V

1. Each client should be sent a letter explaining that the firm is breaking up and informing the client that his or her file may be sent to the lawyer or law firm of the client's choice. Clients are not the property of either lawyer, and there is no proper way for Jones or Yates to compel or even properly encourage a client to remain with one of them.

2. Each partner may keep a copy of whatever material is necessary to protect that partner's interest. As indicated above, the clients are free to go with either partner or with another law firm, and their files must be sent to the selected lawyer or firm. However, if a client has not paid his or her fees, the partners may have a lien for those fees that will allow them to retain some of the files. Likewise, either or both partners may be liable for malpractice with respect to any of the cases that they have been working on, and thus it may be in each partner's interest to retain copies of some or all of the files.

ANSWER TO SAMPLE EXAM QUESTION VI

1. Although the ABA does not specifically prohibit a lawyer's taking this kind of case, some state statutes do, and most lawyers would not try to represent both sides in a case like this.

   A lawyer may take a case involving conflicting interests where both parties understand the potential conflict, consent to the dual representation, *and* the lawyer believes that she can adequately represent the interests of each client. Moreover, the lawyer may counsel Mary and Bill in an uncontested, nonlitigation situation, and it would be proper to draw up an agreement concerning child custody and property settlement. However, the lawyer can act as an intermediary only after full disclosure of the conflicting interests of Mary and Bill and with the express consent of both of them.

Here, even if a lawyer believed at the outset that adequate representation of both Mary and Bill was possible, it would be hard to maintain that belief after Mary's confidence. Once the lawyer knows that Mary's needs are not likely to continue to be as they appear, the lawyer is forced to take a position that will in some sense constitute taking advantage of Bill. As Mary's private counsel, the lawyer probably could seek to get Mary a large alimony payment as long as no affirmative misrepresentations were made. However, as Bill's lawyer, she would presumably also be trying to make those payments as low as possible and would be obliged to use Mary's information on Bill's behalf. Absent Mary's consent, the lawyer cannot disclose confidential information elicited from Mary in preliminary discussions. The lawyer owes a professional duty under the Model Rules and the ABA Code to preserve all client confidences; this obligation is not limited to legal proceedings but applies to any client confidence gained in the course of the lawyer-client relationship. Thus, the lawyer could not make a full disclosure to Bill and so is prohibited from representing him.

Furthermore, a clear conflict of interests is apparent after Mary's disclosure; when a conflict of interest becomes apparent after employment, the lawyer must withdraw from representing one of the clients pursuant to Model Rule 1.7. The lawyer should suggest that Bill get other counsel, since it does not appear that Bill's interest will actually be prejudiced thereby.

2. A fee based on the amount of child support awarded would not be proper. Under the Model Rules a fee contingent on obtaining a divorce or on the amount of alimony or support would be prohibited. Under the ABA Code, there is no absolute prohibition on contingent fees in domestic relations cases, but the practice is strongly discouraged. Particularly in a case in which the lawyer is representing both sides, such a fee might encourage the lawyer to try to increase the amount of child support (to the disadvantage of one party) so as to increase her own fee. Of course lawyers consider a variety of factors in setting the fee they ultimately charge, but to tie the fee directly to a figure such as child support would be improper.

ANSWER TO SAMPLE EXAM QUESTION VII

1. Although the ABA rules do not prohibit Mark from answering in response to the court's order, Mark should probably continue to refuse to answer.

Mark is probably correct in citing the evidentiary attorney-client privilege as a reason not to disclose Pat's address. A communication made in confidence by a client to his lawyer in obtaining legal assistance is generally protected under the privilege. Here, Pat himself "communicated" the address to Mark and disclosure of the address would clearly not be in Pat's interest. Pat has not waived the privilege. Thus, Mark should not disclose the information.

Also, the information certainly qualifies as a "secret" protected by the professional obligation of confidentiality (in the ABA Code and Model Rules). Thus, it is information Mark should not reveal.

If Mark refuses to disclose the information when the court orders him to answer, Mark will probably be sentenced for contempt of court. Mark will then be in a position to appeal the court's order to disclose, which is about the only way that he can get a judicial test of the privilege question. If the appellate court sustains the trial court, then presumably Mark has an obligation to disclose and should do so.

It should be noted that the ABA Code and Model Rules would *permit* Mark to reveal the client's secret when ordered to do so by the trial court, but he is not *required* to do so, and most lawyers believe their duty to their client is somewhat higher than this standard.

2.   Mark should tell the court what he heard. The information about Pat's drug habit is clearly not protected by the attorney-client privilege since the information was not communicated to Mark by the client. However, the information was something Mark heard in the course of representation that could be embarrassing or harmful to Pat. That puts the information again into the category of "secret." However, a lawyer must reveal such information when ordered by the court to do so. Here, Mark has been subpoenaed, and if ordered to do so by the court, should answer the question.

ANSWER TO SAMPLE EXAM QUESTION VIII

Doris should look into this situation more fully to assure herself that she is not perpetrating a fraud.

A lawyer is the client's representative, not her judge. However, the lawyer is neither required nor permitted to assist a client in perpetrating a fraud on someone else. In this situation, Doris has become aware of the possibility that her client may be making a false claim. Doris would not be required to go to the prosecutor and accuse her client of perjury, but she is under an obligation to try to prevent more damage from being done. Doris should not conduct a further search of Mavis's files; she is not permitted to use her role as a trusted advisor to become a self-appointed investigator. However, she should confront Mavis directly about the issue and try to get satisfactory answers. If she is not satisfied that Mavis's claim is legitimate, she should advise Mavis to drop it. If Mavis refuses, Doris should withdraw from the representation.

ANSWER TO SAMPLE EXAM QUESTION IX

Claudia is likely to be denied admission to the bar.

Conviction of a crime involving moral turpitude is often sufficient to deny an applicant admission to the bar. Arson would likely constitute such a crime and in context so might malicious damage to property. The bar admissions committee is not limited by the label of an offense but may investigate all of the surrounding facts. A finding that Claudia consciously engaged in setting fires so as to do damage might be considered to make her a sufficiently "bad person" that admission would be denied.

The charge of perjury would be even more serious. Offenses involving deceit are thought to be particularly serious for potential lawyers. Although the charges were dropped, the bar admissions committee would again be entitled to look into the evidence that the prosecutor had and would not be bound by the fact that the charges were never brought to trial.

Finally, the refusal to fill out the required character and fitness form would probably itself cause denial of admission to the bar. The burden of supplying relevant information is on the applicant for admission. The Supreme Court has held that failure to supply information can be the basis for denial of admission. There may be substantive limits on the criteria that the bar admissions committee can consider in actually ruling on the applicant's case, but there is no excuse for not supplying relevant information.

Since all of Claudia's criminal behavior took place many years ago, it is possible that Claudia has been rehabilitated. However, since Claudia did not bother to fill out the form, she did not raise the rehabilitation argument and so it would not be considered by the committee.

ANSWER TO SAMPLE EXAM QUESTION X

Don could be subject to discipline for improper pretrial publicity.

Lawsuits are to be tried in the courts and not in the media. The Model Rules and ABA Code allow a lawyer to reveal certain basic information about a case that has been filed, but they do not permit the lawyer to argue that case in the media. This problem presents a somewhat closer case because Don is obviously mixing politics with litigation. Some of his remarks are presumably partisan and possibly designed to aid a political comeback. The Model Rules and ABA Code do not prohibit political activity, but they may be read to require Don to do his politicking other than by publicizing a litigated case.

Calling for citizens to join a class action and send in cash also might be prohibited. Traditionally, it was improper for lawyers to initiate the organization of prospective litigants as a means of providing employment for themselves. Soliciting clients for fee-generating work by an announcement on television could be considered improper solicitation.

Advertising on television no longer violates the ABA Code and is acceptable under Model Rules 7.1 and 7.2, but posing under a large sign extolling one's own talents might violate prohibitions on false or misleading advertising.

TABLE OF CITATIONS
ABA CODE OF PROFESSIONAL RESPONSIBILITY

TABLE OF CITATIONS
ABA MODEL RULES OF PROFESSIONAL CONDUCT

TABLE OF CASES

Fellerman v. Bradley - §364
Ferry v. Ackerman - §903
Fine Paper, *In re* - §242
Firestone Tire & Rubber Co. v. Risjord - §491
First Wisconsin Mortgage Trust v. First Wisconsin
   Corp. - §492
Flanagan v. United States - §491
Fletcher v. A. J. Industries - §243
Flores v. Flores - §488
Florida Bar, *In re* - §100
Florida Bar v. Furman - §104
Florida Bar v. McLawhorn - §516
Florida Bar v. Saxon - §694
Florida Bar v. Stupica - §105
Florida Bar v. Wilkes - §898
Foley, Hoag & Eliot - §732
Fracasse v. Brent - §§317, 320
Freeport-McMoRan Oil & Gas Co. v. F.E.R.C. -
   §725
Friday v. State Bar - §887
Fund of Funds, Ltd. v. Arthur Andersen & Co. - §482

G.W.L., *Re* - §47
Gair v. Peck - §263
Gardner v. North Carolina State Bar - §115
Geffen v. State Bar - §809
Gentile v. Nevada State Bar - §598
Giddens v. State Bar - §875
Ginsburg v. Kovrak - §80
Goldfarb v. Virginia State Bar - §§222, 223, 781
Goldsmith v. Pringle - §64
Grand Jury Proceedings, *In re* - §350
Graves v. P.J. Taggares - §166
Green v. Ralston Purina Co. - §623
Greenberg, *In re* - §440
Greene v. Committee of Bar Examiners - §47
Gregory v. United States - §721
Greycas, Inc. v. Proud - §§527, 919
Grievance Committee v. Rottner - §433
Griffiths, *In re* - §30
Grimes, *In re* - §565
Gulbankian, State v. - §398
Gulf Oil v. Bernard - §817
Gullo v. Hirst - §572

Haack v. Great Atlantic & Pacific Tea Co. - §681
Hackin v. Lockwood - §33
Haddad, United States v. - §375
Hallinan v. Committee of Bar Examiners - §§42, 50,
   51
Harris, People v. - §340
Hawk v. Superior Court - §619
Hawkins v. Moss - §64
Hay v. Erwin - §258
Heron v. Jones - §483
Herron v. State Farm Mutual - §322

Heyer v. Flaig - §918
Himmel, *In re* - §893
Himmel v. State Bar - §883
Hishon v. King & Spaulding - §733
Hiss, *In re* - §886
Hobart's Administrator v. Vail - §443
Holloway v. Arkansas - §416
Horan, State v. - §§397, 399
Horne v. Peckham - §176
Huffman v. Montana Supreme Court - §37

In re - *see* name of party
International Business Machines v. United States -
   §537
Iorizzo, United States v. - §475
Isserman, *In re* - §927

Jackson v. State Bar - §218
Jacobson v. National Dairy Products - §618
January 1976 Grand Jury, *In re* - §338
Jedwabny v. Philadelphia Trust Co. - §422
Jeffry v. Pounds - §434
Johns v. Smyth - §200
Johnson, Petition of - §863
Johnson v. Mississippi - §931
Johnson v. Superior Court - §719
Jonathan Corp. v. Prime Computers, Inc. - §341
Jones, State v. - §487

Kamp, *In re* - §440
Kandel v. State - §575
Kaplan, *In re* - §371
Katris v. Immigration & Naturalization Service -
   §660
Kavanaugh, State v. - §67
Keller v. State Bar of California - §12
Kelly v. Greason - §875
Kentucky Bar Association v. Heleringer - §564
Kinnemon v. Staiman & Snyder - §546
Kirsch v. Duryea - §908
Kleiner v. First National Bank of Atlanta - §817
Klemm v. Superior Court - §427
Koffler v. Joint Bar Association - §246
Konigsberg v. Board of Bar Examiners - §46
Kor, People v. - §357
Kreamer, *In re* - §§851, 864, 865
Krieger v. Bulpitt - §254
Kushinsky, *In re* - §435

Lamb, *In re* - §855
Lamberis, *In re* - §855
Lathrop v. Donahue - §11
Law Students Research Council v. Wadmond - §55
Lawline v. American Bar Association - §87
Lewis v. State Bar of California - §174
Lindy Brothers v. American Radiator - §242

INDEX

Subject	Model Rules	ABA Code
with estate of deceased lawyer, §§757-758	5.4(a)(1)	DR 3-102(A)(1), (2)
with forwarding attorney, §§844-845	1.5(e)	DR 2-107
with laypersons, §§753-759	5.4(a),(3)	EC 3-8; DR 3-102(A)

DRAFTING DOCUMENTS, AS CONSTITUTING THE PRACTICE OF LAW, §§95-96

E

EDUCATION

requirement of for bar applicant, §§32-34		EC 1-2

EMPLOYEES OF LAWYER

delegation of tasks, §§736-742	5.3	EC 3-6
duty of lawyer to control, §742	5.1, 5.3(a)	EC 4-2; DR 4-101(D)
engaging in "solicitation," prohibition against, §809	7.2(c)	DR 2-103(A), (C)
payment to, §§754-755		DR 3-102(A)(3)

EMPLOYMENT

See also Advice by lawyer; Accepting employment

acceptance of. *See* Accepting employment

contract of. *See* Contract of employment

duty to accept. *See* Accepting employment

frivolous claims, §§137, 571-573	3.1	DR 2-109(A)(2)

manner of seeking. *See also* Advertising

passive standard, §778		EC 2-9

solicitation. *See* Solicitation of business

public, retirement from, §§506-509	1.11(a)	EC 9-3; DR 9-101(A), (B)

rejection of. *See* Accepting employment

when client already represented, §140		EC 2-30
when violation of law involved, §141	1.2(d)	DR 7-102

withdrawal from. *See* Termination of attorney-client relationship

ENFORCEMENT OF PROFESSIONAL RESPONSIBILITY

See Misconduct; Discipline of lawyer

ETHICAL CONSIDERATIONS, PURPOSE AND FUNCTIONS OF, §21		Col. 2. para. 3 ("Preliminary Statement")
EXPENSES OF CLIENT, ADVANCING OR GUARANTEEING PAYMENT OF, §§642-649	1.8(e)	EC 5-8; DR 5-103(B)

F

FEDERAL CONFLICT OF INTEREST ACT, §§506-509

FEDERAL PRACTICE

See Admission to practice

FEE FOR LEGAL SERVICES

agreement as to, §§224-228	1.5(a), (b)	EC 2-19; DR 2-106(A)

amount of

excessive, clearly, §229	1.5(a)	DR 2-106(A), (B)
in absence of agreement, §234		
reasonableness, desirability of, §§229-233		EC 2-17
class actions, §§241-244		

collection of

avoiding litigation with client, §266		EC 2-23
client's secrets, use of in collecting or establishing, §§375-377	1.6(b)(2)	EC 4-5; DR 4-101(B)(3), (C)(4)
liens, use of, §§267-283		EC 5-7; DR 5-103(A)(1)

contingent fee. *See* Contingent fee

Subject	Model Rules	ABA Code

G

GIFT TO LAWYER BY CLIENT, §§395-400	1.8(c)	EC 5-5
GIFT TO TRIBUNAL OFFICER OR	3.5(a)	EC 7-34, DR 7-110(A)
EMPLOYEE, §§567, 694-696		
See also Judicial conduct		
GOODWILL, SALE OF, §847		
GOVERNMENT ATTORNEY		
conflict of interest, possibility of, §§506-509		
representing private claimants, disqualification from, §§493-501	1.11(a)	DR 9-101(B)
return to private practice, §§494-503	1.11(a)	DR 9-101(B)
GROUP AND PREPAID LEGAL SERVICES		
approval of by ABA, §§776-777		DR 2-103(D)(4)
constitutional protection of, §§769-771		
types of		
closed panel, §774		
open panel, §775		
GUARANTEEING PAYMENT OF CLIENT'S	1.8(e)	EC 5-8; DR 5-103(B)
COSTS AND EXPENSES, §§642-649		
GUARDIAN, APPOINTMENT OF, §171	1.14(b)	

H

HARASSMENT, DUTY TO AVOID LITIGATION	3.1, 4.4	EC 2-30; DR 2-109(A)(1),
INVOLVING, §§136, 292, 571		7-102(A)(1)
HOLDING OUT		
as limiting practice, §§836-839	7.4	EC 2-14; DR 2-102(A)(6), 2-105(A)(1)-(4)
as partnership, §729	7.5(d)	EC 2-11, 2-13; DR 2-102(C)
as specialist, §§829-835	7.4	EC 2-14; DR 2-105(A)(1)-(4)
HONESTY IN COMMUNICATION		
WITH OTHERS		
See also Candor, duty of		
basic obligation, §516	4.1(a)	DR 1-102(A)
duty to come forward, §§517-519	1.6	DR 7-102(A)(3)
evaluator, lawyer as, §§525-528	2.3	
negotiations, §§520-524	4.1	
widely disseminated information, §§529-532		
HUSBAND AND WIFE ATTORNEYS, §489		

I

IDENTITY OF CLIENT		
duty not to disclose, §§369-371		
duty to reveal, §550		EC 7-15, 7-16, 8-4; DR 7-106(B)(2)
ILLEGAL CONDUCT, AS CAUSE FOR	1.2(d)	EC 1-5; DR 1-102(A)(3), (4)
DISCIPLINE, §§850-854		
IMPROPER INFLUENCES		
gift or loan to judicial officer, §§694-696	3.5(a)	EC 7-34; DR 7-110(A)
See also Judicial conduct		
IMPROPER PURPOSE, USE OF LEGAL		
PROCESS FOR		
delay, §§574-583	3.2	DR 7-102(A)(1)
threatening criminal prosecution, §§542-547		DR 7-105
unfounded case, §§571-573	3.1	DR 7-102(A)(2)

Subject	Model Rules	ABA Code
KNOWLEDGE OF INTENDED CRIME, REVEALING, §§353-354	1.6(b)(1)	DR 4-101(C)(3)

L

Subject	Model Rules	ABA Code
LAW SCHOOL, WORKING WITH LEGAL AID OFFICE OR PUBLIC DEFENDER OFFICE SPONSORED BY, §§111-114		DR 2-103(D)(1)(a)
LAW SCHOOLS, ACCREDITATION, §33		
LEGAL AID OFFICES, WORKING WITH, §§763-766	5.4(c)	EC 2-25, 2-33; DR 2-103 (D)(1)(a)-(d)
LEGAL DOCUMENTS OF CLIENT, DUTY TO SAFEGUARD, §219	1.15(a)	DR 9-102(B)
LEGAL SERVICES, FORM OF		
association with nonlawyers, §§749-759	5.4(a), (b)	DR 3-102, 3-103
See also Fee splitting, with nonlawyer; Employment; Partnership, with nonlawyer; Profit sharing with lay employees,		DR 2-103(D)(4)
group legal services, in general, §§767-777		
See also Group and prepaid legal services		
legal aid offices. *See* Legal aid offices, working with		
prepaid legal services. *See* Group and prepaid legal services		DR 2-103(D)(4)
specialization. *See* Specialization		
LEGAL SYSTEM, DUTY TO IMPROVE, §§548-569		EC 8-1, 8-9
LEGISLATURE		
improper influence upon, §557	3.5(a)	EC 8-5; DR 8-10(A)(1)
regulation of fees, §§236-240		
regulation of practice, §§6-8		
representation of client before, §§548-551	3.9	EC 7-15, 7-16, 8-4, 8-5
serving as member of, §§555-561		EC 8-8
LIABILITY TO CLIENT		
See Malpractice suits		
LIENS, ATTORNEY'S, §§267-283		EC 5-7; DR 5-103(A)(1)
LIMITED PRACTICE, HOLDING OUT AS HAVING, §§836-839	7.4	EC 2-14; DR 2-101(B)(2), 2-105(A)(2)
LITIGATION		
acquiring an interest in, §387	1.8(j)	EC 5-7; DR 5-103(A)(1)-(2)
expenses of, advancing or guaranteeing payment of, §§642-649	1.8(e)	EC 5-8; DR 5-103(B)
pending, media discussion of, §§588-590	3.6	DR 7-107(A)-(J)
to harass another, duty to avoid, §§136, 571	3.1, 4.4	EC 2-30; DR 2-109(A)(1), 7-102(A)(1)
to maliciously harm another, duty to avoid, §§136, 571	3.1, 4.4	EC 2-30; DR 2-109(A)(1), 7-102(A)(1)
trial tactics		
arousing emotions of jurors, §§621-625	3.4(e)	EC 7-25; DR 7-106(C)(1)
personal knowledge or opinion, use of, §§619-620		EC 7-24; DR 7-106(C)(3), (4)
reference to matters unsubstantiated by evidence, §§615-618	3.4(e)	DR 7-106(C)(1)
testing validity of rule, §§514, 627	3.1, 3.4(c)	EC 7-25; DR 7-106(A)
violation of rules of evidence or procedure, §§626-629	1.8(e)	EC 7-25; DR 7-106(C)(7)
LIVING EXPENSES OF CLIENT, ADVANCES TO CLIENT OF, §§642-649		EC 5-8; DR 5-103(B)

Subject	Model Rules	ABA Code

Subject	Model Rules	ABA Code

Z

ZEAL

asserting "technicalities," §§199-200
DR 7-101(B)(1)

criminal defendants, §§201-207

general duty of, §§195-207, 549 — 2.1, 3.1 — EC 7-1, 7-19;
  DR 7-101(A)(1)

legislative and administrative proceedings,
  §§548-551 — 3.9 — EC 7-15, 7-16

limitations upon — EC 7-4, 7-6, 7-7, 7-9, 7-10,
  7-36; DR 7-101(A), (B),
  7-102(A)(7), (8)

candor. *See* Candor, duty of

communicating with adverse party, §§533-538 — 4.2, 4.3 — DR 7-104
  See also Adverse party

communication with judge, §§697-700 — 3.5(b) — DR 7-110(B)

communication with jury. *See* Jury

conduct affecting witnesses. *See* Witness

fraud by client. *See* Attorney-client privilege

obligation of courtesy. *See* Courtesy

public statements, §§584-598 — 3.6 — DR 7-107

trial tactics. *See* Litigation

using legal process for improper purpose.
  See Improper purpose

plea bargaining, §§205-207

ZEALOUS REPRESENTATION

See Zeal

gilbert

LAW SUMMARIES

LEGAL ETHICS

Thomas D. Morgan

1996 SUPPLEMENT

HARCOURT BRACE LEGAL AND PROFESSIONAL PUBLICATIONS, INC.

EDITORIAL OFFICES: 176 W. Adams, Suite 2100, Chicago, IL 60603

gilbert
LAW SUMMARIES

REGIONAL OFFICES: New York, Chicago, Los Angeles, Washington, D.C.

Distributed by: **Harcourt Brace & Company** 6277 Sea Harbor Drive, Orlando, FL 32887 (800)787-8717

SUPPLEMENT TO GILBERT "LEGAL ETHICS" SUMMARY
(Seventh Edition)

March 1996

Page   **Revision**

47   **Insert** the following after para. (1) [§314]:

    (a) **And note:** A lawyer may not try to avoid the consequences of discharge by charging a "nonrefundable retainer." Such retainers typically provide that once the lawyer has entered an appearance in a case, even if the lawyer is later terminated, the client owes the entire fee. Nonrefundable retainers violate the fiduciary relationship between lawyer and client and inhibit the client's right to terminate the lawyer; thus, they are both unenforceable and a basis for sanctioning the lawyer. [*In re Cooperman*, 83 N.Y.2d 465 (1994)]

68   **Insert** the following after para. (2) [§435]:

    (3) **Application to members of a corporate family:** A lawyer prohibited from filing suit against a client may also be prohibited from maintaining an action against a parent, subsidiary, or sibling corporation of that client. The kinds of corporate family relationships are too varied to state a bright-line rule forbidding such suits. The lawyer must ask whether: (i) the corporations are in effect one entity; (ii) the lawyer has agreed to treat the corporate family as a single client; *or* (iii) the lawyer's obligations to one of the entities will impair pursuit of the claim against the other. Furthermore, even if the client's consent is not required, telling the client about the representation is simply good client relations. [ABA Opn. 95-390]

81   **Insert** the following at the end of para. a. [§518]:

    A particularly difficult disclosure issue has been the lawyer's obligation to reveal adverse information in the context of a bank examination, the so-called Kaye Scholer problem. Clearly, where a lawyer learns her services have been used to perpetrate a fraud, she *must* withdraw and *may* do so noisily, even though that may have the effect of revealing client confidences. [Model Rule 1.6, Comment] However, the ABA says that while a lawyer may not lie to bank examiners, the lawyer is not affirmatively obliged to warn about problems at the bank. [ABA Opn. 93-375]

84   **Insert** the following at the end of para. 1. [§533]:

    Note: Model Rule 4.2 has been amended to prohibit contact with any "person" represented by counsel, not just any "party." The point of the amendment was more clearly to prohibit contact with individuals prior to the time a suit or charge is actually filed.

93   **Insert** the following at the end of para. (1) [§589]:

    However, the Model Rules have been amended to differentiate between some duties of prosecutors and defense counsel. Prosecutors must now "except for statements that are necessary to inform the public of the nature and extent of the prosecutor's action and that serve a legitimate law enforcement purpose, refrain from making extrajudicial comments that have a substantial likelihood of heightening public condemnation of the accused."

[Model Rule 3.8(c)] Defense lawyers now may "make a statement that a reasonable lawyer would believe is required to protect a client from the substantial undue prejudicial effect of recent publicity not initiated by the lawyer or the lawyer's client." Such a statement must "be limited to such information as is necessary to mitigate the recent adverse publicity." [Model Rule 3.6(c)]

118   **Insert** the following at the end of para. g. [§762]:

The Model Rules have again been amended to regulate ancillary business activities. These activities, now called "law related services," are defined as services that "in substance are related to the provision of legal services, and that are not prohibited as unauthorized practice of law when provided by a nonlawyer." These services might include providing title insurance, financial planning, lobbying, accounting, trust services, real estate counseling, economic analysis, social work, psychological counseling, tax return preparation, and patent, medical, or environmental consulting. The Model Rules provide that a lawyer is "subject to the Rules of Professional Conduct with respect to the provision of" these services unless the lawyer takes reasonable measures to make clear that the services are not legal services and that protections such as the attorney-client privilege do not apply. [Model Rule 5.7]

124   **Insert** the following after para. (b) of §800:

d.   ***Went For It* case:** In 1995, for the first time since *Bates*, the Supreme Court **upheld state limits** on lawyer advertising. [Florida Bar v. Went For It, Inc., 115 S. Ct. 2371 (1995)] The majority opinion in *Went For It* said it applied the substantial government interest standard discussed above but concluded that the state's limitation on advertising was valid.

   (1)   **Example:** The regulation in *Went For It* prohibited lawyers from using targeted direct mail to contact victims and their families within 30 days following an accident or disaster. The Court concluded that the state had a "substantial interest" to justify such a regulation—*i.e.*, "to protect the flagging reputations of Florida lawyers" from conduct that was "universally regarded as deplorable and beneath common decency" because it invaded the privacy of potential clients. Also, the state showed that the regulation advanced its interests "in a direct and material way." Relying on newspaper editorials and a Bar survey of citizen attitudes, the Court concluded that the facts were sufficient to justify regulation of post-accident contact. The fact that recipients of the mailings could just throw them away was not sufficient here since mailings sent to bereaved persons would inflict their pain when first seen (before they could be discarded). Finally, the regulation was found to be a "reasonable fit for the problem the Bar had identified, even if not the "least restrictive means" of addressing the concern, and plenty of other ways exist for lawyers to make their availability known to potential clients, *e.g.*, television, newspapers, billboards, the Yellow Pages, or even untargeted direct mail.

      (a)   **Dissent:** Four Justices dissented, claiming that the majority was not following earlier precedents: The fact that advertising was "offensive" or "undignified" had not been sufficient in the past to ban it. Also, the Bar's "proof" that a problem existed was methodologically flawed and largely anecdotal. Finally, the flat ban on direct mail was too broad because it applied no matter how serious the accident or disaster.

147   **Insert** the following after para. (1) of §960:

    (2)   **And note:** Normally, the judge's alleged bias also must come from an "extra-judicial source"; what the judge learns in the courtroom inevitably is a part of the judge's decision and is not "bias or prejudice." However, a "pervasive bias" exception applies even to the extrajudicial source doctrine. Where the judge has a "clear inability to render fair judgment," the judge's recusal is required. [Liteky v. United States, 114 S. Ct. 1147 (1994)]

Notes

Publications Catalog

Publishers of America's Most Popular Legal Study Aids!

All Titles Available At Your Law School Bookstore.

Gilbert Law Summaries are the best selling outlines in the country, and have set the standard for excellence since they were first introduced more than twenty-five years ago. It's Gilbert's unique combination of features that makes it the one study aid you'll turn to for all your study needs!

Accounting and Finance for Lawyers
Professor Thomas L. Evans, University of Texas

Basic Accounting Principles; Definitions of Accounting Terms; Balance Sheet; Income Statement; Statement of Changes in Financial Position; Consolidated Financial Statements; Accumulation of Financial Data; Financial Statement Analysis.
ISBN: 0-15-900382-2   Pages: 136 $19.95

Administrative Law
By Professor Michael R. Asimow, U.C.L.A.

Separation of Powers and Controls Over Agencies; (including Delegation of Power) Constitutional Right to Hearing (including Liberty and Property Interests Protected by Due Process, and Rulemaking- Adjudication Distinction); Adjudication Under Administrative Procedure Act (APA); Formal Adjudication (including Notice, Discovery, Burden of Proof, Finders of Facts and Reasons); Adjudicatory Decision Makers (including Administrative Law Judges (ALJs), Bias, Improper Influences, Ex Parte Communications, Familiarity with Record, Res Judicata); Rulemaking Procedures (including Notice, Public Participation, Publication, Impartiality of Rulemakers, Rulemaking Record); Obtaining Information (including Subpoena Power, Privilege Against Self-incrimination, Freedom of Information Act, Government in Sunshine Act, Attorneys' Fees); Scope of Judicial Review; Reviewability of Agency Decisions (including Mandamus, Injunction, Sovereign Immunity, Federal Tort Claims Act); Standing to Seek Judicial Review and Timing.
ISBN: 0-15-900000-9   Pages: 278 $20.95

Agency and Partnership
By Professor Richard J. Conviser, Chicago Kent

Agency: Rights and Liabilities Between Principal and Agent (including Agent's Fiduciary Duty, Right to Indemnification); Contractual Rights Between Principal (or Agent) and Third Persons (including Creation of Agency Relationship, Authority of Agent, Scope of Authority, Termination of Authority, Ratification, Liability on

Agents, Contracts); Tort Liability (including Respondeat Superior, Master-Servant Relationship, Scope of Employment). Partnership: Property Rights of Partner; Formation of Partnership; Relations Between Partners (including Fiduciary Duty); Authority of Partner to Bind Partnership; Dissolution and Winding up of Partnership; Limited Partnerships.
ISBN: 0-15-900327-X   Pages: 149 $17.95

Antitrust
By Professor Thomas M. Jorde, U.C. Berkeley, Mark A. Lemley, University of Texas, and Professor Robert H. Mnookin, Harvard University

Common Law Restraints of Trade; Federal Antitrust Laws (including Sherman Act, Clayton Act, Federal Trade Commission Act, Interstate Commerce Requirement, Antitrust Remedies); Monopolization (including Relevant Market, Purposeful Act Requirement, Attempts and Conspiracy to Monopolize); Collaboration Among Competitors (including Horizontal Restraints, Rule of Reason vs. Per Se Violations, Price Fixing, Division of Markets, Group Boycotts); Vertical Restraints (including Tying Arrangements); Mergers and Acquisitions (including Horizontal Mergers, Brown Shoe Analysis, Vertical Mergers, Conglomerate Mergers); Price Discrimination— Robinson-Patman Act; Unfair Methods of Competition; Patent Laws and Their Antitrust Implications; Exemptions From Antitrust Laws (including Motor, Rail, and Interstate Water Carriers, Bank Mergers, Labor Unions, Professional Baseball).
ISBN: 0-15-900328-8   Pages: 210 $18.95

Bankruptcy
By Professor Ned W. Waxman, College of William and Mary

Participants in the Bankruptcy Case; Jurisdiction and Procedure; Commencement and Administration of the Case (including Eligibility, Voluntary Case, Involuntary Case, Meeting of Creditors, Debtor's Duties); Officers of the Estate (including

Trustee, Examiner, United States Trustee); Bankruptcy Estate; Creditor's Right of Setoff; Trustee's Avoiding Powers; Claims of Creditors (including Priority Claims and Tax Claims); Debtor's Exemptions; Nondischargeable Debts; Effects of Discharge; Reaffirmation Agreements; Administrative Powers (including Automatic Stay, Use, Sale, or Lease of Property); Chapter 7- Liquidation; Chapter 11-Reorganization; Chapter 13-Individual With Regular Income; Chapter 12- Family Farmer With Regular Annual Income.
ISBN: 0-15-900442-X   Pages: 311 $21.95

Business Law
By Professor Robert D. Upp, Los Angeles City College

Torts and Crimes in Business; Law of Contracts (including Contract Formation, Consideration, Statute of Frauds, Contract Remedies, Third Parties); Sales (including Transfer of Title and Risk of Loss, Performance and Remedies, Products Liability, Personal Property Security Interest); Property (including Personal Property, Bailments, Real Property, Landlord and Tenant); Agency; Business Organizations (including Partnerships, Corporations); Commercial Paper; Government Regulation of Business (including Taxation, Antitrust, Environmental Protection, and Bankruptcy).
ISBN: 0-15-900005-X   Pages: 277 $17.95

California Bar Performance Test Skills
By Professor Peter J. Honigsberg, University of San Francisco

Hints to Improve Writing; How to Approach the Performance Test; Legal Analysis Documents (including Writing a Memorandum of Law, Writing a Client Letter, Writing Briefs); Fact Gathering and Fact Analysis Documents; Tactical and Ethical Considerations; Sample Interrogatories, Performance Tests, and Memoranda.
ISBN: 0-15-900152-8   Pages: 216 $18.95

Civil Procedure
By Professor Thomas D. Rowe, Jr., Duke University, and Professor Richard L. Marcus, U.C. Hastings

Territorial (Personal) Jurisdiction, including Venue and Forum Non Conveniens; Subject Matter Jurisdiction, covering Diversity Jurisdiction, Federal Question Jurisdiction; Erie Doctrine and Federal Common Law; Pleadings including Counterclaims, Cross-Claims, Supplemental Pleadings; Parties, including Joinder and Class Actions; Discovery, including Devices, Scope, Sanctions, and Discovery Conference; Summary Judgment; Pretrial Conference and Settlements; Trial, including Right to Jury Trial, Motions, Jury Instruction and Arguments, and Post-Verdict Motions; Appeals; Claim Preclusion (Res Judicata) and Issue Preclusion (Collateral Estoppel).
ISBN: 0-15-900429-2   Pages: 410 $22.95

Commercial Paper and Payment Law
By Professor Douglas J. Whaley, Ohio State University

Types of Commercial Paper; Negotiability; Negotiation; Holders in Due Course; Claims and Defenses on Negotiable Instruments (including Real Defenses and Personal Defenses); Liability of the Parties (including Merger Rule, Suits on the Instrument, Warranty Suits, Conversion); Bank Deposits and Collections; Forgery or Alteration of Negotiable Instruments; Electronic Banking.
ISBN: 0-15-900367-9   Pages: 166 $19.95

Community Property
By Professor William A. Reppy, Jr., Duke University

Classifying Property as Community or Separate; Management and Control of Property; Liability for Debts; Division of Property at Divorce; Devolution of Property at Death; Relationships Short of Valid Marriage; Conflict of Laws Problems; Constitutional Law Issues (including Equal Protection Standards, Due Process Issues).
ISBN: 0-15-900422-5   Pages: 161 $18.95

LAW SCHOOL LEGENDS SERIES

America's Greatest Law Professors on Audio Cassette

We found the truly gifted law professors most law students can only dream about — the professors who draw rave reviews not only for their scholarship, but for their ability to make the law easy to understand. We asked these select few professors to condense their courses into a single lecture. And it's these lectures you'll find in the Law School Legends Series. With Law School Legends, you'll get a brilliant law professor explaining an entire subject to you in one simple, dynamic lecture. The Law School Legends make even the most difficult concepts crystal clear. You'll understand the big picture, and how all the concepts fit together. You'll get hundreds of examples and exam tips, honed over decades in the classroom. But best of all, you'll get insights you can only get from America's greatest law professors!

Administrative Law
Professor Patrick J. Borchers
Albany Law School of Union University

TOPICS COVERED: Classification Of Agencies; Adjudicative And Investigative Action; Rulemaking Power; Delegation Doctrine; Control By Executive; Appointment And Removal; Freedom Of Information Act; Rulemaking Procedure; Adjudicative Procedure; Trial-Type Hearings; Administrative Law Judge; Power To Stay Proceedings; Subpoena Power; Physical Inspection; Self Incrimination; Judicial Review Issues; Declaratory Judgment; Sovereign Immunity; Eleventh Amendment; Statutory Limitations; Standing; Exhaustion Of Administrative Remedies; Scope Of Judicial Review.
4 Audio Cassettes
ISBN: 0-15-900189-7 $45.95

Agency & Partnership
Professor Thomas L. Evans
University of Texas

TOPICS COVERED: Agency: Creation; Rights And Duties Of Principal And Agent; Sub-Agents; Contract Liability — Actual Authority: Express And Implied; Apparent Authority; Ratification; Liabilities Of Parties; Tort Liability — Respondeat Superior; Frolic And Detour; Intentional Torts. Partnership: Nature Of Partnership; Formation; Partnership By Estoppel; In Partnership Property; Relations Between Partners To Third Parties; Authority of Partners; Dissolution And Termination; Limited Partnerships.
4 Audio Cassettes
ISBN: 0-15-900351-2 $45.95

Antitrust
Professor Thomas D. Morgan
George Washington University Law School

TOPICS COVERED: Antitrust Law's First Principle; Consumer Welfare Opposes Market Power; Methods of Analysis; Role of Reason, Per Se, Quick Look; Sherman Act §1: Civil & Criminal Conspiracies In Unreasonable Restraint Of Trade; Sherman Act §2: Illegal Monopolization, Attempts To Monopolize; Robinson Patman Act Price Discrimination, Related Distribution Problems; Clayton Act §7: Mengers, Joint Ventures; Antitrust & Intellectual Property; International Competitive Relationships; Exemptions & Regulated Industries; Enforcement; Price & Non-Price Restraints.
4 Audio Cassettes
ISBN: 0-15-900341-5 $39.95

Bankruptcy
Professor Elizabeth Warren
Harvard Law School

TOPICS COVERED: The Debtor/Creditor Relationship; The Commencement, Conversion, Dismissal, and Reopening Of Bankruptcy Proceedings; Property Included In The Bankruptcy Estate; Secured, Priority And Unsecured Claims; The Automatic Stay; Powers Of Avoidance; The Assumption And Rejection Of Executory Contracts; The Protection Of Exempt Property; The Bankruptcy Discharge; Chapter 13 Proceedings; Chapter 11 Proceedings; Bankruptcy Jurisdiction And Procedure.
4 Audio Cassettes
ISBN: 0-15-900273-7 $45.95

Civil Procedure
By Professor Richard D. Freer
Emory University Law School

TOPICS COVERED: Subject Matter Jurisdiction; Personal Jurisdiction; Long-Arm Statutes; Constitutional Limitations; In Rem And Quasi In Rem Jurisdiction; Service Of Process; Venue; Transfer; Forum Non Conveniens; Removal; Waiver; Governing Law; Pleadings; Joinder Of Claims; Permissive And Compulsory Joinder Of Parties; Counter-Claims And Cross-Claims; Ancillary Jurisdiction; Impleader; Class Actions; Discovery; Pretrial Adjudication; Summary Judgment; Trial; Post Trial Motions; Appeals; Res Judicata; Collateral Estoppel.
5 Audio Cassettes
ISBN: 0-15-900322-9 $59.95

Commercial Paper
By Professor Michael I. Spak
Chicago Kent College Of Law

TOPICS COVERED: Types Of Negotiable Instruments; Elements Of Negotiability; Statute Of Limitations; Payment-In-Full Checks; Negotiations Of The Instrument; Becoming A Holder-In-Due Course; Rights Of A Holder In Due Course; Real And Personal Defenses; Jus Teril; Effect Of Instrument On Underlying Obligations; Contracts Of Maker And Indorser; Suretyship; Liability Of Drawer And Drawee; Check Certification; Warranty Liability; Conversion Of Liability; Banks And Their Customers; Properly Payable Rule; Wrongful Dishonor; Stopping Payment; Death Of Customer; Bank Statement; Check Collection; Expedited Funds Availability; Forgery Of Drawer's Name; Alterations; Imposter Rule; Wire Transfers; Electronic Fund Transfers Act.
3 Audio Cassettes
ISBN: 0-15-900275-3 $39.95

Conflict Of Laws
Professor Patrick J. Borchers
Albany Law School

TOPICS COVERED: Domicile; Jurisdiction—In Personam, In Rem, Quasi In Rem; Court Competence; Forum Non Conveniens; Choice Of Law; Foreign Causes Of Action; Territorial Approach To Choice/Tort And Contract; "Escape Devices"; Most Significant Relationship; Governmental Interest Analysis; Recognition Of Judgments; Foreign Country Judgments; Domestic Judgments/Full Faith And Credit; Review Of Judgments; Modifiable Judgments; Defenses To Recognition And Enforcement; Federal/State (Erie) Problems; Constitutional Limits On Choice Of Law.
4 Audio Cassettes
ISBN: 0-15-900352-0 $39.95

Constitutional Law
By Professor John C. Jeffries, Jr.
University of Virginia School of Law

TOPICS COVERED: Introduction; Exam Tactics; Legislative Power; Supremacy; Commerce; State Regulation; Privileges And Immunities; Federal Court Jurisdiction; Separation Of Powers; Civil Liberties; Due Process; Equal Protection; Privacy; Race; Alienage; Gender; Speech And Association; Prior Restraints; Religion—Free Exercise; Establishment Clause.
5 Audio Cassettes
ISBN: 0-15-900373-3 $45.95

Contracts
By Professor Michael I. Spak
Chicago Kent College Of Law

TOPICS COVERED: Offer; Revocation; Acceptance; Consideration; Defenses To Formation; Third Party Beneficiaries; Assignment; Delegation; Conditions; Excuses; Anticipatory Repudiation; Discharge Of Duty; Modifications; Rescission; Accord & Satisfaction; Novation; Breach; Damages; Remedies; UCC Remedies; Parol Evidence Rule.
4 Audio Cassettes
ISBN: 0-15-900318-0 $45.95

Copyright Law
Professor Roger E. Schechter
George Washington University Law School

TOPICS COVERED: Constitution; Patents And Property Ownership Distinguished; Subject Matter Copyright; Duration And Renewal; Ownership And Transfer; Formalities; Introduction; Notice, Registration And Deposit; Infringement; Overview; Reproduction And Derivative Works; Public Distribution; Public Performance And Display; Exemptions; Fair Use; Photocopying; Remedies; Preemption Of State Law.
3 Audio Cassettes
ISBN: 0-15-900295-8 $39.95

Corporations
By Professor Therese H. Maynard
Loyola University Law School

TOPICS COVERED: Ultra Vires Act; Corporate Formation; Piercing The Corporate Veil; Corporate Financial Structure; Stocks; Bonds; Subscription Agreements; Watered Stock; Stock Transactions; Insider Trading; 16(b) & 10b-5 Violations; Promoters; Fiduciary Duties; Shareholder Rights; Meetings; Cumulative Voting; Voting Trusts; Close Corporations; Dividends; Preemptive Rights; Shareholder Derivative Suits; Directors; Duty Of Loyalty; Corporate Opportunity Doctrine; Officers; Amendments; Mergers; Dissolution.
4 Audio Cassettes
ISBN: 0-15-900320-2 $45.95

Criminal Law
By Professor Charles H. Whitebread
USC School of Law

TOPICS COVERED: Exam Tactics; Volitional Acts; Mental States; Specific Intent; Malice; General Intent; Strict Liability; Accomplice Liability; Inchoate Crimes; Impossibility; Defenses; Insanity; Voluntary And Involuntary Intoxication; Infancy; Self-Defense; Defense Of A Dwelling; Duress; Necessity; Mistake Of Fact Or Law; Entrapment; Battery; Assault; Homicide; Common Law Murder; Voluntary And Involuntary Manslaughter; First Degree Murder; Felony Murder; Rape; Larceny; Embezzlement; False Pretenses; Robbery; Extortion; Burglary; Arson.
4 Audio Cassettes
ISBN: 0-15-900279-6 $39.95

Legalines

Legalines gives you authoritative, detailed briefs of every major case in your casebook. You get a clear explanation of the facts, the issues, the court's holding and reasoning, and any significant concurrences or dissents. Even more importantly, you get an authoritative explanation of the significance of each case, and how it relates to other cases in your casebook. And with Legalines' detailed table of contents and table of cases, you can quickly find any case or concept you're looking for. But your professor expects you to know more than just the cases. That's why Legalines gives you more than just case briefs. You get summaries of the black letter law, as well. That's crucial, because some of the most important information in your casebooks isn't in the cases at all ... it's the black letter principles you're expected to glean from those cases. Legalines is the only series that gives you both case briefs and black letter review. With Legalines, you get everything you need to know—whether it's in a case or not!

Administrative Law

Keyed to the Breyer Casebook
ISBN: 0-15-900169-2   176 pages $19.95
Keyed to the Gellhorn Casebook
ISBN: 0-15-900170-6   186 pages $21.95
Keyed to the Schwartz Casebook
ISBN: 0-15-900171-4   145 pages $18.95

Antitrust

Keyed to the Areeda Casebook
ISBN: 0-15-900405-5   165 pages $19.95
Keyed to the Handler Casebook
ISBN: 0-15-900390-3   158 pages $18.95

Civil Procedure

Keyed to the Cound Casebook
ISBN: 0-15-900314-8   241 pages $21.95
Keyed to the Field Casebook
ISBN: 0-15-900415-2   310 pages $23.95
Keyed to the Hazard Casebook
ISBN: 0-15-900324-5   206 pages $21.95
Keyed to the Rosenberg Casebook
ISBN: 0-15-900052-1   284 pages $21.95
Keyed to the Yeazell Casebook
ISBN: 0-15-900241-9   206 pages $20.95

Commercial Law

Keyed to the Farnsworth Casebook
ISBN: 0-15-900176-5   126 pages $18.95

Conflict of Laws

Keyed to the Cramton Casebook
ISBN: 0-15-900331-8   113 pages $16.95
Keyed to the Reese (Rosenberg) Casebook
ISBN: 0-15-900057-2   247 pages $21.95

Constitutional Law

Keyed to the Brest Casebook
ISBN: 0-15-900338-5   172 pages $19.95
Keyed to the Cohen Casebook
ISBN: 0-15-900378-4   301 pages $22.95
Keyed to the Gunther Casebook
ISBN: 0-15-900060-2   367 pages $23.95
Keyed to the Lockhart Casebook
ISBN: 0-15-900242-7   322 pages $22.95

Constitutional Law (cont'd)

Keyed to the Rotunda Casebook
ISBN: 0-15-900363-6   258 pages $21.95
Keyed to the Stone Casebook
ISBN: 0-15-900236-2   281 pages $22.95

Contracts

Keyed to the Calamari Casebook
ISBN: 0-15-900065-3   234 pages $21.95
Keyed to the Dawson Casebook
ISBN: 0-15-900268-0   188 pages $21.95
Keyed to the Farnsworth Casebook
ISBN: 0-15-900332-6   219 pages $19.95
Keyed to the Fuller Casebook
ISBN: 0-15-900237-0   184 pages $19.95
Keyed to the Kessler Casebook
ISBN: 0-15-900070-X   312 pages $22.95
Keyed to the Murphy Casebook
ISBN: 0-15-900387-3   207 pages $21.95

Corporations

Keyed to the Cary Casebook
ISBN: 0-15-900172-2   383 pages $23.95
Keyed to the Choper Casebook
ISBN: 0-15-900173-0   219 pages $21.95
Keyed to the Hamilton Casebook
ISBN: 0-15-900313-X   214 pages $21.95
Keyed to the Vagts Casebook
ISBN: 0-15-900078-5   185 pages $18.95

Criminal Law

Keyed to the Boyce Casebook
ISBN: 0-15-900080-7   290 pages $21.95
Keyed to the Dix Casebook
ISBN: 0-15-900081-5   103 pages $15.95
Keyed to the Johnson Casebook
ISBN: 0-15-900175-7   149 pages $18.95
Keyed to the Kadish Casebook
ISBN: 0-15-900333-4   167 pages $18.95
Keyed to the La Fave Casebook
ISBN: 0-15-900084-X   202 pages $20.95

Criminal Procedure

Keyed to the Kamisar Casebook
ISBN: 0-15-900336-9   256 pages $21.95

Decedents' Estates & Trusts

Keyed to the Ritchie Casebook
ISBN: 0-15-900339-3   204 pages $21.95

Domestic Relations

Keyed to the Clark Casebook
ISBN: 0-15-900168-4   119 pages $16.95
Keyed to the Wadlington Casebook
ISBN: 0-15-900377-6   169 pages $18.95

Estate & Gift Taxation

Keyed to the Surrey Casebook
ISBN: 0-15-900093-9   100 pages $15.95

Evidence

Keyed to the Sutton Casebook
ISBN: 0-15-900096-3   271 pages $19.95
Keyed to the Waltz Casebook
ISBN: 0-15-900334-2   179 pages $19.95
Keyed to the Weinstein Casebook
ISBN: 0-15-900097-1   223 pages $20.95

Family Law

Keyed to the Areen Casebook
ISBN: 0-15-900263-X   262 pages $21.95

Federal Courts

Keyed to the McCormick Casebook
ISBN: 0-15-900101-3   195 pages $18.95

Income Tax

Keyed to the Freeland Casebook
ISBN: 0-15-900361-X   134 pages $18.95
Keyed to the Klein Casebook
ISBN: 0-15-900383-0   150 pages $18.95

Labor Law

Keyed to the Cox Casebook
ISBN: 0-15-900238-9   221 pages $18.95
Keyed to the Merrifield Casebook
ISBN: 0-15-900177-3   195 pages $20.95

Property

Keyed to the Browder Casebook
ISBN: 0-15-900110-2   277 pages $21.95
Keyed to the Casner Casebook
ISBN: 0-15-900111-0   261 pages $21.95
Keyed to the Cribbet Casebook
ISBN: 0-15-900239-7   328 pages $22.95
Keyed to the Dukeminier Casebook
ISBN: 0-15-900432-2   168 pages $18.95
Keyed to the Nelson Casebook
ISBN: 0-15-900228-1   288 pages $19.95

Real Property

Keyed to the Rabin Casebook
ISBN: 0-15-900262-1   180 pages $18.95

Remedies

Keyed to the Re Casebook
ISBN: 0-15-900116-1   245 pages $22.95
Keyed to the York Casebook
ISBN: 0-15-900118-8   265 pages $21.95

Sales & Secured Transactions

Keyed to the Speidel Casebook
ISBN: 0-15-900166-8   202 pages $21.95

Securities Regulation

Keyed to the Jennings Casebook
ISBN: 0-15-900253-2   324 pages $22.95

Torts

Keyed to the Epstein Casebook
ISBN: 0-15-900335-0   193 pages $20.95
Keyed to the Franklin Casebook
ISBN: 0-15-900240-0   146 pages $18.95
Keyed to the Henderson Casebook
ISBN: 0-15-900174-9   162 pages $18.95
Keyed to the Keeton Casebook
ISBN: 0-15-900406-3   252 pages $21.95
Keyed to the Prosser Casebook
ISBN: 0-15-900301-6   334 pages $22.95

Wills, Trusts & Estates

Keyed to the Dukeminier Casebook
ISBN: 0-15-900337-7   145 pages $19.95

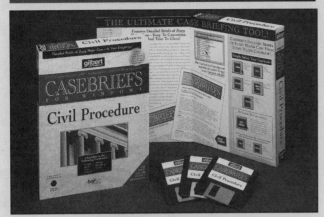
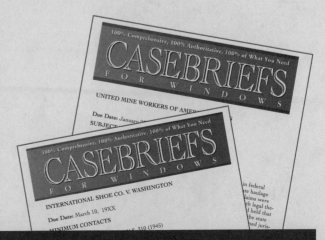

on the Internet!

www.gilbertlaw.com

Pre-Law Center

Learn what law school is really like including what to expect on exams. Order your free 32-page color catalog and a free 88-page sample of Gilbert Law Summaries for Civil Procedure — the most feared first year course!

Bookstore

Review detailed information on over 200 of America's most popular legal study aids — Gilbert Law Summaries, Legalines, Casebriefs, Law School Legends audio tapes and much more. Order on-line!

Past Exam Library

Browse hundreds of past exams from law schools across the country. Test your knowledge with true/false, multiple choice, short answer, essay – all of the question types (with answers!) you'll see on your midterm and final exams. Includes exams from some of the country's greatest law professors. If you can pass their exams — you can pass any exam!

Links to Law Sites

Links to hundreds of law-related sites on the web, including:
- Legal Publications
- International Law
- Legal Research
- Department of Justice
- Legal Employment
- Legal Associations

Order Products On-line!

Fast, easy and secure on-line ordering is now available 24 hours per day, 7 days per week!

Employment Center

E-mail the Job Goddess with your job search questions, and download a free copy of *The Myths of Legal Job Searches: The 9 Biggest Mistakes Law Students Make*. View content from some of America's best selling legal employment guides, including *Guerrilla Tactics For Getting The Legal Job Of Your Dreams* and *The National Directory of Legal Employers*.

Wanted! Student Marketing Reps

Become a campus representative and earn hundreds of dollars of free product from Gilbert Law Summaries, Legalines, Casebriefs and more! Join our national marketing program and help promote America's most popular legal study aids at your law school!

1st Year Survival Manual

A must-read for 1L's! Learn how to prepare for class, how to handle class discussions, and the keys to successful exam performance — plus much more!

Taking the Bar Exam?

Learn how to make the transition from law school exams to the bar exam — including what to expect on the MBE, MPT, MPRE, MEE and state essay exams.

Welcome Center

Whether you're about to enter law school or you're already under way, we've created this site to help you succeed!

Employment Guides

A collection of best selling titles that help you identify and reach your career goals.

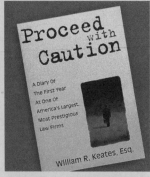

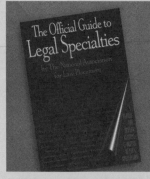

Guerrilla Tactics for Getting the Legal Job of Your Dreams
Kimm Alayne Walton, J.D.

Whether you're looking for a summer clerkship or your first permanent job after school, this revolutionary book is the key to getting the job of your dreams!

Guerrilla Tactics for Getting the Legal Job of Your Dreams leads you step-by-step through everything you need to do to nail down that perfect job! You'll learn hundreds of simple-to-use strategies that will get you exactly where you want to go. You'll Learn:

- The seven magic opening words in cover letters that ensure you'll get a response.
- The secret to successful interviews every time.
- Killer answers to the toughest interview questions they'll ever ask you.
- Plus Much More!

Guerrilla Tactics features the best strategies from the country's most innovative law school career advisors. The strategies in *Guerrilla Tactics* are so powerful that it even comes with a guarantee: Follow the advice in the book, and within one year of graduation you'll have the job of your dreams … or your money back!

Pick up a copy of *Guerrilla Tactics* today … you'll be on your way to the job of your dreams!

ISBN: 0-15-900317-2   **$24.95**

Proceed With Caution: A Diary Of The First Year At One Of America's Largest, Most Prestigious Law Firms
William R. Keates

Prestige. Famous clients. High-profile cases. Not to mention a starting salary approaching six figures.

In *Proceed With Caution*, the author takes you behind the scenes, to show you what it's really like to be a junior associate at a huge law firm. After graduating from an Ivy League law school, he took a job as an associate with one of New York's blue-chip law firms.

He also did something not many people do. He kept a diary, where he spelled out his day-to-day life at the firm in graphic detail.

Proceed With Caution excerpts the diary, from his first day at the firm to the day he quit. From the splashy benefits, to the nitty-gritty on the work junior associates do, to the grind of long and unpredictable hours, to the stress that eventually made him leave the firm — he tells story after story that will make you feel as though you're living the life of a new associate.

Whether you're considering a career with a large firm, or you're just curious about what life at the top firms is all about — *Proceed With Caution* is a must read!

ISBN: 0-15-900181-1   **$17.95**

The Official Guide To Legal Specialties
Lisa Shanholtzer

With *The Official Guide To Legal Specialties* you'll get a behind the scenes glimpse at dozens of legal specialties. Not just lists of what to expect, real life stories from top practitioners in each field. You'll learn exactly what it's like to be in some of America's most desirable professions. You'll get expert advice on what it takes to get a job in each field. How much you'll earn and what the day-to-day life is really like, the challenges you'll face, and the benefits you'll enjoy. With *The Official Guide To Legal Specialties* you'll have a wealth of information at your fingertips!

Includes the following specialties:

Banking	Intellectual Property
Communications	International
Corporate	Labor/Employment
Criminal	Litigation
Entertainment	Public Interest
Environmental	Securities
Government Practice	Sports
Health Care	Tax
Immigration	Trusts & Estates

ISBN: 0-15-900391-1   **$17.95**

Beyond L.A. Law: Inspiring Stories of People Who've Done Fascinating Things With A Law Degree
National Association for Law Placement

Anyone who watches television knows that being a lawyer means working your way up through a law firm — right?

Wrong!

Beyond L.A. Law gives you a fascinating glimpse into the lives of people who've broken the "lawyer" mold. They come from a variety of backgrounds — some had prior careers, others went straight through college and law school, and yet others have overcome poverty and physical handicaps. They got their degrees from all different kinds of law schools, all over the country. But they have one thing in common: they've all pursued their own, unique vision.

As you read their stories, you'll see how they beat the odds to succeed. You'll learn career tips and strategies that work, from people who've put them to the test. And you'll find fascinating insights that you can apply to your own dream, whether it's a career in law or anything else!

From Representing Baseball In Australia. To International Finance. To Children's Advocacy. To Directing a Nonprofit Organization. To Entrepreneur.

If You Think Getting A Law Degree Means Joining A Traditional Law Firm — Think Again!

ISBN: 0-15-900182-X   **$17.95**

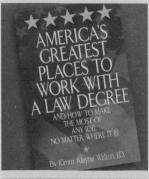

America's Greatest Places To Work With A Law Degree
Kimm Alayne Walton, J.D.

"Where do your happiest graduates work?"

That's the question that author Kimm Alayne Walton asked of law school administrators around the country. Their responses revealed the hundreds of wonderful employers profiled in *America's Greatest Places To Work With A Law Degree*.

In this remarkable book, you'll get to know an incredible variety of great places to work, including:

- Glamorous sports and entertainment employers — the jobs that sound as though they would be great, and they are!
- The 250 best law firms to work for between 20 and 600 attorneys.
- Companies where law school graduates love to work and not just as in-house counsel.
- Wonderful public interest employers – the "white knight" jobs that are so incredibly satisfying.
- Court-related positions, where lawyers entertain fascinating issues, tremendous variety, and an enjoyable lifestyle.
- Outstanding government jobs, at the federal, state, and local level.

Beyond learning about incredible employers, you'll discover:

- The ten traits that define a wonderful place to work … the sometimes surprising qualities that outstanding employers share.
- How to handle law school debt, when your dream job pays less than you think you need to make.
- How to find — and get! — great jobs at firms with fewer than 20 attorneys.

And no matter where you work, you'll learn expert tips for making the most of your job. You'll learn the specific strategies that distinguish people headed for the top … how to position yourself for the most interesting, high-profile work … how to handle difficult personalities … how to negotiate for more money … and what to do now to help you get your next great job!

ISBN: 0-15-900180-3   **$24.95**

About The Author

Kimm Alayne Walton is the author of numerous books and articles including two national best seller's — *America's Greatest Places To Work With A Law Degree* and *Guerrilla Tactics For Getting The Legal Job Of Your Dreams*. She is a renowned motivational speaker, lecturing at law schools and bar associations nationwide, and in her spare time, she has taken up travel writing, which has taken her swimming with crocodiles in Kakadu, and scuba diving with sharks on the Great Barrier Reef.

THE JOB GODDESS

E-mail the Job Goddess with your own legal job search questions!

Visit www.gilbertlaw.com for details.

Call To Order: 1-800-787-8717 or Order On-Line at http://www.gilbertlaw.com

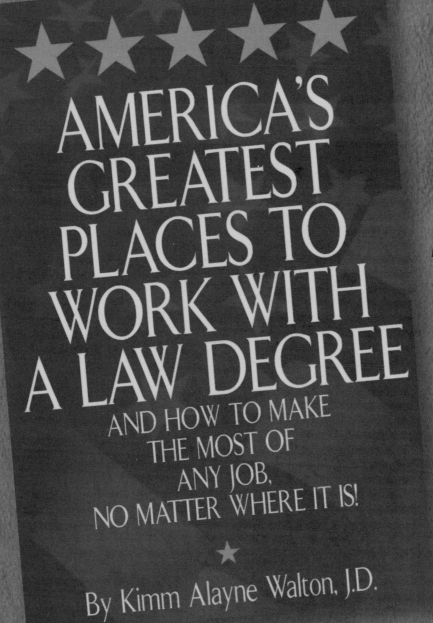

Employment Guides

A collection of best selling titles that help you identify and reach your career goals.

The National Directory Of Legal Employers
National Association for Law Placement

The National Directory of Legal Employers brings you a universe of vital information about 1,000 of the nation's top legal employers— *in one convenient volume!*

It includes:

- Over 22,000 job openings.
- The names, addresses and phone numbers of hiring partners.
- Listings of firms by state, size, kind and practice area.
- What starting salaries are for full time, part time, and summer associates, plus a detailed description of firm benefits.
- The number of employees by gender and race, as well as the number of employees with disabilities.
- A detailed narrative of each firm, plus much more!

The National Directory Of Legal Employers has been the best kept secret of top legal career search professionals for over a decade. Now, for the first time, it is available in a format specifically designed for law students and new graduates. *Pick up your copy of the Directory today!*

ISBN: 0-15-900434-9 $39.95

SAMPLE PAGE

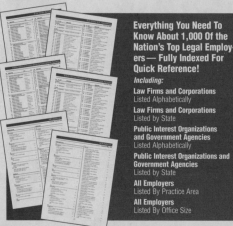

Everything You Need To Know About 1,000 Of the Nation's Top Legal Employers — Fully Indexed For Quick Reference!

Including:

Law Firms and Corporations
Listed Alphabetically

Law Firms and Corporations
Listed by State

Public Interest Organizations and Government Agencies
Listed Alphabetically

Public Interest Organizations and Government Agencies
Listed by State

All Employers
Listed By Practice Area

All Employers
Listed By Office Size

Company Information

1. Name, Address, and Phone Number Of Hiring Partner
2. Demographics
3. Primary Practice Areas
4. Benefits
5. Pro Bono
6. Public Interest Fellowships
7. Minority Recruitment Efforts
8. Non-Discrimination Policy
9. Narrative

Employment Information

10. Office Size
11. Total Firm Size
12. Job Opportunities
13. Summer Associate Information
14. Application Timeline For Summer Associates
15. Hiring Criteria For All Job Openings
16. Salary Information
17. Other Compensation
18. Other Data
19. Partnership Data
20. Other Offices
21. Campus Interviews

The Best Of The Job Goddess
Kimm Alayne Walton, J.D.

In her popular **Dear Job Goddess** column, legal job-search expert Kimm Alayne Walton provides the answers to even the most difficult job search dilemmas facing law students and law school graduates. Relying on career experts from around the country, the Job Goddess provides wise and witty advice for every obstacle that stands between you and your dream job!

ISBN: 0-15-900393-8 $14.95

SAMPLE COLUMN

Business Card Resumes: Good Idea, Or Not?

Dear Job Goddess,

One of my friends showed me something called a "business card resume." What he did was to have these business cards printed up, with his name and phone number on one side, and highlights from his resume on the other side. He said a bunch of people are doing this, so that when they meet potential employers they hand over these cards. Should I bother getting some for myself?

Curious in Chicago

Dear Curious,

Sigh. You know, Curious, that the Job Goddess takes a fairly dim view of resumes as a job-finding tool, even in their full-blown bond-papered, engraved 8-1/2x11" incarnation. And here you ask about a business card resume, two steps further down the resume food chain. So, no, you *shouldn't* bother with business card resumes. Here's why.

Think for a moment, Curious, about the kind of circumstance in which you'd be tempted to whip out one of these incredible shrinking resumes. You're at a social gathering. You happen to meet Will Winken, of the law firm Winken, Blinken, and Nod, and it becomes clear fairly quickly that Will is a) friendly, and b) a potential employer. The surest way to turn this chance encounter into a job is to use it as the basis for future contact. As Carolyn Bregman, Career Services Director at Emory Law School, points out, "Follow up with a phone call or note, mentioning something Winken said to you." You can say that you'd like to follow up on whatever it is he said, or that you've since read more about him and found that he's an expert on phlegm reclamation law and how that's a topic that's always fascinated you, and invite him for coffee at his convenience so you can learn more about it. What have you done? *You've taken a social encounter and* turned it into a potential job opportunity. And that makes the Job Goddess very proud.

But what happens if you, instead, whip out your business card resume, and say, "Gee, Mr. Winken, nice meeting you. Here's my business card resume, in case you ever need anybody like me." *Now* what have you done? You have, with one simple gesture, wiped out any excuse to follow up! Instead of having a phone call or a note from you that is personalized to Winken, you've got a piddling little standardized card with your vital statistics on it. Ugh. I know you're much more memorable, Curious, than anything you could possibly fit on the back of a business card.

So there you have it, Curious. Save the money you'll spend on a business card resume, and spend it later, when you have a *real* business card to print, reading, "Curious, Esq. Winken, Blinken, and Nod, Attorneys at Law."

Yours Eternally,

The Job Goddess

Call To Order: 1-800-787-8717 or Order On-Line at http://www.gilbertlaw.com